Raves about

"Travel can be a nightmare when you find yourself in the wrong place at the wrong time. This subversive masterpiece of travel writing might just save your sanity the next time you go out there. Get it. It makes life fun!"
—Film Director Oliver Stone

"Quirky Chain Pleasers. The small press may not have all the polish or all the marketing surrounding its books, but it can sometimes offer those little gems that set you store apart, says Wilson of Tower Books. One such gem that he seized is World Stompers: A Global Travel Manifesto. He was drawn by the book's funkiness and clear premise."
—Publishers Weekly

"Twentysomethings, especially those who would really hate to be known by that moniker, will love this irreverent, low-gloss guide that intersperses witty cartoons & quotes from such wise sages as Mr. Roarke from Fantasy Island with advice on how to crash for little cash; health tips; & detailed realistic descriptions of work possibilities abroad."
—Bookpaper

"This book has captured the spirit of what long term travel for backpackers (a.k.a. World Stompers) is all about. Reading this book, I caught the travel bug all over again and my feet just won't stop itching! You'll find tons of insider tips that were previously only found out through the hostel travelers' grapevine."
—www.hostels.com Budget Guidebooks

"A traveling guide for a new generation."
—Last Gasp

"Travel need not be expensive, difficult or dangerous. ... The brightly colored post-psychedelic cover conceals what may be more than you ever knew existed about (travel). Looks like fun!"
—Chicago Tribune

"A great addition to your collection."
—Library Journal

A Global Travel Manifesto

fifth edition

Written and Illustrated by:
Brad Olsen

STARFLEET COMMANDER
www.bradolsen.com

CONSORTIUM OF COLLECTIVE CONSCIOUSNESS
Federation Headquarters

San Francisco • Goa • Easter Island • Giza • Stonehenge
www.stompers.com

World Stompers: A Global Travel Manifesto
5th edition
Copyright © 2001 by Bradford C. Olsen
Developed by the Consortium of Collective Consciousness

Published by CCC Publishing
1559 Howard Street
San Francisco, CA 94103
(415) 552-3628

As is common in a reference and checklist-type book such as this, much of the information included on these pages has been collected from diverse sources. When possible, the information has been checked and double-checked. Even with special effort to be accurate and thorough, the author and publisher cannot vouch for each and every reference. Because this is a book about traveling, many specifics can change overnight and without prior warning. The reader will find ample advice collected from an experienced travel writer, and travel industry experts. The author and publisher assume no responsibility or liability for any outcome, loss, arrest, or injury that occurs as a result of information or advice contained in this book. As with the purchase of goods or services, *caveat emptor* is the prevailing responsibility of the purchaser, and the same is true for the traveler.

Library of Congress Cataloging-in-Publication Data:

Olsen, Bradford C.

World Stompers: A Guide to Travel Manifesto/ Bradford C. Olsen

p. cm.

Includes index

ISBN 1-888729-05-8 (Pbk.)

1. Backpacking–Guidebooks. 2. Travel–Guidebooks. I. Title.

Library of Congress Catalog Card Number: 96-86305

Printed in the United States of America.

10 9 8 7 6 5

Author's Karma Statement

Read this book and decide how you want to develop your own trip. *World Stompers* is written to inform and inspire adventurous young people to plan, prepare, and execute their own world tour. This book is about a new way of traveling around the globe – what we call "freestyle traveling." You don't need a lot of money and you don't need a tour guide to show you the way. What you need is a zest for life and the guts to go for it. An insatiable curiosity about the workings of the world helps as well.

World Stompers describes to the reader the multitudinous options of modern independent travel as they really exist. For example, the traveler low on money may work under the table and break the law by doing so. While this may be considered "unethical," it is nonetheless a way of life for some people. Just as other people go abroad to smoke pot or get laid, it is the way people travel, and it is written about in *World Stompers.*

World Stompers is not about "stomping" out other cultures or leaving a heavy mark in the places you visit. Just the opposite. *World Stompers* teaches young people to respect other cultures, to discover the world, and leave minimal impact. As Mother Earth transforms into a new age, for better or for worse, the last thing She needs is irresponsible backpackers making matters more complicated. Observe, entertain, educate, and support the other peoples of the world. You can help people by simply being there. The planet is wide open and yours for the asking – just remember to give back as much as you take.

"Think globally and act locally" never meant so much at such a crucial time. Today's young generation faces unforeseen challenges to reverse the ominous trends of planetary pollution and mass destruction. Individual actions can make a difference. There is a meaningful reason for you to become a World Stomper. Go out into the world and observe the monumental changes our collective humanity faces. Gain a universal awareness. See how the other half lives. Have a great time. Let it change your life.

– **Brad Olsen**

Consortium of Collective Consciousness
Federation Headquarters (San Francisco), CA 2001

Acknowledgments

Over the course of ten years writing, publishing and promoting five editions of *World Stompers*, many friends and fellow travelers contributed in ways too numerous to mention. They are the invisible writers of *World Stompers*, the ones who lived the drama and aided me in my pursuit to get others to live the dream as well. For those reading this and are not mentioned below, rest assured you are in my highest esteem. You know who you are.

The people I can thank by name are a small fraction of those who influenced the writing and artwork, but gave "hands-on" assistance in the most helpful way. In Europe: Caroline "Rockie" Rock, Erik "Munich Madman" Dekker, Katja "Katz" Manders, and Hansy "Belgian Waffle" Swinnen.

In Chicago I would like to thank: Tom "Double L's" Loftus, Bob "Cuzzy" Cockhill, Tommy "Tally" Peloquin, Sharon "Mrs. Moehling" Sassone, Marc "Mr. Beans" Olson, and my loving family: Uncle Bud and Auntie Bonnie, Chris "Big Brother" Olsen and his wife Toni "Love Chicken" Olsen, my dad Marshall and his wife Susan. Pre-development thanks go out to my grandfather Charles "Pa" Hausman.

In California I would like to thank: Jerry "Skeets" Nardini and Beverly "Bevtosh" Cambron for their masterful editing, Mark "Max Stone" Maxam for layout and art direction, Eric "Gzilla" Stampfli for cover assistance, John "Flavor" Faber, Andrew "Drewster" Lawton, and Creighton "Krinsk" Laskey for their Web site support, Stewart "Spear-Boy" Fallin, Kelly "Kelster," Alei "all-is-one" Parker, Charles "Chuck" Brouard, Susan "Hamster-In-Training" Kagan, Paul "Junior" Puntous, Lynne "Pipsqueak" Giandomenico, "Trace + Leaz," Jain "Pain" Martin, my sister Marsi "Mass" Olsen, and my mom Elaine for everything, especially her unfailing support throughout the years.

The real life drama of *World Stompers* and those who helped shape it in the most creative way are my traveling buddies and Aware House colleagues at the Consortium of Collective Consciousness (CCC). Paul "Vladimir Bolenath" Seymour, Wil "Prince William Sound" Gregory, Steve "The Shaman" Burch, Alex "print droid" & Therese "web droid" Seibert, Trevor "Trouble" Zimmer, Jeffrey "Wizard" DiGregorio, Charlotte "ellow luv" Bouchier, Torstin "Omananda" Klimmer, Alec "Fly-Boy" Gordon, Rachel "coffee-in-the-morning" Royer, Carlo "Brocktoon" Latasa, Natalie "Nat" Keegan, David "Shinichi" Templeman, Daniel "Tandava" Polikoff, Joe "Jovis" Bubrowski and Jennifer "Ja Ja" Fahey, I dedicate *World Stompers* to my loving family, both kindred and those at CCC.

BRAD "SANTOSH" OLSEN

Foreword

*W*orld Stompers, while diverse and encompassing in the most objective way possible, remains one writer's point of view. In order to shed light on the wide spectrum of "What Does Traveling Mean To You?" the author has solicited opinions of other travelers. All have spent more than a year abroad and acknowledge that traveling has changed their lives and perception of the world.

Traveling provides an interdimensional portal through which one can leap from one reality to another, traversing the spectrum of cultures to discover in a broader context the meaning of life on earth. Traveling is about overcoming the fear of the unknown, and looking into the face of the strange and exotic to see the magnificent natural pattern which lies beneath.

The traveler leaves the safety and comfort of his home environment and learns to survive in foreign surroundings, empowering one far beyond the narrow capabilities they teach in school. One returns a more independent, informed individual with a greater understanding of the world we live in and a wider range of compassion for those in it.
– Vladimir Bolenath (USA)

I love to talk about traveling. People who want to listen are amazed at all I've seen and done and want to know how I could possibly do all that. It's rather quite easy. Get a passport and a plane ticket, pack a bag, save some money, and bail! – Trevor Zimmer (CAN)

The catalyst for the caterpillar to emerge into the field of fragrances through sensitivity is foremost developed by opening ones scope of narrow limiting physical reality into the source of all creation by experiencing the soul as eternal unchanging love-energy which is pervading all matter transcending time + space, uniting everything on it's microcellular level. Through traveling you will experience insight into different realms of realities all existing at the same time on the basis of the same ultimate life laws which you will only learn to see after observing many different realities at once. The transcendental objective truth is realness in the present moment which is the teaching Dharma and the golden thread that will lead you – if you are able to receive it with your heart – to the ultimate and final freedom of the known with the blessing of Sat Sit Ananda, while experiencing oneness with all of creation. The Shaman path is the time-traveler who is able to break the one-dimensionality of thought and learn how to perform one's actions right – not just think to travel somewhere, but actually have faith and make that first step – go and see what you could not have known before. Buddha was a traveler. Jesus was a traveler. So was Moses. And so are all mystics of the world. – Torsten Klimmer (GER)

Traveling is about changing your mind set. No longer thinking that where you live is the only place to live. It's about being where you are and making that place your temporary home. It's about migration to tropical beaches, it's about meeting and living with people far away and knowing you will return to see them again someday. It's about meeting others who are traveling and then miraculously meeting again in the last place on earth you ever thought you'd see them. It's about learning to be comfortable where you are no matter where you are. It's about language + communication and being forced to change the way you speak + the way you think, adapting to any situation. It's about learning that there's a different way to do things. It's about spending time in the mountains, in strange cities, on a seat in the air. It's about great food and it's about the worst food! It's about Hell and it's about the Highest of Highs. But most of all, it means being Free.
– Alec Gordon (USA)

All that mind-spinning natural beauty aside – Imagine linking fingers with an elderly peasant-farmer somewhere in Asia, somewhere down a dusty orange track. Little or no words are spoken – we don't share a common language. The language of swinging hands and loving hearts. Buffaloes wallow, the sun low and fat. Communication unfolds, Western conditioning stripped away. Loving kindness, and sacred moments in a smile.

When traveling, great teachers appear in the most unexpected ways.
– Wil Gregory (UK)

Movement, challenges, change: contact with the new, facing your fears, blowing away the cobwebs. Finding your own rhythm, and harmonizing it with others. To learn to live and listen among other people – all kinds, all sorts cross your path. Learning to give without giving away, learning to receive and not to judge – always open but always aware. Building strong friendships on the road, having no expectations, but trusting that the right people will be around at the right time. To be out in the fresh air: nature is ridiculously beautiful and awe-inspiring – it blows your fucking mind!

Independence ... freedom to discover the world through your own eyes, to sort out your part in it all. To feel the energy of the earth, the cosmos, to live in tune with the cycles of nature. To release your mind – allow the stars and the moon to work their magic. Vermilion cliffs, the sound of the sea, standing on the peak of a snow-capped mountain, shaking from the intensity of a total solar eclipse, dancing around a fire, finding your voice and sharing it with others, trying things out and discovering they are possible, enjoyable, and invigorating. To get to know your body, nutrition, exercise – staying healthy and strong. Landing in bustling cities, relaxing in hilltop houses, and constantly being stimu - lated by new sights, sounds, and people. Sharing, not hoarding, and feeling useful. Getting involved in human rights or environmental projects. Loving and laughing, crying and hugging, discovering and dancing, supporting and smiling – basically, being alive and being yourself! – Charlotte Bouchier (UK)

Life is a journey, a soul journey; full of excitement, challenges and experiences. Everything in life is in motion, everything in the universe is in motion; change is the only constant. For me, motion is movement is travel; to heighten the excitement, challenges and experiences!

From the earliest days man has moved – tribal flows – in touch with the creators energy – in true respect for Mother Earth and love for the all. Now times have progressed, (or maybe even regressed) and this tribal movement is alive once more. Is the human race looking for more than this false sense of security that the 'societies' trap us with? Touching on the essence of travel is to experience the rhythm of the global family; different cultures of different nations feeling the same pulse of life. For me this rhythm comes through the native music vibrations that can break all boundaries, climb all walls and create a healing energy that can unite all under creation.

So brothers and sisters everywhere, wake up and live, get up and go, and enjoy the won - derful creation of life to the full. Go in a boat, take a plane, jump on a train, hitch a ride, no matter how near or how far, have no fear, travel some + experience: Listen, talk, smell, taste and feel, see as much as possible, let the higher self re-awaken to the all! It can some - times be a lonely path but no one can know, only you! So travel and link up with each other and ourselves and be as one. Travel in peace, enjoy all! – Steve Burch (IRE)

Nothing is quite as opening and bearing as traveling into an unknown land. The con - nections made with people and nature are set deep inside, which can be a shocking reminder of what's important in life and what isn't. – Jeffrey DiGregorio (USA)

F O R E W O R D

Freedom! Learning customs, people, history, education. Smiles. Body language, exotic tongues and ways of communication. Religions; Buddhist, Christian, Hindu, Jewish, Muslim ... the oneness (om) of all of them. Understanding reasons and ways of living, and adjusting to differences. Sampling delicacies and sharing with friends! Everywhere on planet earth and beyond! Creativity for comfortability and survival. Experiencing beautiful nature, flora, fauna, and humanity in native settings = melodious harmony. Patience. Peace. Earth is microscopic in scope with the universe. This earth is my realm, physically. Travel and accumulate knowledge. Freedom to expand understanding and love. Diversity. Open mindfulness. Joy. OM TAT SAT. – Rachel Royer (USA)

By traveling one experiences the expansion of consciousness first hand. The cultures that you come in contact with are actually different realities. In effect, your world view is con-stantly being changed in a dynamic process. One also learns about self reliance, and to believe in all possibilities. Along with these things comes a tangible expansion of time – where a day is a part of the rhythmic cycle of time, and not merely hours strung together. I have found travel to be the most transformative experience of my life. – Jovis (USA)

It's not much different day to day when you're doing someone else's stuff. So what? As long as I'm alive and getting paid, occasionally getting high while the passion fades, feeling time burn as the moment becomes a haze. So what? Everyone else is doing it, right? This is all I need, right? But how come the sky is so big? What does the moon look like from down under? Do people really live in the jungle?

Only a day now and I'm far away. Everything seems so strange because it's all so alive. Going where I want, when I want with a higher force. Each moment is a lifetime. Channeled with cosmic love, I can fly through dimensions seeing people and places I never dreamed of. Slowly tuning into the rhythms of the earth, moon, sun and stars, the moment suddenly vibrates and resonates so strong that all my senses explode.

– Carlo Latasa (USA)

Stepping outside of the normal time frame, being released from a pattern of re-occur-ring known events, to be able to move with the flow of the present moment. Leaving behind your past, and finding yourself in a new skin, with innocent eyes to see as a child each passing image.

Re-awakening your senses as you discover new cultures, their history and mysteries, and in so doing find clarity in your own. It is a time to become in touch with the cycles of nature, and the patterns of the sky. Feeling the motion of chance as you awake to the sunrise and move into the day with no plans or rules – only your intuition to guide you. You become aware of the eagles view, of yourself in relation to this rotating orb, the mother, GAIA that we walk upon. – Natalie Keegan (UK)

A Note From Mom

To the Parents of young adults:

My two sons, Chris and Brad (author of this book), graduated from college a week apart. Chris, with a Masters Degree in Engineering, had a great job lined up and a girl he was serious about. Brad had a backpack and a one-way ticket to Europe.

Chris made me feel safe; college, work, and engaged to be married. (A parents dream, right?) Brad's plan for his immediate future scared me. Where would he stay, eat, be with? And, I'm embarrassed to say, was he "wasting" his college education?

After my initial "fear of the unknown" about Brad, I did some soul searching. Didn't I raise my children to be independent and open to new experiences? College was always stressed while they were growing up – couldn't extensive travel be a big part of that education?

After Europe, Brad returned to the States. My daughter Marsi and I were now living in Santa Cruz, California. Still with no plans "to settle down," Brad lived and worked at Lake Tahoe, CA for 18 months and Lahaina, Maui for seven months. After Hawaii, Brad moved in with me. He created his own business painting houses in a town where it is very difficult to find work. He saved his money, flew to Tokyo, and without knowing how to speak Japanese, found a job teaching English as a second language. Only a college degree was necessary. He saved $10,000.00 in just over a year, and from there took off on his "World Stomp." He documented his trip with travel journals, drawings, photos, and a funny bimonthly newsletter called "B-rad's World Tour Times."

Because of his world travels, Brad is one of the most fascinating people I know. Today, Chris is happily married and is successful in a career he dearly loves. Brad's travels have opened professional avenues which would not have been available to him otherwise. Both brothers respect each others life choices and offer each other help and information in their mutual life goals.

If your son or daughter has read this book and is considering travel, you may want to discuss the following options:

1. They need to finish college. Good jobs without a degree before, during and after travel are hard to come by.

2. Do not finance their trip. Give birthday, Christmas, and graduation gifts such as: plane tickets, cameras, journals, prepaid phone cards, or money in a special travel account.

3. Read this book and other travel matter to understand the broad spectrum of world travel.

4. Help your kids find jobs during school breaks. If they keep their grades up and save their money, let them live with you free until they can afford their world tour.

The world that is open today was not there for you and I when we were young. What they learn along the way will only help them become "Citizens of the World," a prerequisite for the 21st century.

Good Luck!

Elaine Olsen
Santa Cruz, California

EARTHLINGS

**George, Brenda and Larry at the
Picasso model auditions.**

CONTENTS

Part One: Thinking About the Stomp

Part Two: Preparing for the Stomp

Part Three: Stomping Grounds

Part Four: Every Good Thing Comes to an End

Maps

Earthlings

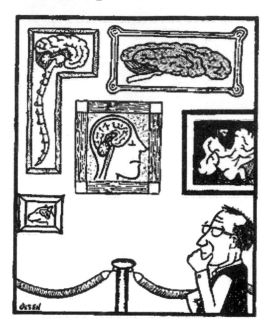

Different frames of mind.

Part

 # 1

Thinking About the Stomp

If the doors of perception were cleansed, everything would appear to man as it is, infinite.
— William Blake

The first step, my son, which we make in this world, is the one on which depends the rest of our days.
— Voltaire

The opportunity to live during the birth of a new geometric model has proven in history to be fortuitous; for it is in these infrequent times that artists have produced the most significant innovations.
— Henri Poincare

You miss 100% of the shots you never take.
— Wayne Gretzky

Travel is fatal to prejudice, bigotry and narrow-mindedness, all foes to real understanding. Likewise tolerance, or broad, wholesome, charitable views of men and things cannot be acquired by vegetating in our little corner of the earth all one's lifetime.
— Mark Twain

Intro to Stomp: 101

I believe that all of us have the capacity for one adventure inside us, but great adventure is facing responsibility day after day.
– William Gordon, *Time*, Nov. 19, 1965

Caution. This is not your typical or entirely serious travel book. *World Stompers* candidly portrays the incredible fun and realities of extended global travel. It is intended to build your confidence and eliminate misconceptions. This book prepares you for your own challenging world tour on less money than you might think. Essentially, it's a graduate program for the wild at heart.

World Stompers is fun to read! Play, learn, and introduce yourself to the planet and its people. The world is like a giant theme park. Get yourself a ticket, enjoy life in perpetual play time, take as many rides as possible, and leave with a giant smile on your face. Where a carnival lasts only a couple of days, a properly planned world tour can last several years. It then becomes your unique memory for a lifetime.

World Stompers reminds us no other generation *in history* has had such freedom to travel. Whenever before could you just get on an airplane and be anywhere on the planet within twenty-four hours? The explorers of yesteryear would be green with envy. Just consider how accessible air transportation has made the world. Never before has a generation had so many open, safe, and welcoming destinations to choose from.

This is the golden age of touring planet earth.

World Stompers celebrates the options of the modern day explorer. New regions of the world open up regularly. Almost nothing inhibits a solo traveler from any global destination, except his or her imagination. It doesn't matter where you were raised or what your background, you are incredibly lucky to be born in the U.S. during a time of no draft and no war. In addition, the English language is commonly spoken and universally recognized.

World Stompers is a hands-on advanced degree in modern world happenings. By observing different cultures, we expand our minds with a new global perspective. We gain an appreciation for our own country, world travel, and planet Earth. We learn more about ourselves.

Finally, *World Stompers* stresses total self-responsibility through complete control of personal finances. It is written and illustrated by a young man who created an exciting three-year adventure on very little money. It helps you overcome the hardships awaiting an ultra-budget traveler, and setbacks that inevitably occur. Not everybody has the courage to go to foreign countries and live out of a backpack for months or years at a time. But to the few that do, this book is for you. See you out there.

"You're never too old to do goofy stuff."
– Ward Cleaver
Leave it to Beaver

My Brief History

The man who makes everything that leads to happiness depends upon himself, and not upon other men, has adopted the very best plan for living happily. This is the man of moderation, the man of manly character and of wisdom.
– Plato, 370 B.C.

So many times I am talking to people about my world travels and a few very basic questions keep coming up. "How much did it cost? What were your favorite/least favorite countries? Were you ever afraid? How did you travel for so long? Why did you travel for so long?" These simple questions are the basis for this book and will be answered, but first, a little of my personal travel history

My life has been very goal-oriented. The ultimate culmination in my twenties was a three-year, self-financed, solo journey to twenty-eight nations, on five continents, above and below the equator.

When I finished college I took a three-month backpack trip around Europe. When I returned from Europe I only wanted to do one other thing – a multi-year world tour. It took me a few years to save the money and make the Renegade Move, but I finally did it. Looking back on my travels, I believe it was perhaps the greatest lesson I, or any young person, could ever receive. My next goal is to get this book into potential world traveler's hands. Just heed this warning: Stomping is not for boneheads. You *must* be prepared ahead of time, and you *must* be able to take responsibility for yourself.

The three essential factors of a world tour are:
Time, Money, and Desire.
When you have all three, the world is your oyster.

From Boy Scouts to Bombay

I had the travel bug from the time I was a little kid, going on family vacations and summer camp as most kids do. I joined the Boy Scouts with my brother and our neighborhood friends to get out into nature and horse around. We changed our name from Apache patrol to the Salamanders much to our leader's disliking, taunting him by being alternative. The Salamanders enjoyed blowing off merit badge duties and going off on our own adventures that were "not allowed" by camp elders. We were just in it for kicks and when the bureaucracy became too heavy, we bailed.

The best thing I got out of the scouts was
their motto: "Be Prepared."

In high school we missed going on summer camping trips, so the Salamanders reunited and began doing our own advoyages (see: Glossary). We chose our favorite place from scouting: the Warren Dunes State Park in southwest Michigan, only two hours from our native Chicago suburbs. We continued going to the dunes well into our college years until the summer we were busted for bringing in three kegs of beer. At this time the guys started giving up on adventures (along with their adolescence) for the job search. Sure, everybody needs to make money, but what's the hurry to grow up so quick? Jobs look for experience, right? So couldn't a few months on the road qualify? It seemed to me then that just being out of college offered the most freedom a lifetime was going to offer, so why not use it? This was a chance to travel wider and farther than ever before, maybe even out of the U.S.

In college, only one friend from that group saw things the way I did; Tommy P. was my roommate at Illinois State University (ISU) and best pal growing up. For spring break, just before I finished my marketing and art degree, he and I decided to hitchhike 3000 km to Matamoros, Mexico, and back. We hitched for the alternative experience, not to mention we were broke. The 11 day trip was very exciting and some of the rides we caught were absolutely classic. Our total cost was $75 each. It proved to me that traveling need not cost a lot of money. When we returned to our school in Normal, Illinois, we became instant campus celebrities after our adventure tales were written up in the student newspaper!

"Don't worry about what's gonna happen next, just roll with it."

Shortly after college, I painted a few houses and saved money for my next dream – Europe. Tommy still had two years in school to finish up, so he couldn't go, and another friend chickened out at the last minute. I wasn't too crazy about going to Europe alone, but that "roll with it" saying from the Mexico trip kept popping up in my head.

Throwing caution to the wind, I arrived in London, England, without knowing anyone and without hotel reservations. I made some calls from the airport and determined the cheapest place to crash was a big back-packer complex called Tent City. Cheapest is my favorite travel word, so I located the place and checked into a circus tent with rows and rows of bunk beds.

Tent City was a great mix of characters: skinheads, punkers, lunatics, hippies, and a wide assortment of travelers from all parts of the world. I met an Australian chap named Richard who had a station wagon. We teamed up and shared car expenses and proceeded to criss-cross our way up the country. To save cash, we cooked meals on a portable stove and crashed in the back of the wagon. After two weeks of touring the beautiful countryside, we arrived in Edinburgh, Scotland. Unfortunately, the car was vandalized while we were in a pub, and both of our backpacks were stolen. The police caught the thief a few days later when he tried to pawn my camera, but our packs were never recovered.

Richard and I decided we were not going to let this bastard-thief ruin both of our adventures of the Old Country. Instead, we resolved to carry on without any luggage (we were wearing our money belts the night we were robbed). I got my camera back, bought some clothes, and quickly routed myself south to the warmth of the Mediterranean. Traveling light took on a whole new meaning. Even with hardly any luggage, the next two and a half months were a total rip-raging good time partying and talking to people from all walks of life. The coolest aspect was that by the time I returned to northern Europe, I had made so many friends, I had free places to stay just about anywhere I showed up.

**Life is like a roller coaster. There are ups and downs
and spirals. All you can do sometimes is just
sit back and enjoy the ride.**

After Europe, I returned to the U.S. on a total travel buzz. I emptied my savings account and bought a one-way ticket to Lake Tahoe, California, for the beginning of the ski season. In two days I found a place to live and landed a job selling skis for Heavenly Ski Resort. That job allowed me to ski for free and buy top of the line equipment for half price. When the season ended I got a much better paying job as a time-share rep. I stayed for the summer and another ski-season raking in the cash. At that time I hoped to begin my fabled world tour, but my girlfriend talked me into moving to the coastal town of Santa Cruz, California. I spent much of the summer in Santa Cruz working on cartoons, some of which are featured in this book (Earthlings).

My girlfriend and I broke up a few months later, most of my money was gone, and I wanted badly to travel again. So I called up my old pal Tommy P. who had just finished college and we decided to move to Maui, Hawaii. It was great to travel with a friend like Tommy who loved adventure as much as I did. We both got set up in a house and found jobs rather soon. I stayed on the island for seven months until my brother was to be married, and returned to Chicago in 1991. I stumbled across a woman who suggested I go to Japan and teach English. After my bro's wedding, I had no plans and that sounded like an ideal way to fund my long dreamed of world tour. I painted a few houses again, packed a backpack along with my mountain bike, and set off for Japan on another one-way solo voyage.

**The best travel advice comes from other
travelers who have been there.**

I decided I could be comfortable in the ancient and beautiful Japanese city of Kyoto. Through word-of-mouth, I found a great job teaching English and a decent place to live. At first it was awkward living in an Asian city, but after I made some Japanese and foreigner friends I really began enjoying my new life. For the next year I focused on working full-time, getting in top physical shape, and saving the mighty Yen for my long awaited world tour.

Setting goals and sticking to them pays off.

Finally, after four years in the planning and much anticipation, a glorious day arrived. With ten thousand dollars saved, all my business finalized, and the go-for-it-attitude instilled in my brain, I set sail for China on November 26, 1992 – my own personal history in the making.

The next 19 months were nothing less than solid touring around the globe and glorious good times. Internet users see: *www.stompers.com* for the complete story of my world tour. Final tally: seven circuits covered, one rip-off, one illness, zero run-ins with the police, and a million stories to tell. I worked a few small jobs in Australia, but other than that, I financed the entire trip on the money I saved in Japan.

Now I'm 28 at the time of this writing, catching my breath and review-ing the blizzard of adventure memories swirling in my head. It was a blast, let me tell you, but it's time for me to mellow out and pass the torch on to you. I have learned and recorded vast amounts of data concerning the do's and don'ts of World Stomping. My collection technique was largely obser-vation, reflection, talking to people, and trial and error. A book like this could have given me a much clearer view of what to expect, and saved me a lot of headaches, not to mention money. Looking back, I would do it all over again without even flinching.

After world touring, I feel quite confident with my life and my ability to succeed at anything I really want to achieve. No doubt I attribute this to my success as a Stomper. I also feel as if there is a stabilizing rudder in my life allowing me to be content and happy with the little things in life, where before I was rather unsure and restless.

Assert your independence. Cherish your freedom. Enjoy your youth.

The day I rounded the planet, I felt like I was in a special club, something extremely exhilarating and yet equally esoteric. The exclusive fraternity of World Stompers. I felt as if I was living life for the sole propose of living life, and what else was it for? I did something in my 20s so few people will ever do in their entire lifetimes, how could I not feel great about myself? I was amazed at the ease of traveling which was so free to find, yet sought by so few. Why wasn't every able-bodied young person of the affluent nations doing exactly what I was doing? It seemed as if my peers were thinking more about security instead of opportunity. They seemed more afraid of life than death.

Where are all the Yanks?

I was really surprised at how few Americans I met abroad. We, as young people of one of the most prosperous nations on earth, have more advan-tages to make money than anyone else. But it doesn't seem to work that way. Many Americans equate making money to buying more and more things, thus trapping themselves in the vicious cycle of work, produce, and consume ... work, produce, and consume. Before most people realize it, they are locked into car payments, credit cards, mortgages, investments, and so on, giving up the chance to see the world at a young and zestful age.

Do not miss out on life's most golden opportunity! Keep your commit-ments to a minimum and all of your options open. The wisest people are those who have themselves in their own power. Take control of your own life and do it! Nobody else can make things happen except you.

Life does not have to be complicated and stressful at all. Life can be as carefree and boundless as you want it. You just have to *want* it. This is true for traveling and everything else in life.

Top Ten U.S. Excuses For Not Traveling:

10. "My parents and friends don't encourage me."

9. "I'm too preoccupied chasing material goods."

8. "I'll be too lonely, I have no one to go with."

7. "If I didn't have family / career commitments."

6. "I think the world is a dangerous place."

5. "America's such a big place to see, why leave?"

4. "I don't know anything about travel in foreign countries."

3. "I'd miss all my favorite TV shows."

2. "I've never met any world travelers."

1. "OK, I'm just plain chicken."

Embarking   *Returning*

"If you speak three languages, you are trilingual. If you speak two languages, you're bilingual. If you speak one language, you're American."
Sonny Spoon

A Young Reader's Guide

*There is far too much talk about making life easy. It is all right to take the
pain and bitterness out of a struggle; but were you to take the struggle out,
there would be no adequate chance for young Americans.*
– Paul Shoup

World travel begins as a personal dream and a magnificent vision.
There is no doubt you can achieve whatever you put your mind to
doing, but many things must take place before the ball actually gets
rolling. The younger the reader, the more time the person has to make the
plans and set the goals. Indeed, evolution requires time. Just remember,
Pablo Picasso did not learn how to paint when he was an old man, he
started painting when he was quite young. If traveling seems viable in your
future, start setting goals today and you will be World Stomping in the not
too distant future.

**Nothing big happens overnight. Dreams become visions,
visions mature into goals, and goals finally become
actualizations – never without some struggle, however.**

Very few people are ambitious in the sense of having a specific image of
what they want to achieve. Their future vision is myopic and they see only
toward the next run, the next increment of money. This view is fatal to
putting together an overseas trip, and the biggest hurdle to jump. The key
is to clearly fix yourself onto goals for the long run and stick to them. Give
up and the race is over. Keep jumping, and you will surprise yourself by
what you can achieve.

Remember this fact: the longer you wait, the harder it gets.

Time, Money, and Desire. Set goals for each of these. The perfect time to
travel is just after graduation from high school or college. Having a college
degree is ideal because it will open many employment opportunities
abroad and give you a better knowledge base to reflect upon. If your desire
to begin traveling starts early or between semesters, that's okay too. Just
think it out carefully, and "Be Prepared."

Another way to set time goals is to begin acquiring primary items for
your Stomp when you are young. A backpack for Christmas, a camera as
a birthday present, or a plane ticket for graduation. And always be on the
lookout for garage sales to collect the little things: pocketknife, sleeping
bag, lightweight flashlight, money belt, etc.

Earn and save the money yourself. This will allow you maximum
freedom and a great sense of pride. Don't ever borrow the money to travel,
unless it's an extreme emergency. You would be severely jeopardizing your
financial future if you maxed out a credit card on your trip. Don't even

bring a credit card – they are just too damn tempting. Simple rule: when the traveler's checks or ATM account runs low, time to head home or get a job on the road.

It is equally important to have a high self-esteem about yourself before setting off than it is to have the money to pay for it. Be secure and know thyself. Emotional breakdowns are not conducive to World Stomping. Traveling is nothing more than a learning process. While no one is expected to be Lewis and Clark on their first expedition, those people who whine and bitch on a regular basis are not going to be making a lot of friends. Real confidence comes from knowing and accepting yourself – your strengths and limitations, in contrast to depending on affirmations from others.

Traveling, like learning anything, is a process of trial and error.

It is easy to "learn travel" by observing what it takes to get around. You have done it already – family vacations, camp outings, college roadtrips – they all materialize with some semblance of planning. Develop trips on your own, like to a friend's college in another state, or a vacation in a neighboring country. Get some friends together and go camping for a few days. Follow the Rainbow Tribe for a while. Take your boyfriend or girlfriend to Mexico for a week. Whatever. The important thing is to feel it out and then expand on what you learn. Learning is just discovering something is possible.

When the best student hears about the way
He practices it assiduously;

When the average student hears about
the way
It seems to him one moment there
and gone the next;

When the worst student hears about the way
He laughs out loud.

If he did not laugh
It would not be worthy of being the way.

– Lao Tzu, *Tao te Ching*

This book should also get you motivated to personally better yourself, take a greater interest in school, and understand what it takes to live on your own in a faraway place. While there is nothing more important than a healthy curiosity, it is the street-wise people who get by with the fewest problems. You gain an education as you travel, but it doesn't hurt to have a decent knowledge base before setting out. Every subject you study in school is relevant to Stomping. Math is useful for quick exchange-rate computations. History brings relevance to the relics you see. Psychology helps you understand people. Reading will further enhance your experience. Geography will facilitate better interpretation of maps. The metric system will acquaint you with distances, weights, volumes, and temperatures. Environmental studies will give insight into the planetary destruction taking place. Knowledge is power on the road.

Although English is becoming the common language of the world, learning a second language enables you not only to converse with native speakers but also with travelers who speak it as a first or second language. Traveling is a great way to start studying a new language; especially when you are immersed in a new culture. Once abroad, every interaction becomes a free language lesson, and most foreigners are eager to practice their English in exchange.

Top Ten Ways Travelers Differ From Tourists

10. "Tourist" implies being on a tour, led by a tour guide, in a tour group. Travelers need no one to show them the way, or wipe their asses, either.

9. Tourists wear trendy and new clothes; travelers don ethnic threads and/or patches.

8. A tourist goes abroad to discover foreign sights, the traveler goes abroad to discover himself.

7. The tourist crowd spends much, parties fast, and passes out soon. The traveler spends less on more, and stays up all night for the amazing sunrise.

6. The tourist sees what she has come to see, while the traveler is content seeing what she sees.

5. Tourists meet other tour companions and their guide — that's about it. Travelers meet the world.

4. Locals usually heckle tourists, hang out with travelers.

3. Short-term tourists are on tight itineraries, visiting awesome places for only days or hours per visit; long-term travelers live at those places for weeks or months at a time.

2. Tourism is consumer driven while traveling is do-it-yourself.

1. Tourists follow, travelers freestyle.

By being a World Stomper you are assuming total responsibility for yourself and your actions. There are no baby sitters and no therapists to whine to. The rest of this book is going on the premise that the reader is educated and intelligent enough to manage his or her own financial affairs and emotional balance. All destinations can easily be reached by working and saving and not being dependent on others to make it happen.

First things first, get yourself educated. The world does not cater to boneheads.

Earthlings

Mass-Produced Children

"We know that a dream can be real, but who ever thought that reality could be a dream? We exist, of course, but how, in what way? As we believe, as flesh-and-blood human beings, or are we simply part of someone's feverish, complicated nightmare? Think about it, and then ask yourself, do you live here, in this country, in this world, or do you live instead ... in the Twilight Zone?"
Rod Serling
The Twilight Zone

Time

Lost time is never found again.
— Benjamin Franklin, *Poor Richard's Almanac*, 1748

Do your days go by quickly? Do you fear your life may go by quickly? Like sands in the hourglass, these are the days of our lives, and every moment we are alive counts. Make the most of your days; stop the hourglass; enjoy your time; travel the world. William James observed some time ago, "Most men lead a life of quiet desperation." Break the mold and take account for yourself.

Here's a concept for you: time expands when you travel. It's a bizarre notion, but when everything is so new and happens so quickly, the days become much longer than when you were living in the rat race. Every day is a new experience and usually a whole lot of fun, so certainly time expands.

Life is all about changes. It is how you deal with these changes that determine how you deal with life.

Consider the life-span of an average American person in years of age:

Child-hood	Elementary and High School	College	Career and Family						Retirement
0 5	10 15	20	25 30 35 40 45 50 55 60 65						70 75 80

Child-Hood	Elementary and High School	College	World Tour	Career and Family					Retirement
0 5	10 15	20	25	30 35 40 45 50 55 60 65					70 75 80

Think about the big picture. Fitting in a few years of travel right out of college is the most opportune time in a person's life. Why not take a little of that retirement now? After four years of busting ass and cramming for exams, you deserve to blow off a little steam. Besides, why wait until you are old and retired? Unlike young people, old folks don't have the stamina and vigor to do a major World Stomp.

This is the best time in your life to travel. You are young, healthy, curious, smart, and free. Once you begin a career and a family you give up on your chance to up and go, to start anew, to challenge the world, to exhibit your freedom. Basically, you pass on a golden, once-in-a-lifetime opportunity to check out the planet. Remember, there is always a spouse and job waiting for you in your chosen field if you elect to move back home. If it's there now, it'll still be there in five years.

Make yourself more marketable. Postpone the career. Travel now.

Finish your educational pursuits and wrap up all commitments before setting off on a long-term advoyage. A college degree will open many doors when job hunting overseas, but it's not necessary if you're just going abroad to travel. Your chosen major is insignificant to teach English abroad for example, but having a college degree is required in almost all cases.

A curiosity into the workings of the world and a good knowledge base is the most important factor. As we emerge into the Information Age, those with a clue will be the ones who make it big. Today, in this fast-changing world we live in, despite all inequalities of wealth, the coming exertion for power will increasingly turn into a struggle over the distribution of and access to knowledge. Social commentators note we are drowning in information but starving for knowledge. Take some time off and learn about the world; it can only make you a better person.

There may never be another chance to see the planet so full of life.

The new millennium, for many people, is an age of transition. These people, from religious fundamentalists to doomsday prophets, from environmentalists to politicians, are saying the twenty-first century is going to be crunch time for civilization as we know it. Do, or perhaps quite literally, die. Social thinkers from Toynbee to Wells have long debated that our global society is in a race between education and catastrophe.

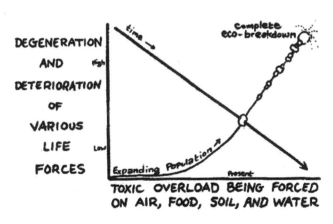

DEGENERATION AND DETERIORATION OF VARIOUS LIFE FORCES

TOXIC OVERLOAD BEING FORCED ON AIR, FOOD, SOIL, AND WATER

Are we going to cut down all the trees and pollute all the oceans to the point we cannot breathe or feed ourselves any more? Will the madmen of the world, who are ever increasingly gaining the capacity to launch weapons of mass destruction anywhere on earth, be kept in check? Can overpopulation be leveled off before the planet is totally overrun with humans? Or will the expanding holes in the ozone make it too dangerous to be outdoors anymore? Global warming, new diseases, acid rain, and species extinction top the list, just as new problems continue to sprout up every year. One thing is certain, our planet is changing at an alarming pace and these are all real problems our generation will have to confront, no matter how depressing they seem.

On the other hand, there is great hope in some of our leaders. The intellectual and artistic Czech president Vaclav Havel writes that we have entered a "postmodern" age where "everything is possible and almost nothing is certain." He believes "a single interconnected civilization" is emerging where human beings "are mysteriously connected to the universe ... just as the entire evolution of the universe is mirrored in us." He also puts forth the ancient Greek "Gaia hypothesis," which describes Earth as a "mega-organism" on which we all depend.

Men and women who are in power and dwell upon these deepest issues will be twentieth century history makers to future generations. Former Vice President Al Gore wrote in his book *Earth in the Balance*, "As we continue to expand into every conceivable environmental niche, the fragility of our own civilization becomes more apparent ... In the course of a single generation, we are in danger of changing the makeup of the global atmosphere far more dramatically than any volcano in history, and the effects may persist for centuries to come."

Recognition is the key to understanding.

The Chain of Life

If one is to truly understand interconnectedness and environmental niches, would it not help tremendously if one could see these things for oneself? Havel tells us, "We enjoy all the achievements of modern civilization, yet we do not know exactly what to do with ourselves." How about some World Stomping?

Al Gore continues; "At the current rate of deforestation, virtually all of the tropical rainforests will be gone partway through the next century. If we allow this destruction to take place, the world will lose the richest storehouse of genetic information on the planet, and along with it possible cures for many of the diseases that afflict us. Indeed, hundreds of important medicines now in common use are derived from plants and animals of the tropical forests." Wouldn't it be wild to tell your grandchildren you actually walked in a virgin rainforest?

A university professor named Chuck K. has been World Stomping since the end of W.W.II, and gave this advice; "Many things have changed over the years and continue to change ever so rapidly. Forests are cut down, national corruption, good places go bad and new ones open up. The ultimate goal of capitalism is a Westernized globe, and that is happening as we become a global society."

In our sheltered TV society it is so easy to have tunnel vision. Film director Oliver Stone sums it up well, "TV can have a totalitarian effect; it makes you passive. We're becoming more and more inured — because the Gulf War is treated the same way as Michael Jackson. One shock after another. You become inured to the concept of suffering. You lose empathy. However, when you go to Asia, you notice the media bombardment is no longer part of your life. And you relax."

Right now is the time to travel, like never before.

With the collapse of communism and the emergence of a "New World Order" based on democracy, world travelers have advantages never before seen. Never before in human history has there been this much technology in transportation to get us around. Never before have there been so many financial opportunities available to Americans (of all ages) to reside and work abroad. Never before in the past, and perhaps never in the future, will this world be so open and accessible. The coming millennium change will prove to be the most exciting and challenging moment in all of humankind's tumultuous advances in civilization. Go abroad and witness this incredible transitional phase of human history. Don't miss this golden opportunity to be a living part of it!

Being from a native English-speaking country is a fantastic advantage.

The fact that the English language is universally recognized and the most frequently spoken language around the globe gives us a great advantage for being understood on the Stomp. The Brits were damn good colonialists spreading their language for four hundred years into every conceivable corner on earth. Now the Americans are the major super-influencers, spreading our TV and Hollywood products to eager viewers. Developing nations love our programs!

The English language is changing the way people communicate in so many other ways too. Already it is the language of international commerce and business. You must know how to read English to tap into the vast wealth of information on the Internet. English is the official language, or preferred foreign language, in 90% of all countries worldwide. Speaking English is very trendy with East Asian and Southeast Asian students. European children receive a decade of English classes in school. In fact, Euro-kids are quite proficient speakers, and some tests indicate even more so than American kids. One identical exam was given to Dutch teens and American teens a few years ago, testing their vocabularies and verbal skills. The Dutch teens won.

Make the time to Stomp soon. You will never regret it.

EARTHLINGS

Weaponry of the Cold War.

"Cling to your youth. Time has a habit of moving forward, never backward, never motionless."
Jim Anderson
Father Knows Best

Money

It is not the volume of money but the activity of money that counts.
– W. Bourke Cockran, speech, 1896

Of the three elements of world travel: Time, Money, and Desire; perhaps money is the greatest challenge for young travelers. Saving a large amount of money is difficult for most people, but absolutely essential if you wish to travel. You will need to adopt a new mind-set towards accumulating money. Your new relationship should include disciplined saving habits, achievable financial objectives, and good old-fashioned hard work. Every dollar saved should represent a step closer to your world tour. The first wise financial move is destroy all credit cards and sell the car.

Before departure, your new saving and thrift habits will come in handy. Initial travel expenses include: your passport and visa fees, Eurail pass, backpack, and airline ticket. What's left over represents your bankroll for travel expenses. This is the largest and most varied cost on any world tour. Budget yourself carefully. Roughly plan on $1,200 per month on the expensive circuits, half that for developing nations.

Credit Card Prison

Do not finance a world tour on credit. Misused credit card debt is the number one excuse for not traveling. Burying yourself in revolving debt will deter any hopes of extended world travel. A small charge "now and then" has left far too many persons stuck with enormous debts and obscene interest rates. Research indicates fully one-third of all college students believe their credit card balances have gotten out of hand. Don't be in this group. Shred it now or leave it at home for the "emergency/just in case" scenario.

Used and Abused Benji was an 18-year-old New Zealand lad I met in India. His spending habits illustrate the danger of using credit on the Stomp. Benji was having a good old time as we all were. Problem was, his traveler's checks were all used up. A wise traveler would call it a day and head on home. Not Benji, he had a credit card. He started taking cash advances for another two weeks in India, then he was off to Thailand for more fun in the sun, and then home. He financed his airline tickets, party money and another month of traveling on the card. When I asked him if he had any clue about the 18.5 % interest grave he was digging for himself, he just shrugged and said, "I'm having too much fun now; why should I go home?"

Today, he's trapped paying off his travel debts. He will remember the debt that got him into years of struggle, and the long attempt to get "out from under." His great adventure memories will be blurred by the credit card prison that will take him years escape.

M O N E Y

**A much better idea than credit cards: Savings
accounts earning interest before departure.
Traveler's checks and cash on the Stomp.**

Owning an Auto is a Deep Money Pit

Some will argue that a car is a necessity, and this may be true for people
in L.A. or rural areas. Don't believe the myth that you need a car to get to
work, school, or wherever. Using public transportation, a bike, or the folks'
car, will, in time, save you a small fortune. Get used to not having a car.
Certainly you won't need one on your world tour.

Money saved is money earned for travel.

Consider what you pay to own a car. The vehicle's purchase price, expensive insurance (especially for the young), repair and upkeep bills, traffic
tickets, gasoline, and the risk of a huge DUI fine. These costs can easily tap
just about any world tour fund and make the reality of travel just a dream.
Get rides with friends or use public transport.

Quit the Car, Buy a Bike

Investing in a bike serves several purposes. First, it's a cost-free mode of
transportation that never requires a parking fee. Bike riding adds no
noxious gases into the atmosphere. It's healthy, fun, and great exercise.
Bikes are easily transportable on airplanes and usually do not require an
extra fee. Mountain bikes are great for off-road exploration trips. You can
travel on rough terrain where most vehicles can't. Bikes are very efficient
and ubiquitous worldwide. They are emerging as the best mode of travel
within many congested traffic cities. In most inner city instances, bike
riding is faster than driving or public transportation – <u>with no cost!</u> Repairs
and upkeep are elementary and inexpensive.

A solid, sturdy mountain bike is recommended, along with a kryptonite
lock. Shoot for good components such as brakes, gears, and derailer. A
beat-up looking frame will help deter theft. A repair kit with tools is also
important, as well as a helmet.

**Do not get caught in the auto trap. It's a vicious
cycle that can be difficult to escape.**

Note to Parents:

Why not invest in a World Stomper education rather than his or her first
auto? Christmas, graduation, and birthday presents such as an airline
ticket, books on travel, backpacks, a nice camera ... you get the picture.
After all, what's more dangerous: a wild kid behind the wheel of a car, or
a youngster on a bike in a youth hostel?

Ways to Make Money

in the U.S.A.

Work is hard. Distractions are plentiful. And time is short.
– Adam Hochschild, New York Times, 1985

The American dream was founded on the principle that every person can succeed if they work hard, or take the opportunity to start their own enterprise. Most other countries do not offer this luxury. America was built on the entrepreneurial spirit, regardless of one's age, race or gender. The only limitation to making money in this country is your imagination, and capacity for hard work.

Invent your own summer job.

Here's a few time-honored money-making ideas for the enterprising to consider: Odd jobs, mowing lawns, washing windows, cleaning gutters, building decks and/or retaining walls, gardening, washing cars, raking leaves, landscaping, baby-sitting, tutoring, auto repairs and painting houses.

Whatever you think you'd be good at, or enjoy, try it for a summer. For other options, check school bulletin boards for jobs, the newspaper, or there is always McDonalds.

Starting your own short-term business can be the most rewarding experience of all. You'll acquire practical business skills, and usually higher pay. Most service jobs allow you to be out of doors.

It usually requires more patience and discipline than skill to succeed, as the initial task of prospecting and finding potential clients does not provide any   financial rewards.

Profits do not just happen – they must be planned. Find a boss who can give you experience and observe what it takes to run a business. A novice messing up on the first few jobs will have a hard time keeping the ball rolling because references are the best form of advertising. Make friends with your clients and do exactly what you said you would do. Remember, a fair shake goes both ways.

Starting your own enterprise is a great way to make the money to travel. The best advice for a new business: keep your overhead low.

A Self-Employment Model

The following are the basics for starting up a house painting business. Apply some of these concepts to your own business ideas.

A few house painting jobs in the spring can easily pay for a few months traveling in the summer. To get started, you must have a large vehicle (borrow it; don't buy it if possible). Also borrow a ladder; design some clever advertising; know how to budget your money; and have a good idea how to paint a house.

First of all, look around your neighborhood to determine what services could be in demand. Ask a few neighbors if they need any specific work done. Look for houses with peeling paint.

As independent contractors we can undercut the competitor's bid by minimizing our overhead. We work for a lower wage, hire our friends cheaply, avoid licensing and bonding costs, and insurance premiums (optional). This saves tons of cash for you and your clients. Furthermore, it is easy to do short-term, under-the-table jobs and avoid paying taxes (also optional).

Use the sympathy angle when creating your advertising and business name: "Student Home Painters," or Outgoing Dependable Diploma-seekers, Job Opportunities to Benefit Students (O.D.D. J.O.B.S. for short) Homeowners, especially the elderly, like the idea of employing students. It also implies: "students work for less."

The biggest key to landing contracts is to make your business look legit. It's not enough to offer a great price. You'll need to convince your client you can do the job well and are covered with insurance. Most college students are covered under their parents' homeowner insurance policy, so to say you are insured is not lying. Of course, that is not the kind they mean, but sometimes you have to stretch the truth to get going.

Cheap and clever advertising

By far the cheapest way to promote your business is with flyers. Design something like this:

Student Home Painters

* All jobs done by hand *

* Two years' experience *

* References available *

* Satisfaction guaranteed *

* Call for a free estimate *

* Quality work, affordable prices *

Create and distribute inexpensive advertising by Xeroxing two or four ads per page. Catch your prospective client's eye by adding an illustration, or color highlight certain words. Start in your own neighborhood and systematically put a leaflet in every door – not the mailbox.

If you encounter the homeowner, smile, introduce yourself and the business, and ask, "would you know of anyone in the neighborhood who may need my services or a free estimate?" Set the person at ease.

Use an answering machine; it is an indispensable and critical tool.

Follow up your calls on the machine right away. Even waiting longer than a day may be too late. Set up one day to deliver proposals and give the client a time you will be there — do not be late! First impressions mean a lot, so be on time and greet the client with a smile and a sincere compliment on their house or pet or something. This is especially effective in gaining trust with the elderly.

Next, reassure the client with the importance of the work to be done. Something like, "You know, Mr. Jones, the rain and the upcoming winter will do a lot of damage to that exposed wood." Or, "Yes, Mrs. Willie, this house will look so beautiful again with a fresh coat of paint." The degree of sappiness will vary from client to client.

The hardest part of the painting business is not so much the work, but the bottom figure on your proposal. There are times you will make out like a bandit and other times you will lose your ass by that bottom figure. This comes with trial and error and if you know someone in the field to acquaint you with typical prices and going rates, it will save you much grief. Sometimes you can ask the client what the lowest bid has been. Use discretion.

The best way to estimate the cost of the job is by estimating the hours of scraping, prepping (sanding, washing, and primer coat), and the actual painting of the house. Multiply this by your rate salary (say, $15 an hour) and the cost of supplies. The only way to know these time estimates is by painting a house first; then estimating will come much more easily. Specify all work to be performed on your proposal form (available at any office supply store) and then sign it.

Your supplies are simple and can be used over and over again if you take care of them. They include: a large brush and a detail brush, five or six tarps, a roller and a tray, two scrapers, a few rags, window putty, and a ladder. If these items can be borrowed, that reduces your overhead even more. A car will be needed to transport the materials to the work site. If you can get away with borrowing the folks' car and biking it thereafter, you are laughing all the way to the bank.

Make a sign to put in front of the worksite. People driving by will take notice and further jobs will come from it. Another great way to get free publicity is to call your local newspaper and introduce yourself and the business. Most papers run feature stories on new enterprises (though only once, of course).

After the bid has been accepted and a start date agreed upon, ask the clients' advice as to where exactly on the house they would like you to start, and if they would mind if you listened to the radio while you work. Be considerate and maintain rapport with the clients by giving them progress

STUDENT PAINTERS WORK FOR LESS! 555-1212

reports as you go along. If they change the game plan along the way, go with the flow – because the customer is always right.

When the job is completed, there shouldn't ever be a problem getting paid. Honesty is a two-way street. Keep your word on doing a quality job, attention to detail, and being neat and efficient. These factors will be evident upon completion. If your clients are satisfied, they will usually agree to serve as a reference for you. Perhaps the best marketing tool is word-of-mouth recommendations from satisfied customers, as well as the houses you have already painted to show future clients.

<u>Endnote</u>: When I was nearly finished writing *World Stompers*, I needed a little extra cash to get by. I called forty painting companies out of the San Francisco yellow pages, and the next day I was working for $12 an hour. It just goes to show, knowing a trade or labor task lasts a lifetime and can get you out of a financial tight spot quickly.

The world of thought and action overlap. What you think has a way of becoming true. If you make it your goal to travel, only you can make it happen, and only you will ultimately benefit. The key is to discipline yourself on spending money, and concentrate on saving it. Play the revolutionary and challenge the rules.

Earthlings

Minimum wage on the high seas.

"Money speaks all languages."
J.R. Ewing
Dallas

Desire

People are always blaming their circumstances for what they are. I don't believe in circumstances. The people who get on in this world are the people who get up and look for the circumstances they want, and if they can't find them, make them.
– George Bernard Shaw (1856-1950)

Desire is the most revealing aspect of who we are as individuals. Because it is completely subjective, desire differs from person to person. Everyone has their own personal desires for something or another. The person who determines how he or she wants to live, is the person who can *actualize* individual wishes and wantings. The difference is in doing. A strong ambition to travel the world begins with a strong desire.

Desire is also about maintaining positivity. The positive mind-set of leaving the security of home behind and setting off into the great unknown. Positive thinking is the ability to contain your emotions in stressful and unpleasant situations. Keeping an open mind while you travel usually leads to a wonderful state of bliss and overall happiness as you go about experiencing the joys and beauty of the world firsthand.

Desire is something that must come from within and manifest into action and goals. Desire is the prime motivator. It leads to hard work, commitment, sacrifice. It's about doing *whatever it takes* to follow through on your goals until you are at that destination across the world and can say:

"Hey! Only *I* did this and only *I* made this happen!"

The Roman poet Spirella:

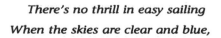

There's no thrill in easy sailing
When the skies are clear and blue,

There's no joy in merely doing
Things which anyone can do.

But there is some satisfaction
That is mighty sweet to take,

When you reach a destination
That you thought you'd never make.

No Regrets, no Sorrow

When travelers from around the world were asked *why* they were doing what they were doing, most would agree: A very strong motivating factor was *regret*.

The regret of missing out on one of life's greatest opportunities... the regret of reflecting in middle age that their life was incomplete... the regret of not living life to its fullest... the regret of not taking the chance when it was possible.

No regret in life equates to optimum happiness. On the other hand, nothing eats away at your insides more hungrily than regret – the wistful wonderings, the "what might have beens."

"Jonathan Livingston Seagull spent the rest of his days alone, but he flew way out beyond the Far Cliffs. His one sorrow was not solitude... it was that the other gulls refused to believe the glory of flight that awaited them; they refused to open their eyes and see." – Richard Bach, *Jonathan Livingston Seagull.*

Desire Comes from Challenge

Many times, before I left on my journeys, I found myself being judged by hometown friends. I would say to them, "I'm thinking about going to Japan for a year." Or, "I'm going to backpack around Europe for a couple of months." After the initial shock wore off and the "What do you want to do that for" questions were answered (why not?), I found myself in a sort of challenge.

The next time I saw them the usual response was, "Are you still going to Japan? (chuckle, chuckle)." I'd retort, "Hell yes! After I save enough money and get my things together, I'm gone!"

Upon returning from a few trips, my friends began to take my travel plans more seriously. They offered constructive advice rather than doubts and sarcasm. Some friends were astonished at how easily I could just up and do it without hesitation. Coming home and seeing these friends again, I was always secretly amazed at how little had changed in their lives, while mine seemed to expand exponentially.

When time, money, and desire are clear in your mind, make the announcement that you are taking off on your chosen trip. Many will offer their advice, comments, criticisms, doubts and fears, which will be up to you to sift through. Be strong and hold steadfast. When these people see you achieving your departure goals, their disposition will change. Attitudes transform from the doomsday scenario and deep concern to genuine support and enthusiasm, frequently with a dash of envy. Stick to your time goals and do not let negative attitudes drag you down. If you can do this, you will be harnessing an incredible driving force.

You don't need to have all the answers before you leave. It's amazing what ordinary people can achieve when they set fourth without preconceived notions. You are going out to challenge the great unknown! Even if you do believe some of the doubt and failure stories, just remember, there is more dignity in failure than taking no action at all.

At least go down swinging; this carries a lot more respect in life than never making the effort.

In college, a professor advised our business class, "We need to teach the highly-educated person that it is not a disgrace to fail. The individual must analyze every failure to find its cause. One must learn how to fail intelligently, for failing is one of the finest art forms in the world."

The desire to jump right into a world tour and embrace the enormous changes before us should be on par with getting a Masters degree. There has never been such an exciting time to travel.

Changes around the globe happen instantaneously in this Information Age. Consider these excerpts from the book *Megatrends 2000* by John Naisbitt and Patricia Aburdene:

•The further the information economy evolves, the better the jobs, and the more they pay.

• If the West's influence decreases, it will only have itself to blame – for ignoring Asia's markets, for becoming paranoid over Asian investment (in the West) instead of welcoming the influx of Asian dollars. In the end, as ever, what we are moving toward is an increasingly interdependent world.

• The new era of the individual is happening simultaneously with the new era of globalization. The 1990s will be largely devoted to the full realization of one, single global economy. As we globalize, individuals – paradoxically – become more important, more powerful.

• The most exciting breakthroughs of the 21st Century will occur not because of technology, but because of an expanding concept of what it means to be human.

**Learning about the world is learning about life.
Dream it and it will come true.**

"Dreams are the true interpreters of our desires."
Dr. Smith
Lost in Space

Out of College: Out of Country

In the business world, everyone is paid in two coins: cash and experience.
Take the experience first; the cash will come later.
— Harold Geneen, *Managing,* 1984

So you are about to finish college and you don't know what your future has in store for you? Hey, take a number and join the club. Our generation of college graduates is looking at one of the most intense job markets there has ever been. Mostly this is due to an instable economy, and the Baby Boomers glutting the market and creating a log jam for fresh opportunities. Most Boomers are ahead of us in management jobs and won't be retiring for another 15 years. While opportunities in technology related fields continue to expand, these are highly specialized positions for trained individuals. What to do in the meantime?

Consider the Gloom:

- "There are about 12 million students in colleges across the country, and this economy cannot absorb all of them," according to Michael Kahan, a political science professor at Brooklyn College of the City University of New York.

- Six thousand seniors graduated from Michigan State in 1992 and of those, only 10% to 15% were expected to have job offers at graduation, reported Patrick Scheetz, Director of the Collegiate Employment Research Institute at Michigan State.

- "I've never seen a tougher market for college grads," Victor Lindquist, Northwestern University's Director of Placement, said recently, "and I've been in the field since 1958."

- All around the nation, from the University of Virginia, to Texas A&M, to Bryant College in Smithfield, R.I., college recruitment offices are placing 10% to 35% less graduating seniors into desired jobs, according to recent statistics from college recruiting boards.

- Real earnings for white-collar workers have been in a downward spiral since 1987. Inflation-adjusted wages of college-educated workers fell 3.1 percent between 1987 and 1991, with male college-educated workers experiencing a steeper 4.4 percent decline during that period, according to a recent study by the nonprofit Economic Policy Institute.

- A four-year study conducted by the University of Alberta reveals a gradual, prolonged school-to-work transition. Rather than a quick jump from one to the other, the study concludes, students will have to face intermittent periods of employment – often at low-paying jobs – with more years of schooling, before settling into a long-term career.

Consider the Options:

- Work abroad. There are many ways to find work overseas, both while in college or out on the Stomp. While still in school, one can check with the university jobs abroad program or the Council on International Educational Exchange (CIEE). CIEE operates a series of work-exchange programs, allowing students temporary employment in other countries, primarily during summer vacation. Post-graduation jobs, found almost always when you are living in the country, will be described extensively in: "Work Around the Planet," and "Work and Money" in each specific circuit.

- Study abroad. Each college or university has its own overseas-study programs. CIEE also works in voluntary cooperation with participating schools and their programs for high school and college students. CIEE operates 41 Council Travel offices, and more than 450 issuing offices at college and universities in the U.S. alone.

- Volunteer abroad. The Peace Corps is always looking for volunteers and CIEE also organizes an International Voluntary Service. There are dozens of other nonprofit and private organizations that place volunteers in positions abroad.

- Travel abroad. Make your money in the U.S. and design your own trip. Freestyle Stomping offers the most possibilities because any combination of the above can be found en route, if so desired.

Consider the Outcome:

- Business leaders and academics who are watching the work-abroad trend are optimistic. "It is not a brain drain but an enhancement of the brain power of the U.S.," says William Glavin, a former vice chairman of Xerox and now president of Boston College. Glavin also believes the returning expatriates are receiving and returning with invaluable training they cannot get at home.

- "A major problem in corporate America is a lack of global management knowledge. They are not going to learn much from managers in the U.S.," says William Hasler, the dean of the Haas School of Business at the University of California, Berkeley. He feels his recent grads who opt for overseas options are "very positive, because most of these people will end up working for American companies and will be able to make those more successful and globalized."

- "Any businessperson who doesn't have a global perspective is either dead or dumb," says Abraham Krasnoff, the CEO of Pall Corporation.

What did you go to college for, anyway?
To get a good education, to make yourself
more marketable, and to increase the
prospects of getting a good job.

Go abroad for the exact same reasons.

OUT OF COLLEGE: OUT OF COUNTRY

Today's job prerequisites are becoming more and more specialized and demanding. The days of finishing college and just walking into a good job are now almost all technology specific. Besides experience, it is the intangible assets of an individual that job interviewers are keenly looking for.

Such intangibles include: a basic knowledge of technology; general skills in oral and written communications; critical thinking and flexibility; the ability to work as part of a team; to get along well with others; and to focus on a task. Essentially, being an adaptable person is key.

Traveling, perhaps better than college, teaches you all of these.

Everyday in non-English-speaking counties you will have to strive to make yourself understood. Writing in your journal helps you to improve penmanship skills. The ability to read maps and navigate for yourself, as well as comprehend local customs, will make you a more flexible thinker. Traveling with other Stompers naturally makes you more apt to compromise and get along with others. Planning and executing a world tour requires considerable focus, and adapting to travel conditions as they arise are perhaps a traveler's greatest asset.

Traveling enriches like nothing else. Self-betterment, cultural enhancement, and a certain esoteric perspective coalesce, resulting in a more well-rounded person.

Earthlings

Low man on the totem pole.

"It is said a man's life can be measured by the dreams he fulfills."
Mr. Roarke
Fantasy Island

Freedom

*In my youth I stressed freedom, and in my old age I stress order.
I have made the great discovery that liberty is a product of order.*
— Will Durant, *Time*, 1965

Freedom is just another word for nothing left to lose. In Stomping terms, when the time, money, and desire goals are in place, and the decision to live life to the fullest is made, freedom comes very naturally. Just because it isn't the norm doesn't mean that it can not nor should not be done. John F. Kennedy once said in an address, "Conformity is the jailer of freedom and the enemy of growth."

Freedom is synonymous with America. It was fought for in the American revolution and confirmed in the Civil War. It was the catalyst for women's equality and the civil rights movement. Even today it remains the most powerful and compelling ideal keeping this nation whole. Many Americans live and die for that word. So why do so few of us exercise our freedom in terms of world travel?

The modern-age enlightened mystic Osho says, "Nobody can make you free. Freedom is your choice."

Why are we meant to walk this planet? To stay in one place, grow up, get a job, raise a family, retire, and die? What does it really mean to be human? To Stompers, it means meeting interesting people and exploring the monuments and relics of humankind's glorious past. A climb into an Egyptian pyramid tomb, an exploration of the ancient Roman Forum, meditation in front of the Taj Mahal, or a stroll along the Great Wall of China. To stare out into the great expanse of the Australian desert and wonder how it is you arrived there. To be totally portable to go anywhere, at anytime, and have all the possessions you need to tour the planet on your back. These advoyages and many other transcendental experiences abroad introduce one's imagination to the magnificence of our civilization and collective consciousness. It is seeing the planet on your own terms that epitomizes World Stomping.

To be conscious of what's happening in the world, past and present, makes a person feel more aware and in tune with the complexities of life. The slow death of planet Earth is rather evident on all the circuits, and to see for yourself the abused environment is somehow sadly enlightening. You never know if you might be the final person to trek in a particular ancient rainforest, or observe a primitive tribe for the last time in their native habitat. And, strange as it may sound, it also allows an individual to feel more human (if not depressed) to see our human made tragedies. The real casualty, after all, is humanity, and all we have allowed ourselves to become.

F R E E D O M

In essence, freedom is a state of mind. Freedom must be worked for, but it starts with your belief system and it shows in your actions. Sometimes it takes time away from your hometown family and friends to realize how diverse and free the world really is. It takes time to evolve into the person you want to be. And it takes a great amount of desire to get there. The eminent German writer and scientist Goethe once said, "From the power that binds all beings, that man frees himself who overcomes himself."

Freedom is also exhibited in one's ability to make the money to travel, and then execute the desired trip. Very few people of the world have the money-making possibilities as U.S. citizens have. Freedom means unlimited potential, which explains why so many would-be immigrants wish to enter this country.

Traveling should be an individual statement; don't rely on a guide book too much.

Get a general idea of what part of the world, or country, you want to see from a travel guide book. Use it for maps, history, statistics, basic layout of the land, and travel info. The restaurant guide is usually worthless, and lodging recommendations are only rarely worth consulting.

Rely on your feelings and what you hear from others. Some of the best-kept secrets are usually well off the beaten track and not featured in travel guide books at all. Mostly when the guide books tell you to go somewhere, that place is swarmed with tourists reading the same book. Some veteran Stompers go into countries without a guide book at all, and feel even more liberated as a result. Don't try this until you have traveled a bit and basically know what to expect. However, after a few circuits, you'll see it's all pretty much the same song and dance the world 'round.

People go on world tours for totally different reasons. The following is a top ten list of those different personality types and their motivations for being out there. Every traveler falls into one or most of these categories. All exhibit their freedom in one way or another.

Top Ten Types of Travelers:

10. The Escapist – Needs to get away from a present situation.

9. The Travel Snob – Goes to exotic places just to come home and brag about them.

8. Thrill Sex-Seeker – Goes abroad to get laid.

7. The Partier – Goes abroad to get wasted.

6. Spiritual Seekers – Specifically travels to holy sites, sacred places, or ashrams.

5. The Learner – Either an academic or just-plain-curious type.

4. Professionals – Travels on business or is an expatriate living abroad.

3. The Adventurer – Enjoys physical trips like canoeing down the Congo River in Africa or trekking in Nepal.

2. Tourists – Arrive in tour busses and leave shortly thereafter. Tourists snap a lot of photos, cover a lot of ground, but don't stay long enough to observe natural patterns emerge.

1. Students – Still in school or just out of school, learning about life and learning about themselves.

EARTHLINGS

Bazooka Joe takes off.

"To seek freedom, a man must struggle. To win it, he must choose wisely where and when he struggles, or it is like spitting in the wind."
Caine
Kung Fu

The Renegade Move

Look with favor upon a bold beginning.
– Virgil, 30 B.C.

Try something new. Take the great escape. Venture into *terra incognita*. Travel around the planet. Set off on an adventure of a lifetime. These things can only happen after making the commitment to the word "Go!" Make the Renegade Move.

The break from old ways is always difficult, but absolutely necessary in making a world tour come true. To leave behind the security of home and set off into unknown territories is a big jump for a lot of people, but there is no way to discover new oceans unless you have the courage to lose sight of the shore. An old maritime proverb notes that the sailor who will not put to sea until all dangers are over, will never put to sea.

**The hardest thing about long-term travel is just
getting all affairs settled and busting out.
That is making the Renegade Move.**

Start with a Positive Mind-Set

One month before my graduation from Illinois State University, the College of Business I was attending sponsored "Career Day," and all my lectures had been canceled as a result. It was a beautiful spring day outside and I was delighted to have the day free to play Hackey-Sack and Frisbee.

When my senior classmates from the College of Business walked by in their three-piece suits, they were astonished to see me having a good time on such an important day. "Olsen!" some of them shouted, "Why aren't you dressed? Why are you blowing this off?" Laughing at them, I exclaimed I was not into making good impressions and phony self-promotions. I also said, "I'm just not interested in starting a career... yet. I've got my whole life to work away, what is the damn hurry to start so soon?" When they asked what I was going to do with my life, I told them, "Get out of the Midwest and travel."

Confused by my lack of priorities, they marched off to shove some résumés around. I kept myself blissfully uncommitted to anything, except fulfilling my curiosities about the world.

**Do not think you are necessarily on the right track just
because it is a well-beaten path.**

The enlightened mystic Osho has some good words on this. "It is easy to become part of the society and get into the rut; it is difficult to get out of it. And once you are in the rut, you start becoming afraid. What will happen if you get out of it? You will lose money, you will lose this, you will lose that. But you are losing your life all the time! Life should be the supreme value. Nothing should be put above life. Never sacrifice your life for any-thing! Sacrifice everything for life! Life is the ultimate goal – greater than any god, greater than any scripture. But no leader is going to say that to you, because then their whole business is gone. No priest is going to say that to you, because then their whole business is gone."

Challenge the Unknown

Setting off into unknown lands is very difficult for many people. This is especially tough if the traveler has no contacts, job offers, or is going solo. These were real fears I had setting out, and after I overcame them, the old Franklin D. Roosevelt saying, "We have nothing to fear but fear itself" made a lot more sense. I never let the fear of the unknown hinder my travel dreams; rather, I allowed it only to enhance and challenge me. My conclusion is that nothing in life is to be feared. It is only to be understood.

Pre-Stomp jitters affect us all. Good advice is this: don't think about it too much. Make your preparations, research your destination, finalize your business, say your good-byes and just get on the plane and bail. Do not let the unknown scare you. Instead, make it your greatest thrill, your biggest challenge and your driving force to succeed.

Mark Twain once wrote in a letter, "All you need to know in this life is ignorance and confidence, and then success is sure." Worrying will only give you an ulcer, nothing else. There is just no way to know how everything on your trip is going to turn out.

**Sometimes you are better off not knowing everything –
it *increases* your excitement and freedom.**

When you arrive at your destination, it is remarkable how fast the mind collects data on what needs to be known. *Just put yourself in a situation that requires results and you will get results.* Accommodations are found, friends are quickly made, information discovered, jobs located, apartments set up, and good times had. Inquiring minds want to know, and this is ever so true on the Stomp.

The important thing is simply getting yourself over there, and then figuring things out. It's not that hard. Aristotle advised, "For the things we have to learn before we can do them, we learn by doing them."

Traveling is like the acorn that grows into the mighty oak. First, get the seed into fertile soil, and give it what it needs. When the young tree grows, it branches out and establishes roots. Soon enough the trunk is solid enough to survive the harshest weather *and* continue growing. Point is, start small and let it grow. Don't expect everything overnight.

It is amazing how many times things seem to fall into place just by asking politely or by being in the right place at the right time. Swami Dyhan Santosh waxing poetic:

Good restaurants, a place to stay.
A drag off a joint, a good lay.
A hike up a mountain or a job to be had,
A free ride to town with a girl scantily clad.

A friendly and positive attitude goes a very long way when you are Stomping solo. There is no reason to bring along your anxieties on a world tour. No one wants to hear about self-pitying slop. A popular travel proverb advises; "If you wish to travel far and fast, travel light. Take off all your jealousies, unforgiveness, selfishness and fears."

Top Ten Things Extensive Travel Helps People Overcome:

10. **Neurotic tendencies and hang-ups.** (Crybabies don't last long.)

9. **Despair.** (Don't worry, be happy!)

8. **Inability to be assertive or confrontational.** (Only if necessary.)

7. **Prejudice.** (Black, white, yellow, red, green – we're all the same.)

6. **Shyness.** (Make friends or be lonely, it's your choice.)

5. **Attitude problems.** (Hardasses are ignored.)

4. **Western society's short-sighted goals on an individuals future.** (The meaning of the good life in reflection to how others live.)

3. **Poor money management skills.** (Blow your money quick and it's all over quick.)

2. **Reliance on other people.** (Anyone but yourself.)

1. **Fear of the unknown.** (Stompers' greatest challenge!)

No one can predict the outcome of a long adventure. There are inevitably going to be good times, bad times, and ugly times. The important thing is just doing it, having a good time, and not being afraid. This is character building that will enrich you for the rest of your life.

Live by the Go-For-It-Attitude and roll with the punches.

Forget all those self-help gurus and their multi-level marketing schemes. Go abroad to learn about yourself. There is nothing in the world that can make you a better person than the world itself. The amount of money people waste on psychiatrists could pay for many years of World Stomping.

Osho further advocates, "Go out! The world is beautiful, adventurous; it is a challenge, it enriches. Don't lose that opportunity! Whenever the world knocks at your door and calls you, go out! Go out fearlessly... there is nothing to lose, there is everything to gain."

"Time and Ed wait for no man."
Mr. Ed

The American Image: Cultural Champions

Feel by turns the bitter change
Of fierce extremes, extremes by change more fierce.
— John Milton, *Paradise Lost* (1667)

Until you leave the United States and observe the changing attitudes and cultures abroad, this may be very hard to believe: The world is becoming American.

Nobody's forcing anything on anyone. In fact, quite the opposite is true. The American Image is welcomed and admired and cool in the global community. The freedom we represent and the look of Hollywood is incredibly alluring to the masses of TV viewers worldwide. Global consumerism is the ultimate goal of capitalism and is actualizing before our very eyes, before we can understand its far-reaching implications. As multinational companies continue their relentless power search for new markets abroad, they are unwittingly changing the make-up of cultures around the planet.

Clothes, MTV, fast food, music, glamour magazines, Coca-Cola, Mickey Mouse, cigarettes, plastic surgery, and television are all sweeping the globe. The entertainment industry is now one of America's top exports. What *we* as Americans take for granted every day is destroying traditional customs, rituals, religion, clothing, and attitudes worldwide. The biggest casualty of all are the hundreds of ancient traditions and isolated languages around the planet which are falling into complete obscurity, in some cases within a single generation. These are the perils of a globalized civilization. It can't be helped. After all, change is inevitable and constant in a progressive society.

It's just that nowadays it is happening so damn quick.

Lifestyles and customs that have fiercely resisted the attempts of foreign powers to dominate and subvert them over many centuries have fallen to Hollywood in a decade. Thailand is the perfect example.

Except for their wearing kimonos on certain holidays, the Japanese dress and consume almost identically to their American big brothers — including gala Christmas celebrations — despite the fact that fewer than one percent of the population is Christian. Societies in Africa which passed on folklore through song and dance for centuries now prefer Michael Jackson. English is spoken in almost every corner of the globe. The dollar is king. Blue jeans are everywhere — just ask any Russian what he wants the most. *The Bold and the Beautiful* in India. The world's largest McDonalds in Beijing. Disneyland in France?!?

A homogeneous global lifestyle

As our world becomes more closely linked and culturally homogenized through trade, travel, films, music, and TV, the less likely it becomes that vulnerable cultures will retain their original essence and character. Although some will try to prevent this, or make the full-swing back to their identities, once the people embrace "Westernization," the ball is in motion.

Every day, over four million people fly from one place on the globe to another. By the year 2004, predicts the International Air Transport Association of Washington, D.C., that figure will be up to six million per day. This is good news for the Stomper because increased competition lowers airfares – and bad news for isolated cultures suddenly swamped with tourists.

Indeed, TV is the great equalizer, and it is portraying the U.S. lifestyle as glamorous, wealthy, violent – a decadent paradise the likes of which these people would like to call their own but will likely never realize. Nevertheless, emerging economic nations imitating the West love the American Image, and do not want to give it up. In 1983, the Tuareg tribe, the largest primitive group in the Sahara, delayed their yearly annual migration for 10 days in order to catch the last episode of *Dallas*. According to the distributors of *Baywatch,* the world's most pervasive TV show, the program reaches 2.4 billion people per week and is broadcast in 110 countries on every continent except Antarctica. People's lives are generally boring and TV delivers false fantasy. That's when the mighty marketers hawk our products and the whole cycle comes to life. Everyone dreams of a better life, and the American media "delivers."

But there can be a backlash. Ethnocentric Americans – who ironically do not even *see* America as an ethnic group in and of itself (and a monster one at that) – are regularly scorned for loud voices and strong opinions in Europe. France recently passed laws outlawing the usage of English in advertising. In the 1970s and 80s, Western hostage-taking was popular in the Middle East because of a perceived lack of respect for Islam, among other things. During the 1994 World Cup the audiences in Iran were shown dubbed-in scenes of fans dressed in winter clothing despite blazing hot temperatures. The Iranian censors did not want to corrupt the masses with images of Western women in halter tops, people drinking booze, and soccer fans just plain having fun.

Totalitarian governments like Iran can isolate their people for only so long. When it finally loosens up, the floodgates will pour. Iran will quickly find itself in a race to acquire Western goods and standards of living much in the same way that the Russians did. Everyone knows that whenever you tell someone they cannot have something, they only want it more.

John Naisbitt, in his famous book *Megatrends*, states:
"Change occurs when there is a confluence of both
changing values and economic necessity, not before."

Naisbitt expands on the theme in *Megatrends 2000*: "The emerging global lifestyle walks a thin line between greater options and greater homogenization, which decreases options.

"Unlike cheeseburgers and jeans, the globalization of TV is explosive and controversial because it conveys deeper values the way literature does. It goes right to the (heart) of a culture, addressing fundamentalist spirit that informs its beliefs and practices."

With the flick of a switch, a farmer in a mud-brick hut is transported into *The Lifestyles of the Rich and Famous*. These lifestyles of previously unimaginable opulence suddenly come to life on a little screen in front of him and plants the seed of living a better life and acquiring material wealth. Such images have helped fuel a tide of rural migration to already overcrowded cities, further exacerbating strains on resources, living space and standards of living. In addition, these images of luxury are enticing the best and the brightest to seek that better life abroad.

So what if some things like religion, old traditions, and lousy food are not desired or respected anymore by a young and more liberated generation?

Who or what can stop them from shutting out the old and embracing the new?

Shouldn't everyone have the freedom to choose?

The only problem is that the Western lifestyle is emerging as a false Eden. Powerfully alluring on the outside, but empty, superficial, and materialistic at its core, fueled by a never-ending odyssey called "consumerism" that the developing world wishes to emulate.

Imagine the state of atmospheric pollution if every Indian and Chinese person had his own car like us Americans?

The desire certainly exists, and the reality is not too far off. And the dilemma is this: You cannot deny them. No, instead the West embraces India's and China's and other developing countries' newly realized craving to consume. India has 400 million TV viewers and China has an audience of 600 million. Market potential is enormous.

A Snickers bar is one thing, a rainforest another. The vicious cycle is catching up and we are all the ultimate victims. The greater the demand by the people of the world to have what Americans have, the more the environment will suffer.

The American Dream, with all the elements of conspicuous consumption, could quickly become Planet Earth's nightmare. Overzealous consumerism is not meant for six billion people, except in the minds of greedy profiteers and manufacturers.

When a country sheds traditional dress for miniskirts in Vietnam, banana leaves for plastic in Thailand, chats with grandpa for *Beverly Hills 90210* in Brazil, religious icons for Bugs Bunny in India ...

What is being lost here?

Lure a generation or two away from centuries of cultural evolution, and will they ever again rediscover their lost heritage?

It's an ever-changing world that is rapidly attaining a rather boring feel and generic flavor – and there is nothing the mass media and multinational companies want to do about it.

Stomp the world now – before the shadow of the Golden Arches stretches completely across 24 time zones – and we cosume the planet into oblivion.

Earthlings

The Bushmen of McDonalds.

"Hey Alex – you know the really great thing about television? If something important happens, anywhere in the world, night or day... you can always change the channel."
Reverend Jim Ignatowski
Taxi

Women Stompers

If you think you can, you can. And if you think you can't, you're right.
— Mary Kay Ash, *New York Times*, 1985

Who ever said adventure travel was just for men? No one! As more women in Western nations assert their independence and discover their lack of limitations, industry experts predict women will increasingly turn to adventure travel. Research from McRand International indicates more women alone and more women with families are looking for adventure travel than ever before. Michael McClure, the president of McRand, shows data in the last few years of the growing percentage of women-to-men travelers. Growth rates are expected to expand from 45-65, to 50-50, to 60-40 in the coming future.

Susan Eckert, the owner of Rainbow Adventures in Evanston Illinois built her agency exclusively around women-only adventure traveling. She says more women are drifting away from a tendency to move into gender roles, such as men making the fire and women doing the cooking. Gone also are frets over makeup, hair and nails, and the idea that women must have their best friend come along.

"Most essential," Eckert says, "are a sense of humor and a willingness to be flexible and accept situations as they occur." She also believes women often discover something new about themselves, their bodies and become intimate with other cultures when they travel solo.

Women Stompers Testify

Women's attitudes about traveling differ as much as the people and places they go abroad to experience. Some are tough and rugged travelers who do just fine on their own. Others prefer to travel with a man, or in a large group of men and women. Some like to play up their femininity for special attention. Different women travel in different ways.

The following viewpoints attempt to span the wide array of Women Stomper pros and cons.

Unfortunately, gender *is* an issue, and women *are* treated differently in certain countries. The following is exactly how it was reported, and in no way should it come across as condescending or offending.

Caroline "Rockie" is from London, England, and she bought a one-year, around-the-world airline ticket with a friend. "I left initially with someone I knew to get over the fear of traveling alone. The girl I left with was kinda weird so we made an agreement to split up if either of us wanted to. After a month, I wanted to." For the next eleven months Rockie went solo, hooking up with other travelers when she felt like having company, enjoying her privacy when she didn't.

WOMEN STOMPERS

Pros:
- Meeting very cool guys is rarely a problem.
- It is men who usually run bars and guesthouses so you can use your femininity to score discounts.
- Traveling alone you will meet way more people.
- Good credibility when hitchhiking (with a man), or rapport with locals.

Cons:
- Might find Stomping harder work than men, and have to deal with very different situations than men.
- Lack of safety, security, and sexual harassment. Grabby guys when alone in crowded places, or macho locals may approach and hassle you. But if you stand up and be bold to them they will back down. Or better yet, just ignore them.
- May hold back from adventure and risks unless there is a man in the group.
- Women may get odd treatment in different societies. For example, Turkish men find harassing women normal, second class status is common in most Asian nations, and conservative dress is a necessity in Muslim countries.

Kelly D. is an Australian who prefers to travel solo. Personally, she feels traveling is extremely stimulating and kills apathy. She says, "Extensive travel makes you curious and want to learn about different cultures, ways of life, languages, etc. It can also put your own everyday life into perspective, often revealing how absurd the Western rat-race really is. Best of all, traveling is a major buzz!!!"

Pros:
- Traveling alone gives you a real feeling of achievement because of the challenges you face.
- You become street-wise very quickly.
- Traveling can be a truly liberating experience.

Cons:
- You have to deal with all the negatives a guy has to, and many other ridiculously sleazy situations!
- You are always aware of your gender and reminded of your sexuality in a Muslim country.
- You want to be friendly, but friendliness towards a man can often be taken the wrong way.
- Possible harassment from men and threats to personal safety can limit what decisions you make. This also makes you self-conscious and a little too suspicious of people.

Sue K. is an American from Florida who sees solo traveling as a woman's ultimate expression of her freedom. Her advice for young women thinking of traveling, "DO IT! No matter how many downs there are, there are always more ups. Go with a positive mind set and be prepared for anything. It is well worth it, don't even be afraid to go alone!"

Pros:

- On most travel circuits there are tons of cute guys, far outnumbering girls. I have met way more really cool people from all over the world than I ever did in college.

- Superficially you get preferential treatment, like the lady's sleeper on trains, or rickshaw drivers who will carry your backpack door to door.

Cons:

- Access is limited in chauvinistic societies, such as some parts of Asia, Latin America, or Muslim nations.

- A chance to meet locals are occasionally inhibited by being a woman. Men pay attention to men; local women sometimes see Western women as intruders, hence cold receptions.

- There are times you must change your demeanor and avoid eye-contact for fear of giving a man a come on. This can give you tunnel vision and make you less observant.

- Hard to get exercise. Cannot just go for a jog anytime.

Katja M. is from the Netherlands and did most of her Stomping with her boyfriend. When they broke up in India, she was happy to see a bit of the country solo. Her advice, "Maybe take a self-defense course if you are going solo, or a bitchy attitude also works well. If a man ever touches me, I hit him immediately. I do it instinctively." No one has ever hit her back and it usually surprises Asian men so much they begin apologizing profusely.

Pros:

- You can play the helpless woman sometimes. Most men don't mind helping out a woman in trouble.

- Never a problem meeting really nice guys when traveling.

- Easy to hitch with a man or girlfriend.

Cons:

- Hassles from local men, just a smile can get a guy going.

- Potential harassment in public places (bus stands, markets, beaches) can be frustrating.

- Does not like to be touched by strangers.

- A solo Western woman in other cultures may be seen as "easy," or in need of a man.

In retrospect, all four have no doubt traveling was considerably easier than they had once thought. Rape is extremely rare, and none of these women ever feared it might happen to them. Rockie says, "It was the best year of my life. Now I'd definitely go traveling alone, unless there was someone I was really compatible with." Katja finds a much greater appreciation for the native land she comes from and her family. She also feels a lot more confident with herself, and has some amazing stories to tell for the rest of her life.

The Human Aspect

One is never done with knowing the greatest men or the greatest works of art
— they carry you on and on, and at last you feel that you are only beginning.
— T.R. Glover

Surprises Around Every Corner

From the Travel Journal (Apr. 6, '94) Dahab, Egypt

A normal day of getting things done on the Sinai Peninsula. Today I went into town with my girlfriend Katja to change money and pick up a few things from the market. As we were walking along, a local Egyptian in a pickup truck stopped and offered us a lift to town in the back with two brothers from South Africa. We accepted, jumped in back, and started chatting with the brothers. They told us about their travels and recent jobs on an Israeli kibbutz (I always made it my business to ask others about their work and adventures abroad).

On the way back to the beach, the driver unexpectedly pulled into his home and beckoned us to come inside. Unbeknown to Katja and myself, the Afrikaans brothers wanted to purchase some ganja. Inside the mud hut, the shesha water pipe came out and we began sampling some Dahab local yield, while the brothers haggled over prices. Joining us in the cool clay dwelling was the driver's family: the daughter pouring us tea, the wife breast-feeding a newborn, and several kids staring wide-eyed from the doorway. It was so wild getting stoned with a Bedouin family that probably look, dress, and live the same way today as they have for centuries (apart from the pickup truck).

These are the kind of spontaneous moments indicative of what World Stomping really means. Do not misunderstand, Dahab was a wonderful place. Here travelers discover the rugged Sinai desert meeting the crystal clear waters of the Red Sea, lazy days on the beach, scuba diving at the Blue Hole, and climbing nearby Mt. Sinai where Moses received the Ten Commandments. Certainly all these things are fond recollections, but it is the personal encounters that imprint the deepest travel memories.

The impressions of how the other half lives and how they go about their day-to-day existence is when traveling becomes the most enriching. The people of the world are the interactive aspect which reveal the most color. Reflecting upon so many travel memories: hitchhiking around Australia, the craziness of everything in Vietnam, backpacking across Europe, teaching English in Japan, trekking the Himalayas. All these places and activities were a total blast, but looking back on these wonderful times, it is almost invariably the Human Aspect — the friends and the wacky people — that comes to mind. The fact that you meet the coolest people while playing and partying in the most beautiful scenery around the world makes it even all the better.

Looking back on my photos I flip past the postcard shots of beautiful scenes. What I linger over are the portraits of the people I've met abroad – the Human Aspect.

Every conscientious traveler sets out with the goal of getting to know a few locals in the country they are visiting. Kudos to those who do, but it's not always that easy. In touristy areas the locals view you as a walking dollar sign and are not so interested in talking to you unless you are spending money. In rural and less touristed areas the language differences often create insurmountable barriers. Some people have a hard time overcoming their shyness to break the ice and start a conversation. But in any case at all, a smile and a sense of humor are the best ways to get along with locals, everything falling into place later.

The most regular and funniest travel encounters come from other travelers, especially other Americans, Canadians, Europeans, or Australians. A veteran Stomper is typically on guard when first talking to a local; he is much more relaxed and at ease around people in his own circumstances. Communication is easy with Western travelers, backgrounds are similar, and travel stories relate. Encounters with locals become all the more interesting, and safer, in the company of Western travel friends.

Getting to Know a Local

Having an inside connection makes the experience of being in a strange place even better, but more times than not, there is some sort of hustle involved (sorry as I am to report this). I'm usually cautious when it comes to befriending locals. Maybe I missed some golden opportunities to meet really cool natives, or maybe I avoided being let down. Nevertheless, one genuine local beat my skepticism and is someone I shall never forget.

Peema was his name and he was a descendant of the Sherpa mountain clan of Nepal. The Sherpas were porters for Sir Edmund Hillary and Tenzing Norkay on their historic ascent of Mt. Everest in 1953. Peema can recall as a child the excitement in the village when the climbers returned.

I met Peema in a small restaurant in Darjeeling, a village high up in the Indian Himalayas. We talked about Buddhism in the mountain villages and he told me how he would like to become a monk someday. I really enjoyed his stories and accepted his invitation to meet his Sherpa family over some tea. On the way to his home, many of his friends and village merchants greeted us. Later, the merchants gave me "local prices" on foodstuffs I needed to buy. Peema's home resembled a Buddhist shrine and the family was delighted to meet me. The next day, Peema helped me arrange a permit to trek in Sikkim, which can be difficult to get. The more I thanked Peema for helping me, the more he shied away. He would not even allow me to buy him a meal, and his family gave me some nice gifts when I departed. I sent them a few family portraits, and still keep in touch with Peema.

Drinking With Foreign Men

The best way to get along with Asian men, or men of developing countries, is to be their over-friendly drinking pal. Drinking booze is a chauvinistic man's thing in many parts of the world, but it can be a really funny experience for both Western men and women.

When Far-East Asian men are getting drunk and buying drinks, they like a somewhat belligerent friend who is endearing to them. Kinda like the drunk uncle at a wedding. Give 'em hugs, punch their shoulder, and dance really bad. When there are no women around, all they want to talk about is girls. For best results (them buying more drinks), spin a tall tale and share a hearty laugh.

Talk the Talk, Walk the Walk

Naturally it helps to meet quality locals if you can speak some of their native language. Each country you visit, you'll pick up a few basic things like, "hello, how much? Good-bye." No one ever has any trouble buying things by using gestures, sign-language or simply showing money. Just speak slowly and clearly, and keep eye contact.

Speaking any language conversationally requires a lot of discipline and rote memory skills. A further problem is there can be many different languages in each circuit or country you visit, each breaking down further into regional dialects.

To help overcome the language barrier try to: learn as much of the region's language before visiting; use sign language; speak simple English slowly; point to phrases in a guidebook; and simplify your words and gestures as much as possible.

Numbers, apart from Arab countries and China, are all in English or show the equivalent. Nearly everyone, especially merchants, can count one to a hundred in English. But you should still enunciate just the same, "Soda, ten rupee, yea?"

Proper English in some parts will not do and locals won't know what you're saying. Listen and imitate their version of pidgin English. Everyone worldwide knows these: "Good, no good. No have. Yes? Is possible? I can pay?" Abbreviate everything, and end sentences with, "Yea?" to make sure you're understood.

Quite paradoxically, sometimes locals wish for you to speak to them in English so they can listen and learn and improve their skills. Teaching friendly locals a bit of English is a great way to make pals – with children and adults alike.

EARTHLINGS

Epics of Man.

Earthlings

**Young Papillion makes his
first escape.**

Part

2

Preparing for the Stomp

When you look at the world in a narrow way, how narrow it seems! ... When you look at it selfishly, how selfish it is! But when you look at it in a broad, generous, friendly spirit, what wonderful people you then find in it.
— Horace Rutledge

Life is what happens while you are making other plans.
— John Lennon

If you have no money, be polite.
— Danish proverb

Your mother was a hamster and your father smelt of elderberries. Now go away before I taunt you for a second time.
— French Tower Guard, 1104 AD

'O brave new world that has such people in it. Let's start at once.
— Aldous Huxley

Staying Fit

Don't compromise yourself. You are all you've got.
– Janis Joplin

While you are out world touring you will find that being young is a great advantage – if you are in shape. This is an edge young people have over, say, the average retired bluehair tourist. Because our bodies are newer and stronger, we are more resilient to sickness. We also have greater endurance to do and see more per day, and we are quicker to adapt to different climates without incident. We can also recover from hangovers faster.

If you give little regard to your body now, it will not help you later on down the road. Sure, a lazy and unfit person can still have a great time and get around well enough, and hell, being lazy is sometimes the most fun of traveling. But the point is to keep your edge and have the option of being active open. Besides, this book is not for unmotivated couch potatoes anyhow.

Let's face it, traveling can be tough work sometimes. Lugging your backpack around place to place, sightseeing on foot or by bike, climbing, running, hitchhiking, playing on the beach, whatever. You will need to be in shape and you will want to look and feel good, especially when chatting up the babes in a far away place.

Lofty station is, like one's body,
a source of great trouble.
The reason one has great trouble is that
he has a body. When he no longer
has a body, what trouble will he have?
Thus: he who values his body more than
dominion over the empire
Can be entrusted with the empire.
And he who loves his body more than
dominion over the empire
Can be given custody of the empire.

– Lao-Tzu - Tao Te Ching-

Get in Shape

Physical requirements vary greatly according to the type of trip planned. A brisk 20 minute walk or jog, three times a week for two months before departure would be the minimum required regimen. An exercise bicycle, treadmill, or aerobic classes' offer alternative options to cardiovascular strength. Yoga is also highly recommended.

If you plan on doing some trekking, extend your weekly walks to a couple of hours with extra time walking up hills, or join a health club and use the stair machine. Wear a day pack and fill it with 10 kilograms of weight to simulate a typical load on the trail.

Sit-ups, or crunches, strengthen the stomach muscles and reduce the risk of back problems. Roll-ups are good too. Lie on your back, with feet flat on the floor and knees angled at 90 degrees. Then, with hands behind the head, raise your torso as far as you can. Repeat several times until you feel a good "burn" in your stomach muscles. It won't take long.

If you are in good physical condition already, try harder to reach your optimum state. If you are in poor shape now – *do not wait* – start a workout program immediately.

Pre-Stomp Workouts

Since walking is a major part of world touring, I suggest you become used to it. While riding my mountain bike to work every day in Japan was healthy, it was not a proper workout for the upcoming Stomp. I forced myself to jog three times a week for cardiovascular strength and to prepare my legs for the long walk ahead. I also lifted weights and played basketball regularly, and it paid off. When I left Japan for my world tour I was in the best shape of my life. Apart from an occasional cold, only once did I get sick on my three year journey (see: Setbacks). I largely attribute this good fortune to my pre-travel dedication to regular workouts.

Wasteoids

Some people travel with the sole expressed purpose of being wasted on booze and drugs the entire time. Hey, it's their life and to each his own. However, being sucked into a party animal lifestyle is not a difficult thing to do when you're far away from home and life is but a dream.

Moderation is the key to anything on the Stomp, or even life for that matter. There is nothing wrong with "Going Sai." It keeps your immune system strong and your senses alert for potential danger.

The personification to remember is the Hindu God Shree Sai Baba. He appears all over India and seems to be gesturing, "No thank you, I'm already very high."

Staying fit on the Stomp

Workouts you had done on a regular basis will be tough to continue while traveling, because now you're leading irregular days. This is payoff time anyhow. I found sit-ups, squats, push-ups, and pull-ups kept me quite fit along the way. A frequent beach jog (when available) and long daily walks afforded me new sights and a great overall feeling.

Additionally, each new spot offered a variety of activities and the local popular sport to sample. Canoeing in Thailand, surfing in Indonesia, scuba diving in Australia, volleyball in Goa, horseback riding in Egypt, trekking in Nepal, windsurfing in Maui, and bike riding in China. Nearly every beach offered some combination of snorkeling, frisbee, body-surfing, paddle-ball, and swimming. And don't forget sex – that's a workout too. Being into many kinds of sports, I enjoyed them all on my world tour.

Top Ten Things To Avoid on the Stomp

10. **Altitude Sickness.** From hiking too high too fast.

9. **Bedbugs.** Check the mattresses in new rooms for blood spots before you agree to stay there.

8. **Rabies.** Dogs sometimes chase you when jogging, and bite you if they can.

7. **Scorpions.** Scorpion stings are hideously painful and they are known to shelter in clothes or shoes.

6. **Leeches and Ticks.** Leeches and ticks lurk in damp rainforest conditions, attach themselves to you, and suck your blood. Both should be removed immediately, but not pulled off. Remove leeches with salt or a lighted cigarette end, and ticks with Vaseline, alcohol, or oil.

5. **Bike Riding Accidents.** Drivers around the world are notoriously spastic and speed way too fast on narrow streets. Always play it safe and give way to lunatics.

4. **Parasites.** Always get a room with a mosquito net in tropical zones and get in the habit of putting on insect repellent. Those nasty bugs not only bite, they spread malaria and dengue fever.

3. **Snake and Spider Bites.** On any wilderness trek, no matter how hot it is, wear boots, socks and a shirt. This will minimize the risk of a bite breaking the skin.

2. **Decompression Sickness.** When scuba diving, it is very important to ascend slowly and allow the body to release excess nitrogen. If you come up too fast you can get "the bends" and become very sick or possibly die.

1. **Sexually Transmitted Diseases.** When you're feeling cocky, use a socky! AIDS is rampant in parts of Asia and Africa, and you just never know who is a carrier anymore.

Inscribed on the Greek temple of Apollo at Delphi are the words, "Know thyself." Good advice on Preparing for the Stomp.

EARTHLINGS

Leonardo da Vinci. Florentine artist, engineer, musician, and inventor of the jumping jacks.

Setbacks

To conquer without risk is to triumph without glory.
– Pierre Corneille, Le Cid, 1636

John F. Kennedy once said in a speech, "When written in Chinese, the word *crisis* is composed of two characters. One represents danger and the other represents opportunity." When traveling, and so in life, crises always seem to come up at one time or another. That's life. Shit happens. Murphy's law. Whatever. Inevitable setbacks happen on the road.

Yet, things rarely turn out as bad as they first might seem. "Never find your delight in another's misfortune," said the Roman statesman, Publilius Syrus; but learning through examples is the best teacher. So, here's a collection of some miserable setback stories from the front lines.

Ripped-off in Europe

My first solo journey was to backpack all around Europe in the summer of 1988. I set off on a one-way ticket to London, England, holding my passport, a two-month Eurail pass, two thousand dollars in traveler's checks, a Walkman with 10 tapes, a camera, a suitcase full of clothes, a toiletry kit, and a sleeping bag. I hooked up with a cool Australian guy named Richard who had bought a station wagon car the month before. After we became friends, he asked me to tour with him in the car, so we split expenses on gas and zigzagged our way up England, through Wales, and into Scotland, having a jolly ol' time.

It was in Edinburgh where our luck changed. We stopped at a pub for a pint and a few laughs with the locals, and when we returned to the car we discovered a broken window and two absent backpacks. I lost all my possessions for the entire trip except the clothes I was wearing and my money belt. No more change of clothes, no camera, no travel guide or map, no sleeping bag, no Walkman, not even my toothbrush! Worst of all, no insurance. What luck; I was only into the second week of my three-month advoyage! Richard was in the same boat as me, except he had a car with a broken window now. We slept in the back of the wagon that night clenching our fists, vowing to kill the mofo who ripped us off in the remote chance he would return to the scene of the crime. Of course, he never did.

In the morning we soberly began considering our options. We contacted the police immediately after the break-in, and they asked if we could stay in town for a few days to see if anything would come up. So we had to hang out for a bit longer, but what to do? Should I get on the first plane back to the States? Scrap all my plans and chalk up one misadventure? What would I tell everyone when I got back so soon? I'm a quitter? *No way!* The go-for-it attitude got me out here alone, it will get me through this setback as well.

The police called a few days later with news that they had caught the thief trying to sell my camera in a pawn shop. I got my camera back but everything else was lost in the trash. With a new resolve to carry on, I bought a duffel bag and filled it with a few shirts, socks, a blanket, some underwear, shorts, and a Scottish sweater. I hurried through Ireland and made my way south to the warm Mediterranean climate as soon as I could. Needless to say, during the next three months I traveled Europe and the eastern U.S. *very* lightly!

As it turned out, although I hated losing my stuff, traveling light was really the way to go. The rest of the trip was very eye-opening. I had a great time and made many new friends who gave me the inspiration to plan – and eventually do – my fantastic world tour.

One thing is true when traveling: setbacks will occur, however large or small, in many different forms and fashions, and just about to everyone. This is not intended to scare, but rather to prepare. That way, when setbacks inevitably happen to you – and they will – the bite won't seem so painful. First, try to visualize your worst case scenarios and list what you can do to prevent them. Yes, death would be the worst – but death could also happen anytime to anyone, even non-travelers. So, that doesn't count. More realistically, the worst case is severe illness, or losing the life-supporting money belt. Stay very paranoid about your money belt at all times and have a back-up plan in case of severe illness. Otherwise, be aware of the pitfalls you may encounter and then you'll be all the more prepared when they come along.

Robbed of possessions and breath

Severe illness is something I've had to deal with overseas, and it's *not* one of the glamorous aspects of traveling. In my last year of college I developed a nasal dust allergy and bronchial asthma simultaneously. Both have proved to be a major pain (literally) and my hardest personal setback, particularly while traveling. Either symptom can be triggered at anytime, and without the proper medication, my life becomes a living hell. But let me stress again: only a setback, not a defeat. Both can be dealt with if I have an inhaler, but in European countries, like America, you need a prescription.

Imagine, if you will, every breath you take being uncomfortable and extremely painful ... wheezing ... and not being able to sleep. Not having (or wanting) to spend a lot of money to see a doctor and be told what you already know just to get a prescribed inhaler. Or groveling and pleading to chemists (pharmacists) all over Scotland and Ireland to sell you what you so desperately need (one finally took sympathy and sold me a unit in Dublin, Ireland). This was my situation when my pack was stolen and in two words, *it sucked*.

But, it *was* overcome, proving to me once again that where there's a will, there is indeed a way, no matter how hard it is to breathe.

Sickness in Varanassi, India

I was warned by Nadine, a fellow English teacher I knew in Japan, *not* to go to Varanassi, India. She told me how she became sick for weeks, and nearly died, after breathing the crematorium fumes from her hotel near the Ganges river. I ignored her warning and went to Varanassi anyway. Nadine was nearly 60 years old, so I figured there was no way she could possibly have the stamina I had, a young buck in the prime of my life. Besides, I really wanted to see the holy bathers on pilgrimage and the human remains being thrown into the river.

So anyway, I checked into a hotel far away from the river (heeding part of her warning), but still went on a boat cruise along the Ganges to see the burning ghats and floating body parts which, gruesome as it was, were quite fascinating. The next day the "Curse of Nadine" hit me hard and I became sick as a bastard. Maybe it was the pollution in the air, the Indian food, the filth on the streets, bad water, or the hex of Nadine's burning corpses. Whatever the cause was I still do not know, but I do know that I was afflicted by the worst health setback of my three-year world tour.

One ailment hit me after another for two weeks: the shits, the flu, razors in my stomach, asthma, severe chest bronchitis, weight loss, loss of appetite, no energy, heavy coughing, and brutal lung pains. It was no fun, especially the back-to-back night bus trips up to Katmandu, Nepal, in order to escape the cesspool called Varanassi. The bus ride from hell would not be complete without huge potholes every few minutes, crappy Indian music blaring all night, and extremely crammed conditions, which all worked to break my resistance even further.

By the time we reached Katmandu, I was extremely exhausted and bedridden for a week. I was traveling all this time with a British guy named Paul, who became sick as a dog the day after the boat ride in Varanassi as well. At least misery enjoyed some company. Neither one of us trusted the doctors in Varanassi nor Katmandu, so we bought and prescribed our own medicine. By the time I was well enough to travel again I did not have enough time on my one-month Nepalese visa to do the three-week trek I was looking forward to doing. I settled for an 11-day trek, and that workout finally restored my strength fully back to normal.

Get over a setback and move on – it's the only way.

People always make mistakes. The reassuring thing about making them while traveling is the environment is very forgiving. There are far more nice people out there than assholes. Most fellow travelers will help you out in a crisis (see: Traveler's Support Group). The locals want to see you leave okay too, because as a traveler you are one of their main sources of income. Besides, you are on vacation and you are supposed to be having fun!

Life is a Joke

Hotei the Laughing Buddha

Observe the shaman, monks, priests, and holy men on your world tour. You will see most of them living a life of poverty with no possessions and no money. Ask them how they can remain so blissfully happy under such harsh conditions. Their likely response is that life is one gigantic, elaborately funny joke, and they are merely playing a role in some twisted supernatural game. Why should they take life seriously?

If you can understand yourself as they do, life can seem to be a big charade. The holy men do not let petty things piss them off; they rejoice in being alive and accept any and all inevitable cosmic changes. Likewise, negative people and bad vibes bounce right off and do not affect their spirit.

Adopt the holy man credo: never take life too seriously. If a setback does occur, just remember, tomorrow is another day.

Con-Men Scams

All around the world there are con artists looking to pull a fast one on unsuspecting travelers.

Never believe any stories about the resale value of gems. The salesmen dress like native tourists and they greet you at temples, monuments or on the streets in many Asian cities. They come across like kind and swell chaps who want to let you in on a little secret. They will entice you with something like, "Did you know you can triple your money by buying gems here and reselling them in any jewelry store back in the States? Come to my shop and I'll show you many letters of satisfied customers and the profit scales you can make." Lies and scams.

One girl in Thailand bought a small satchel of gems from some slick salesdude and the next day realized she paid way too much for stones she didn't know anything about. She returned to the shop and the owner refused a refund. When she said she was going to the police, he pulled out a gun and advised against it. She began crying and one way or another finally got her money back.

Don't believe any quick buck stories from foreigners, either. Unscrupulous gemshop owners and con-artists are now using dishonest travelers to lure in native foreigners. Remember, there is no such thing as a government gemshop in Thailand.

Airline tickets are another big scam. Would you hand over $400 to someone whose "office" is a portable table in the back of a restaurant? Do you think he will be there tomorrow when you come back for a refund? Many a gullible traveler found that one out the hard way.

If it sounds too good to be true, it most definitely is!

Con-Men Scams from my Travel Journal

(Oct. 3, '93) As I was walking to the Taj Mahal in Agra, India, a boy on a scooter pulled up to say hello. This is not uncommon on an Asia street, because Western people usually draw a lot of attention. He seemed like a nice kid and asked me if I wanted a lift to the Taj on the back of his scooter. I said yes, and he drove me to the monument.

We got to talking and I learned he was Nepalese and from the village of Pokhara. I was planning to go trekking around the Pokhara area in a few weeks, so I agreed to meet him in the evening to continue our conversation over a few drinks and a spliff. He picked me up at my guesthouse and we went to meet his rich uncle in the textile business. The uncle was very kind and hospitable and asked me if I had time tomorrow, would I like to see his factory? I agreed.

(Oct. 4, '93) I tour the factory of virtual slave-laborers, and afterwards the uncle asks me if I would like to make some money. I listen, and he tells me how his dealers in Chicago have to pay heavy taxes when they order from him. Indian law states only so many rugs can go out before being hit by high taxes, and his dealers need more! If I put up $300 he can ship them in my name and avoid the taxes. When the dealer picks them up from my dad in three months, the dealer will pay my dad $900, tripling my investment! It sounded rather fishy, but I liked their rugs so I picked out my two favorites and signed over $300 in traveler's checks.

The uncle assured me of his integrity and gave me two different written guarantees. My plan was to stay in India until March, so I would have the time to see if he cheats me (I did not tell the uncle my schedule).

(Nov. 7, '93) The uncle sent me the postage receipt for the rugs to my Poste Restante address in Katmandu as he said he would. Maybe it's not a scam I think, but the Nepalese boy cannot be located so I have to wonder.

(Feb. 10, '94) Three months later I call my dad and he tells me the carpets have not arrived.

(Feb. 24, '94) I call my dad and he tells me that one carpet has arrived, but no dealer has come to pick it up. There is no such business at the Chicago address the uncle gave me, either.

(Mar. 13, '94) I call my dad one more time and still only one rug and no agent. If the uncle had sent the two carpets I picked out, I would have let it go at that, but he only sent one, and it was not even the one I chose. The uncle conned me and unless I go back to Agra, he wins and I get a crappy rug for $300. There is no way to avoid the 26-hour train ride, so I buy a second-class sleeper ticket back to Agra.

(Mar. 15, '94) After breakfast and a workout (100 push-ups and 100 squats) I get on a rickshaw and return to the shop in a rather pissed-off mood. I march into the office unexpectedly and surprise the shit out of uncle. I demand my money back plus expenses or I will go to the police. He said, "What about the expense of the carpet we sent you? You must consider that." I stood firm and said, "Look, I never wanted your carpet in the first place. You lied to me about the dealer, and you only sent one rug. I want all of my money back plus travel expenses. Here it is all written in your guarantee." After about ten minutes I had all the money back I had demanded. In a few days, I left Agra and took a train to Bombay. But wait, the story is not over.

(Mar. 19, '94) I'm in Bombay and I've got some time to kill before my evening flight to Cairo, Egypt. I check out a local art exhibition and go for a walk along the waterfront and take a power nap on the beach. On my way back to the station to collect my pack and leave for the airport, a man approaches me.

Normally I'd blow him off, but today I'm in a good mood. We talk for a short while and he asks me if I would help him. He needs to buy traveler's checks in a foreigners name to transfer money to London in order to avoid taxes on cash for his business. If I'd buy him $1000 worth of checks with his cash, he would pay me $200. Nothing illegal at all, I'm just a tourist buying more checks. "Sounds good," I said, "as long as I don't have to put up my own money." "No, no," he said, "come to the cafe and meet an Australian guy who did it for me yesterday."

I did, and the Aussie's story checked out, and today the Aussie was going to do it again for four grand. So we go near a bank all clandestine, like we are pulling off some great heist, and the Aussie goes first. He gives him his own 4K as collateral because I was told a French guy ripped-off the Indian a week ago by keeping the signed checks and telling the Indian to fuck off. There was nothing the Indian could do to the Frenchman to get his money back.

Well, it worked out for the Australian, who got his money back plus $800 for turning the trick. So I don't know how I fell for it, but I hand over all my traveler's checks and the wad of cash I got back in Agra as collateral to this fat Indian fuck, believing his story, and he disappears.

I could not believe I got burned after all I went through with the carpet scam! Anyway, 45 minutes later I finally gave up trying to find the Indian and the Australian, who were obviously con-men cohorts. I was extremely pissed off and very desperate because I only had two dollars to my name and a plane to catch in a few hours.

I wandered down the streets until I come upon a police station. The police drive me to the American Embassy, whose personnel were very helpful. Top marks. They helped me place my calls to Citicorp so I could recover my stolen checks in Cairo; they loaned me money to pay the airport tax; they gave me two bottles of water, bought me dinner, tried to find the guy who ripped me off, and drove me out to the airport. Saved my ass, basically. I lost almost all the $300 I recovered in Agra after all, but I kept the one rug.

<u>Endnote:</u> the carpet was later stolen out of my car in San Francisco (Nov. '94) along with my film negatives from Egypt and several original pieces of artwork that were in my backpack. Karma is a funny thing sometimes.

If a stranger proposes a deal to you concerning money, most likely there is something fishy. Don't ever become involved. You have much better things to do.

SETBACKS

Other Travelers' Woes

There was a jovial Swede named Michael in the German Bakery at Pune, India, who told me his setback story. He met an Indian man, seemingly rich, up in New Delhi who told him a sorrowful tale about his wife recently passing away. Could he travel with Michael to get over his blues? Michael liked the man and was going alone, so they both went to Agra to see the Taj Mahal. A few days pass and a friendship came about between the two, until one night when the man gave Michael a cookie laced with sleeping medicine.

When he came out of his slumber 12 hours later with a crashing headache, he discovered his Walkman, camera, cash, traveler's checks, and jewelry all taken. Of course, the address he gave Michael was bogus and the cops were hardly interested.

Michael, still the jolly Swede, gives this advice: "I hate to say this, but don't ever trust a native-country person, not even if they give you the most convincing sob story you've ever heard. Looks can be deceiving, and you must never let your skepticism wane or let your guard down. I did once, and got burned badly. He could have raped me or killed me, and I considered the guy a friend.

"One more thing. Someone told me once to keep a small amount of money hidden in a non obvious spot. I kept mine in the sole of my shoe. A hundred dollar bill tucked away for emergencies. When I woke up finally and realized what happened, it was this money that held me over until I could recover my stolen checks and contact the insurance company. I would advise other travelers to do the same."

A dude in a Hong Kong youth hostel was very angry with his recent video camera purchase. He spent over a grand on a new camera that didn't tape anything when he tried it out. He took it back to the store and insisted on a refund. The same guy that sold it to him only the day before denied any knowledge of the sale. Enraged, he stormed out and got the police. The cops returned to the store with him and the dude produced the bunk camera and sales receipt. The owner came out and told the police to look at the receipt heading. It was clearly not the same as the store's name and address out front, and could the police please get this confused foreigner out of his shop? There was nothing else the poor dude could do and he was stuck with a non-working camera. The moral of this story is: check out any shop or agent thoroughly before putting any money down.

Do not forget Mr. Brady's advice to Greg when he wanted to buy a car: "*Caveat emptor* – let the buyer beware."

Now, don't get paranoid by all these sad tales; there are still plenty of honest people in Asia and the rest of the world. This is just a warning to make you to be aware of the worst of the lot, so you will approach your adventure with some degree of caution.

Theft

When traveling you should *always* keep your guard up for potential theft. Losing personal belongings can be a real buzzkill, especially when a few small habits could have prevented it. Make these theft-guard mental notes:

- Always, no matter what, know where your money belt is at all times. If you are going to the beach or somewhere and you don't want to bring it along, hide it somewhere it would take a thief some time to find (under the bed, up on a rafter beam, attached to the back of your pack).

- Always *assume* your guesthouse room will be broken into. Use your own padlock on the door, and leave valuables with the guesthouse only if you think the room is unsafe and the people at the front desk can be trusted.

- When traveling on a long bus trip or overnight train, attach the straps of the pack to the rack or lock it in place with your padlock. If you leave your pack easy to be removed, it will be.

- Don't trust people, even other travelers, until you get to know them fairly well. There is always a joker in the deck who supports his trip by ripping-off other travelers.

- Make friends with the guesthouse owner so they will keep an eye on your room when you are not there.

- Be observant and aware. Thieves look for victims engrossed in sightseeing or involved in discussions. Stay alert if a distraction might occur, like a fight or little kids pestering you. Be wary whenever anyone touches you.

More tips to prevent room break-ins and rip-offs

Some guesthouses and hostels urge you to leave your valuables with them to prevent room break-ins. In communal hostel rooms, that is a wise move. If your rent your *own* room, however, your odds of not getting ripped-off might improve if you use your own security "system," since you are never 100% sure if you can trust the hostel workers ... on rare occasions, the staff has dipped into the tourist safe-box.

A good system for ensuring the security of your private room starts with checking the windows and door lock(s). If they seem secure and you can use you own lock on the latch, take the room.

Detour thieves by making it hard for them to steal anything.

Added security measures include hiding your valuables throughout the room. If a potential thief looks in the window and sees only non-valuables lying around, he won't have an incentive to burglarize. And in case he does break in, make him search. Seconds are very valuable, they may represent the margin by which he gets away – or panics and gives up, leaving empty-handed.

Make a dummy-pile of dirty clothes with your camera underneath. Keep your Walkman in an old plastic bag under toiletry items in the bathroom. Put your traveler's checks in a nondescript envelope and mix it in with letters from home, photographs, or in a magazine. Empty your pack and scatter your things about. It is the one time you are encouraged to have a messy room!

SETBACKS

Be one with your money belt at all times

Stories go on ad infinitum about people who take off their money belts in public places and how quickly they disappear. Europe is notorious for money belt thievery. Desperate bandits (usually junkies) have been known to run by travelers sitting in a cafe and grab their money belts right off the table. People sleeping on the beach have been awaken by thieves cutting the bottom of their sleeping bags in search of a money belt. People taking a dump have reported hands from under the stalls trying to grab their money belts on the floor. The most common way to lose a money belt is to take it off at night on a sleeper train. No matter how uncomfortable, become used to sleeping with it on when you are camping or in public places.

The U.S. State Department offers an excellent brochure entitled *A Safe Trip Abroad* for $1. This offers tips on guarding valuables, personal security, and what to do in terrorist or hijack situations. It also informs Americans on the extent of assistance our embassies and consulates offer abroad.

For contact addresses of all U.S. embassies, missions, and consulates abroad, obtain the *Key Officers of Foreign Service Posts* pamphlet. For copies of both, contact the U.S. Government Printing Office, P.O. Box 371954, Pittsburgh, PA 15250, (202) 512-1800 (M-F 7:30 to 5 pm eastern time).

Captain Kirk: "Well there it is – war. We didn't want it, but we got it."
Spock: "Curious how often you humans manage to obtain
that which you do not want."
Star Trek

The Good, the Bad, and the Ugly

The beauty of the world, which is so soon to perish, has two edges, one of laughter, one of anguish, cutting the heart asunder.
— Virginia Woolf (1882-1941)

Traveling has its fair share of thorns. To expect the unexpected, here's a short list of bad and ugly things you can readily anticipate: Long hours in airport waiting rooms. Tiresome searches for a room. Poor, pathetic beggars. Border and visa hassles. No place to change money. A drunk bus driver on a bumpy road. Environmental catastrophes. Assholes. Illness. Broken hearts. Rip-offs. Lousy weather.

A strong will and a stable mind are essential, just as essential as having the time and money to travel. The best way, and perhaps the only way, to preserve your sanity is to maintain a positive attitude. Having a broken spirit is no state of mind to be in thousands of miles away from home. Sometimes when it rains it pours, and that is the day you forgot an umbrella.

Setbacks happen and you will have to deal with them. Period. Get that in your head right now.

To mentally prepare yourself for harsh situations, start by considering worst-case scenarios and work backwards. Have a backup plan for getting injured, losing all of your money, and feeling estranged or lonely. You're relying on your own wits now. You won't have mommy or daddy's shoulder to cry on when an overwhelming situation confronts you.

The lessons learned through the trials and tribulations you'll inevitably encounter will strengthen your character. When you pull yourself out of a jam in a far-away place it builds your confidence, it makes you stronger, and strangely enough, gives you a new outlook on life. Resolving difficulties on your own can be incredibly empowering. You'll also be far more prepared to handle the next setback. After all, character is not made in a crisis, it is only exhibited.

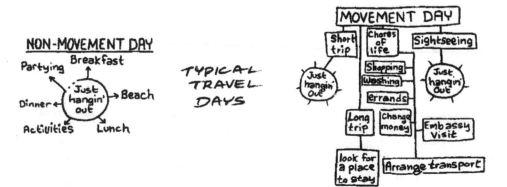

THE GOOD, THE BAD, AND THE UGLY

**Rejoice in the good, endure the bad, and
come to understand the ugly.**

Most days on world tour are a total blast. Your only worries on non-movement days are keeping yourself fed and occupied. Not much problem at all. Most of the hassles of traveling happen on movement days. This is when the good, the bad, and the ugliness of travel become apparent. The following journal entry from India typifies the inequities you can expect to encounter on a movement day in a poor country.

From Order to Chaos

From the travel journal, Puri Beach, India. 5 Dec. '93.

This morning is not unlike many others on the Stomp; I go for a jog along the beach and go swimming in the ocean. After catching some good bodysurfing waves I take my requisite 30-minute massage from a beach masseuse for 30 cents (!), and snack on fresh fruit and coffee from the beach vendors for pennies. I meet my German friend Stephen at Brady's restaurant for a final game of chess over lunch and a spliff. We exchange addresses and bear hug good-bye, and the Brady boys are bummed to see me leave too, especially after I gave them all wristbands as gifts.

It is a travel day, time to move on. I've got to get to Goa a few weeks before the Christmas crowd does in order to get a cheap room. The pack is assembled and I sling it on my shoulders and walk out to the road. I've just spent two fun-filled weeks of non-movement days here on the beaches of Puri, and it is kinda sad saying good-bye to all the cool people I've gotten to know. I flag down a cycle rickshaw and he takes me to the Puri bus station for 50 cents.

I have a ticket on the second-class sleeper train to Madras, but first I must catch a bus to another town where the train is leaving in the evening. I ask the bus fare and the driver says, "40 rupees ($1.20), get on, get on." I do so with my pack, and 10 minutes out of town the ticket collector comes down the aisle and says I have to pay double fare for bringing my pack on the bus. "No way," I said, holding out 40 rupees, "driver said bring pack on bus. One fare. Here."

The ticket collector refuses to take my single fare and we argue back and fourth for 10 minutes. Now, another buck-twenty is nothing to me, but I protested vehemently out of principle. You can't let hustlers like this take advantage of travelers, and I knew I was in the right. Finally, the driver stopped the bus and told me to get off. I wouldn't get off and after a few minutes the other passengers began complaining, so the ticket collector reluctantly took my 40 rupees.

I get to town, grab some fruit, munches, and a bottled water for the long train ride down to the southern end of the continent. At a food stand a merchant tries to sell me a bottled water with a broken seal. I tell him he's an asshole and spend my money at another stand. There are always chances to buy food en route, but I like to have supplies beforehand so I can just lie on my cot, crank out my Walkman, and chill out.

I board the crowded train and find someone else sleeping on my bunk. I wake him up and he is not too pleased to see me waving my ticket, insisting he bail now. I padlock my backpack to the bedpost, pop a Valium and snooze off. Wearing my boots and moneybelt in bed is not the most comfortable way to travel, but the safest. Any sneaky Indian trying to bust into my pack is gonna get a Doc Marten kick to the jaw (fortunately it never happened).

En route to Madras 6 Dec. '93.

I wake up slowly and amuse myself for the rest of the trip by talking to curious Indians, reading my book and news magazines, and sitting in the open doorway watching the country pass by.

We get to hot, stinking, and grimy Madras right at sunset. At the station I immediately get my ticket for the first train out, but there is no train to Goa for another two days, so I'll have to find a room here. My travel guide lists a few cheap hostels near the station, so I walk it. What a royal shithole! Camps of homeless people sleeping on the sidewalks, and hopeless beggars scrounging for food scraps in garbage piles. A dead dog lying in the gutter. Merchants trying to sell me worthless crap, and all the rooms are full.

I wander the streets for an hour until a bald old man wearing a bed sheet and no front teeth approaches me: "You need room? Come, come I show you." "How much?" I ask. "Cheap, cheap, special for you," he says. I tell him how much I want to pay and he assures me that is an okay price. When we get to his hotel it is twice as much. I complain, but they shrug off the old man, and I'm so damn tired I take the room. I still tipped the old man because he was on his knees nearly crying; the 50 cents I gave him will feed his family tonight, even if he gave me bunk advice. Thank Fuck the day is over and I have a real bed to sleep in!

Earthlings

Keeping your cool and maintaining patience is key. Do not let the bastards piss you off – that's how they get off. Good concepts to keep in mind are: the customer is always king, you are living a perpetual vacation, and when things are bad they can only get better.

The black market sock syndicate.

THE GOOD, THE BAD, AND THE UGLY

In order to prepare you for other bad and ugly days of travel, let's get over these:

Top Ten Biggest Misconceptions of World Stompin'

10. **I'd Get Lost.** If you can read a road map and find your way around your nearest U.S. city, you can figure out foreign cities too.

9. **Nowhere to Stay.** Finding a place to crash is usually as easy as showing up and inquiring around.

8. **Worries About Diseases and Accidents.** Pre-travel vaccinations cover most diseases; accidents can happen to anyone at anytime anywhere.

7. **Work is Hard to Get Abroad.** I won't say it's easy, but finding work abroad is definitely possible.

6. **Homesickness.** Every traveler misses their friends and family sometimes. However, while traveling everything is so new and exciting, there's rarely time or a reason to think of home.

5. **Wouldn't Know What to Do.** What do you do on the beach? What do you do when you see an awesome monument? What do you do on a trek? You have fun, that's the whole idea.

4. **I Would Be Lonely.** That depends on you. The opportunities to meet very cool people are no better than when traveling.

3. **The World is a Dangerous Place.** That is exactly what people outside of America think of this country. I believe the world, excluding war zones, is safer for travel than the U.S. The NRA is only an American aberration.

2. **Communication Will Be Difficult.** English is spoken globally and is the most common second language taught in foreign schools. While phrase books and gestures are the best form of communication when English is difficult, money talks any language when you need something.

1. **World Travel is Expensive.** Getting there is the biggest expense, day to day living in Asia (excluding Japan and the Tiger Nations) is a fraction of the cost of living in this country.

A Professor at John Hopkins has come forth with an intriguing thought about a perennial question: He says that if an infinite number of monkeys sat typing at an infinite number of typewriters, the smell in the room would be unbearable."
David Letterman
Late Night with David Letterman

Major Screwups

Great blunders are often made, like large ropes, of a multitude of fibers.
— Victor Hugo, *Les Miserables*, 1862

There was a Greek guy named Eriko who used to hang around the stoner's duney on a Goa beach in India. Everyone liked the way he tried so hard to be nice, and he was quite intelligent.

Yet, unfortunately, he snorted drugs. One day his money ran out. He tried to get some cash from his dad back in Greece, but his dad said no, probably due to his track record.

Eriko disappeared for a few days, and when he came back to the beach all pumped up and with an agenda, it was quite obvious he was up to no good. He told his friends he had to split for Greece as soon as possible, and those that cared for him pleaded with him not to go. He didn't listen and didn't get farther than the local bus terminal before the cops busted him for smuggling heroin. From what travelers have reported about the horrible conditions inside Indian jails, Eriko's not going to be enjoying life for the next 10 to 20 years.

Tarnished Galahad

*What the judge called him at his trial —
written later in Mexico:*

*Down to five pesos from five thousand
dollars
Down to the dregs from
the lip-smacking foam
Down to a dope fiend from
a prize winning scholar
Down to the bush from a civilized home.*

*What people once called a promising talent
What used to be known as an upstanding
lad
Now hounded and hunted by the law of
two countries
And judged to be only a Tarnished Galahad.*

*Tarnished Galahad — did your sword
get rusted?
Tarnished Galahad — there's no better
name!
Keep running and hiding 'til the next time
you're busted
And locked away to suffer your guilt,
and shame.*

Pretty much what happened.

— Ken Kesey, *The Demon Box*

MAJOR SCREWUPS

The U.S. Embassy says there is nothing they can do for people arrested smuggling drugs. Foreign governments have their own laws and visitors breaking them are subject to the consequences.

The horrors of *Midnight Express* are more than real when it's you behind bars. Scattered in jails all over the world are a large number of Westerners serving long sentences in extremely unpleasant conditions for various drug crimes. Many countries have harsh laws concerning dope users – not just smugglers. Yet, the drug problem will not end as long as there continues to be a demand and people's greed gets the most of their rational mind. Most economists agree, easy money equals high risk. Do not chance smuggling or you may regret it for the rest of your life.

Pricey Cab Fare

Holly was a girl I met at my brother's wedding. We had a short fling and she liked the way I traveled, so a year later she decided to live in Japan for the summer. I made it clear to her beforehand that I had a Japanese girlfriend, so if she wanted to come it should be for herself. She agreed, and bought a plane ticket. She called me collect at 3:00 a.m. from Seoul, South Korea, and said she would be arriving at Osaka in a few more hours. I mentioned I'd be teaching in the morning so she would have to figure out her ride into Kyoto. I repeated to her several times to catch the $5.00, No. 19 airport bus to Kyoto.

As expected, Holly arrived while I was teaching. However, she failed to catch the No. 19 bus and had yet to exchange any of her money either. Against my advice, Holly had taken an expensive cab ride without the $150.00 in yen, presently demanded by the angry cab driver. My boss was forced to run down to the bank and loan me the money to get the cab driver out of our school. Later, I was informed by Holly, some guy at the airport had told her "cabs were cheap in Japan."

Top Ten Bonehead Moves of the World Stomper

10. **Taking a taxi in Japan.** $150.00 for a 40-minute ride.
9. **Overstay visa without an extension.** Fines, heavy in corrupt countries.
8. **Complacent with food and water.** Unnecessary sickness. (See: Staying Well)
7. **Get in a fight with a local.** A beehive frenzy of angry relatives to deal with.
6. **Run out of money.** Other travelers will always lend a hand, rarely cash. (See: Travelers Support Group)
5. **Lose your temper while applying for a visa.** One squabble and you're not granted the visa. (See: Patience)
4. **Neglecting health precautions.** Sickness, possibly death. (See: Staying Well)
3 **Financing your trip on a credit card.** 19% hell-hole upon return to reality. (See: Money)
2. **Being careless with your money belt.** Lose your money belt and lose your trip. (See: Setbacks)
1. **Smuggling drugs.** A chunk of forgotten hash could mean a 10-year sentence in a closet-sized, mud-floored cell.

Gang Bang

When I lived on Maui, I was occasionally called "haole" (white jerk) by macho Hawaiian locals. It was derogatory, but I didn't let it bother me. Rex, a tough guy I worked with from L.A., hated being called haole. Rex thought it degrading, equivalent to a black person hearing the "N" word. I told him, "look, it's their island and they have large egos like you. Don't let them bug you. Just laugh at them."

One night Rex and I were out drinking in a local cantina and some little wormy guy called us haole fuckers. I laughed at him, but Rex got all pissed off and called him a Hawaiian asshole. The worm then challenged Rex to a fight. They went outside and Rex beat him up bad. I saw trouble brewing and the No. 7 Bonehead rule actualizing, so I left Rex with his own mess. Sure enough, the wormy local later returned with a pack of cousins and brothers. When Rex walked home they jumped him and beat the shit out of him.

Earthlings

Wally: "Hey, Eddie – How come you're always givin' Beaver the business?" **Eddie:** "I'm not givin' him the business. I'm just tryin' to wise him up. I don't want him goin' out in the world and gettin' slaughtered."
Leave it to Beaver

The Traveler's Support Group

Have no friends not equal to yourself.
– Confucius, *Analects*, 500 B.C.

Imagine you are traveling solo, in say, China. Everything's going fine, but tonight you feel like meeting some new people, partying, or just having a few drinks. No troubles; in nearly every city where there are travelers, there is at least one cafe catering to foreigners. Simply walk into town, spot the local travelers' restaurant or a hip-looking group and ask if you can sit down and join them. Start with a friendly hello and see if you are interrupting anything. If they take notice of you, talk. If not, wait until the conversation lags and then ask a question like, "Excuse me, does anyone know the best way to Hong Kong?" Or "Is there anything special to eat here?" Or "Where have you guys already been?" Before long, you are having that drink and picking up some helpful information for yourself with some new-found friends.

New travel friends are there if you want them, easy to turn away from if you don't.

Making new friends and meeting interesting people is one of traveling's greatest rewards. Typically, you'll find other Stompers to be a whole lot more interesting than the person who has never traveled. So don't ever worry about starting out on your own, before long you'll find yourself part of a large and stimulating group.

Spontaneous Fun

While backpacking through southern Europe in 1988, I hooked up with three hilarious Australian dudes, each having started out solo themselves. During our tour of Italy, we continued to meet other cool Stompers along the way. When we finally arrived in Florence, our international group of new friends totaled fourteen.

After a full day of sightseeing, we all sat and watched a beautiful sunset from a famous city bridge. We started drinking red wine and happily chatting to passersby. As night fell, someone in the group suggested we start looking for a room. The Aussie boys and I decided we would rather spend our daily budget on more wine than pay for a room. The others asked where we intended to crash and we said we would figure it out when the time came. Everyone stayed to drink with us, except a couple who needed a room to *root* (see: Australia Glossary). When the booze finally ran out, we returned to the train station to collect our packs and ended up passing out in front of a fifteenth century church ... one of the funniest nights on that trip.

Making friends with Westerners is even easier in remote regions. In certain countries with few travelers, like Latin America, Africa and Asia, meeting a fellow Westerner instantly creates a common bond. Being a minority makes friend-making especially easy.

Travelers are known to be gregarious. People travel abroad to meet other people. While meeting new friends they love to talk about the country they are in, share stories, engage in current events, or just chat about anything under the sun. English speakers tend to stick together like glue, and there is definitely safety and companionship in numbers.

Backpackers hang out together, share information, and generally look out for one another.

It is fun and easy to start up conversations and build relationships with other travelers, especially those you would like to know intimately. Here are some excellent ways to break the ice with someone you find attractive. At the beach, put your things down next to a babe and ask him or her to watch your stuff while you go for a swim. Other ice breaking situations include: sharing complaints on a crowded bus trip; strolling through a museum; walking around a monument; and sitting in the lounge of a guesthouse or youth hostel on a rainy day. Misery always enjoys company when the weather is foul.

It's quite easy to spark up a conversation about where you are going or where you have been. If you are both going the same way, team up. Almost everyone likes to travel in a group or with someone from another part of the world. It's all part of the adventure. Travelers are generous, too. Whether it is sharing aspirin or reading from the other person's guidebook or splitting a room to cut expenses, travelers like to support one other.

Of all my years World Stomping, it's still a toss-up between the places I've been to or the people I've met. Neither ceases to amaze me or fail to give me a great feeling for what I'm doing.

When travel partners split up, they almost always exchange addresses. Keeping in touch with old Stompin' mates will increase future travel opportunities when visiting their home countries. The important thing is to continue writing letters so they don't forget you. Every traveler will agree, knowing someone in the town you're going to is the ultimate way to experience that destination. Old friends love to rehash travel tales and play host while showing off their hometowns. They'll almost always put you up, feed you, and roll out the red carpet.

Pen Pals Payoff

Five years after our red wine party in Florence, Italy, I finally made it *Down Under* to Australia. I was fortunate to meet up with two of my three Aussies mates who still had current addresses. I found them incredibly hospitable, partly due to the letters I had written. One gave me a free house in Sydney for six entire weeks. In another part of the country, the second pal put me up and paid me wages for helping him with his electrical business. I had a great time for three weeks with his two little kids and American wife, as well as picking up some spare cash, too. Good on 'ya mates!

Support Group To The Rescue

On a trip to Venezuela, my Dutch girlfriend, Katja, had the following experience at the Caracas airport: While collecting her backpack, two men approached the group of passengers from her flight. They claimed to be working for a local hotel providing free luggage transportation for guests. A young couple said they were staying at that hotel and unwittingly handed over their packs. That was the last they saw of their belongings. Within the first hour of their three month trip, they had lost everything but their money belts. Distraught, they strongly considered returning home. Fortunately, the Travelers Support Group came to their rescue. Nearly all the people from their flight donated clothes, toiletries, books, and blankets. They only had to buy new backpacks and malaria pills and soon went on to have a great trip.

On another occasion, my British girlfriend, Rockie, had the following experience at the Australian embassy in Singapore: In order to get an Aussie visa, Rockie was required to show sufficient funds. Out of the blue, a benevolent traveler demonstrated incredible trust by lending her the necessary $500 for over an hour.

At home you have friends who will naturally help you, but when you are traveling, something wonderful happens. Complete strangers become concerned. "We're all in this together" is the prevailing attitude.

Exception to this rule: if you run out of cash, it's your own damn fault and time to go home. Cash handouts to unorganized travelers are where the support group draws the line.

Hitchhiking Perks

Hitchhiking reveals the good in people. On many occasions, it results in more than just a free ride. A bus ticket to move you on, a meal, or even a place to stay can result from hitching. The driver usually thinks, "if this guy is hitching, he must be desperate." Another reason to hitchhike is to meet the locals in the region you are going through and listen to their stories. They are usually quite entertaining.

Japanese Hospitality

One middle-aged couple picked me up hitching in southern Japan. Despite our language barrier, we instantly hit it off. At the end of my hour-long ride, they graciously insisted that I stay the night, so I could meet their teenage son who was studying English. When I agreed, they took me out for an expensive dinner and back to their home for the royal treatment. Sake wine, use of their phone, a comfortable bed, and a great breakfast in the morning. After we ate and the boy went to school, we got back in the car and they drove me to a secret temple in the woods I would never have known about. They even bought me lunch and gave me a few gifts before we departed. *Domo Arigato.*

Traveling overland is rarely a solo activity unless you prefer it that way. Setting off alone is the quickest way to meet like minded others headed in the same direction. Crossroads where other travelers congregate are the best places to team up with other Stompers. Travelers also commonly meet on planes, boats, busses, or trains. When arriving at a new destination it is nice to have a new friend watch your backpack or share a room.

If you would rather find someone before setting off, check the classified ads in national newspapers or the notice boards at colleges and universities before the summer break. If you are in London, the best travel publications are *Time Out* and *TNT*. In the eastern U.S. try the New York Student Center at Hotel Empire, Broadway and 63rd Street, or try the ads in the *Village Voice*. The Lonely Planet website has a link to "Thorn Tree" where travelers communicate and post messages.

E.T. phones home.

"I've never felt closer to a group of people. Not even in the portable johns of Woodstock."
Reverend Jim Ignatowski
Taxi

Backpacker Responsibility

Everyone is really responsible to all men for all men and for everything.
– Fyodor Dostoyevski, *The Brothers Karamazov*, 1880

Many Stompers perceive a long trip as a holiday away from social responsibilities. Yes, extensive traveling is conducive to partying hard and having a blast. However, never forget, you are a visitor in someone else's country and, like it or not, you're a pseudo-ambassador with a backpack. Don't fit the stereotype of a loud-mouthed, inconsiderate jack-ass. The money you spend traveling may seem like a fortune to poor people, so don't flaunt it. John D. Rockefeller, once said in a speech, "I believe that every right implies a responsibility; every opportunity an obligation; every possession, a duty."

I always remind myself that I am extremely privileged to be able to travel. It is a privilege after all, not a right.

Travelers interact with locals much more than package tourists, so we become the impression they keep. We hang around for weeks or months at length, where your average tourist will zip in and zip out in a matter of days or even hours. We rely on locals to help us by providing meals, housing, directions, services, and the ever comforting friendly smile. Respect yourself by respecting the people and cultures you encounter. Be proud to be an emissary. Appreciate the community serving you so the locals won't resent the next dude who comes along. This is an entirely unwritten rule: do your part for future generations of World Stompers. It's all a karma thing that comes back around when you arrive at the next destination and expect a fair shake.

Social behavior varies widely around the world. Conduct you've been conditioned to believe is correct and proper may not apply elsewhere. While every social group is unique in certain ways, outspoken Americans scream their differences. Academics call this "ethnocentrism," people around the world call it "Ugly Americans."

Stomper Code of Conduct

Minimize your impact. Live by the camper's motto: "Pack it in, pack it out." Use recyclable and biodegradable products, such as soap for outdoor bathing. Never litter, the world has enough trash already.

Encourage the old ways. Be a socially conscious representative of your country, not a modern day imperialist (see: American Image: Cultural Champions). Some parts of the world encounter very few foreigners, and in these places, first impressions mean a lot.

Understand local customs and some language. Pick up some words and phrases in the language and the locals will appreciate your making the effort. Watch and imitate greetings, like the Thai hand prayer welcome, or the Australian "G'day mate."

Have a clue where you are going. It is your responsibility to research your next destination. Going in blind can make you seriously lost. Educate yourself regarding local health risks, border checks, geography, history, and customs to name a few.

Be friendly to locals. In heavily touristed areas, it may seem everyone has something to sell or promote. This can be unnerving after a while, but don't let it upset you. You can sometimes turn their game around by haggling yourself to save some cash. Be assertive, not an asshole.

Take nothing, leave nothing. Do not take anything but pictures and only after first asking permission.

How Places Transform when they Become Over Touristed

New countries and regions open up around the globe every year. Once isolated places quickly transform after becoming inundated with travelers and tourists. Local people see the allure of materialism through the eyes of foreigners and want it for themselves. While comfort of rooms, quality of food and services improve over time, prices always go up. The culture soon becomes watered down and the native attitudes change. Crime and safety then become an important issue.

Bad News Bali

The once pristine Indonesian island of Bali has today been transformed into an over-rated tourist ghetto. While still steeped in natural beauty and Hindu folklore, farmers of the age-old rice terraces that grace the island have been lured away from the land and into the tourist centers. The money is much better, particularly if you are a thief breaking into rooms. A stolen camcorder can represent a year's worth of backbreaking farm labor.

Since Bali remains Indonesia's top tourist destination, the crime and sprawling beach developments are not expected to go away anytime soon. But loyalties will change as travelers begin to discover the many other amazing islands along the archipelago. Unfortunately, the Balinese people will soon learn the hard way ... you cannot bite too hard on the hand that feeds you.

Ultimately, the responsibility to care and look out for yourself is entirely up to you. Have your act together; physically, mentally, and financially. Respect other people of the world, just as you would endear their respect for you. Have a conscience when you travel and do your part in keeping the backpacker circuits of the world cool for Stomping. This is the edge that allows us to travel ultra-cheaply because there are no paid baby sitters showing us the way – as with the tourist set. Let's keep it that way.

> "Dig right in and do it now, whatever should be done.
> "You're a dope to sit and mope, when everything is fun."
> **Mouseketeer Tommy**
> *The Mickey Mouse Club*

Patience

A handful of patience is worth more than a bushel of brains.
— Dutch proverb

Patience plays a big part in even the smallest of situations. Little things and big things will come up and certainly test you, but just weather the storm and stay calm. Keeping an even temper and not blowing up means adjusting to the tempo of the situation. It will eventually result in avoiding unpleasant situations, having your way, paying less, and generally enjoying yourself much more. After all, you are on an extended vacation!

In remote, hard to reach areas, patience typically plays an even larger role. In the slow going islands of Indonesia, the term *jamkaret* means rubber-time; literally time s-t-r-e-t-c-h-e-s. In India they say *shanti shanti* meaning slow and easy; or no rush. In Mexico it's *manana*, tomorrow; no hurry.

The hotter the climate = the slower things go

Conventional wisdom relates a travel story involving a mellow and an uptight dude waiting for a bus. When they arrived at the station they both asked when the next bus would leave. "One hour" was the answer. The mellow dude pulled out his sleeping bag and crashed, while the uptight dude kept checking every 20 minutes. "One hour" was the answer they kept giving him.

"What the hell!?" screamed the uptight dude, "That is what you said one hour ago, and one hour before that, AND ONE HOUR BEFORE THAT!"

Fuming, the uptight dude woke up the mellow dude and spoke his grievances. "They keep telling me one hour! I'm freaking out, I can't believe how incompetent they are! This sucks!"

Looking around more carefully, and inquiring politely, the mellow dude discovered the buses leave *every* hour. The man was, in fact, attempting to convey this to the uptight dude all along. A few minutes later they found the right bus and boarded together.

In most Asian countries losing your temper or being aggressive is not respected behavior. "Losing face" applies to locals and foreigners alike.

Long, painful and bitter. A day in visa Hell!

From the travel journal (23, Sept. '93) Kuala Lumpur, Malaysia

Today was indeed the truest test of my patience.

Six long hours standing in sweltering Malaysian heat was no way to spend a day. I approach the Indian Embassy clerk and asked politely once again, " has any progress been made on my visa?" An apathetic "no" was all I received. "Look," pointing to my plane ticket, "I've come here every day for the past seven days and today my flight leaves in three hours!"

"Sir, your visa is not ready," I was told. "We will call you when it is, next in line please."

Frantic, I sat and watched as my flight left without me. Later, I witnessed a Nigerian man lose his temper and scream through the clerk's window, "I can't wait any longer, I demand my visa NOW!"

Shoving his passport and application back he heard a callous, "Your application has been turned down. Next please." Calming down, he tried again patiently, to no avail. His three minute diatribe had cost him a six month trip.

Hours later, at the expense of my flight, I had finally received a six-month visa. Relieved, I walked out and was able to add three days to my flight schedule. Wanting badly to get out of the boring smog-filled city, I caught the first bus toward the Cameron Highlands. As bad luck would have it, this bus arrived 10 minutes too late to catch the last interchange, leaving me stuck in a remote village. I'll tell ya', my timing was really off today.

Desperate to get to the Highlands and end this hectic day, I found two Danish guys also stranded from the same late bus. Anxious to share a ride with me, we started negotiating with the local cabbies.

Due to darkness, the cabbies insisted on charging us double the approximate five dollar normal rate.

After 10 minutes of playing coy, the one driver who seemed most eager finally said "Okay," and called me over. He offered to knock off almost half of the inflated rate; I countered by proposing to pay three *ringgits* over the going rate, and we ultimately settled in the middle.

Traveling without a guide book, I needed some information from the driver and hard feelings from the haggling session would not help matters. After we got going I complimented his driving, the mountains, his car. When we drove past his village and he pointed out his home and some relatives near the road, I knew that we were becoming friends. I started asking him pertinent questions: where the local's chow down; the best hiking trails; and a good guesthouse. He was a wealth of information, talking and describing the region all the way up to the lofty mountain heights.

It was pitch dark out when we reached the village he recommended, yet he went out of his way to take us to a very cool guesthouse in the woods. We shook hands and a long day thankfully came to a mellow end.

P A T I E N C E

**Having patience and good manners can sometimes make
a bad situation tolerable.**

The Art of Chaotic Street Crossing

In developing countries the key to crossing a busy street is to go slow and be patient. From a first impression, it appears to be a random mess of motor scooters, rickshaws, cars, trucks, and ox-carts. Some people wait for the opening and make a run for it, but there are stories of those people getting whacked.

Take a few steps and stop. Let the traffic see you and they will go around you. Make a break when it comes, but never run out of control. The disordered state becomes a pattern once you are in the thick of it, and it becomes easily understood.

Earthlings

**"Omar! Chill out! You cannot
be angry if you want to be a
nomad!"**

Staying Well

Almost anything is easier to get into than to get out of.
– Agnes Allen, Omni, 1979

Western medicine and treatment are quite widespread around the globe nowadays, and competent doctors can be found wherever there are tourists.

However, venture off the beaten track, like the remote Altiplano in Bolivia or the rugged terrain in Zaire, and you could be in a pickle if you got really sick or injured. Far away places can seem daunting and uncertain when you consider finding treatment for an illness. Fortunately, there will always be another traveler or local to aid you in times of distress (see: Travelers Support Group). Folks are folks in the realm of Stomping.

Hospital conditions in developing countries have gotten the "adequate" rating, yet cost a small fraction of the Western rate. Foreign doctors have been known to over prescribe for aliments they know little about. Some minor problems can be treated with natural local remedies. Ask a lot of questions and try to tend to your own minor wounds.

Any town or city in the developing countries will have a pharmacy (mostly called Chemists). You can buy nearly any prescription or non-prescription drug sold in the West. Commonly found over the counter items are: asthma inhalers, Valium, strong painkillers, cold capsules, malaria pills, antibiotics, Pepto-Bismol, antihistamines, calamine lotions, peroxide, and bandages. Bring a few of your own personal items, but stock up your medical kit when you get to a developing country because these things are so much cheaper over there. Practice good hygiene and watch what you eat and drink.

Natural Remedies

If you get motion sickness on boats, planes, or buses, the best natural prevention that will not cause sleepiness is powdered ginger root. This root is available in capsule form in most health food stores. Researchers have shown that two capsules with a big glass of water an hour before departure is 50% more effective than other remedies.

Echinacia and Goldenseal are both great at keeping your immune system strong, preventing illnesses, and also work well when you are sick. Goldenseal powder is also an excellent antiseptic for cuts. Just apply the powder to the cut like a paste, and bandage over it.

Primary parasite killing herbs are: wormwood, cloves, and black walnut tincture. The dosages differ for each specific ailment. A good source book is *The Cure for All Cancers*, or consult your local health food store.

Golden Rule for staying well in developing countries:
Do not drink local tap water!

Upset stomachs from unsafe water is the most common travel ailment. Bottled water and soda are available nearly everywhere, as are freshly squeezed juices, coffee, and tea. However, milk may not always be pasteurized, so ask for it to be boiled, or just avoid it. Remember to ask for your fruit or salad to be washed with iodine-purified or boiled water. Be sure to check the seal on the cap of all bottled water to insure a false cap wasn't just popped on.

Another reason to be paranoid about the water you drink or food you eat is the potential for getting worms. If you suffer long-term from loose stools, diarrhea, and digestion problems, you might have a worm living in your stomach. Consult a travel doctor who will likely prescribe Vermox. Don't be surprised if you shit out a worm as big as your middle finger after three or four days.

Important Health Precautions

Travelers in developing countries can be exposed to dangerous, and potentially fatal diseases and parasites. The biggest health risks to Stompers are: hepatitis A, cholera, typhoid fever, tetanus, meningitis, yellow fever, malaria, dengue fever, and sexually transmitted diseases. These can all be avoided with preventative measures.

The trick is to get your shots and medications *just before* leaving a Western nation. This will prevent them from wearing off over the months you are not at risk. If your first stop was to New Zealand before Southeast Asia, consult the U.S. Embassy in Auckland for the nearest travel doctor, or look in any Kiwi city phone book.

It is very important to confer with a doctor about the reach and intensities of regional illnesses in the countries you plan to visit. In all major Western cities, and some international airports there are specialized travel doctors who can give vaccinations and immunizations on the spot with a record card for verification. Some countries require this record card to be shown in order to enter the country. Again, if in doubt, contact a travel doctor in the yellow pages or the international health information line: Centers for Disease Control, 888-232-3228.

If you have not had a dental checkup recently, get one before departure. A toothache caused by a cavity or a lost filling can turn into a painful ordeal when you are days from the nearest town. If you wear contact lenses, consider bringing extended-wear disposables. They are cheap, can be worn overnight, and it's not a big deal if you lose one. All contact lens wearers should be aware that high altitudes may affect your vision. This is where having a back-up pair of glasses comes in handy.

In the event of serious illness, contact the embassy or consular office of your country. They can assist in locating appropriate medical services, inform family or friends, and assist in the transfer of funds. However, payment of hospital and other expenses is the responsibility of the traveler. The Social Security Medicare program and most national health insurance policies do not provide coverage for hospital or medical costs outside their country. Several private organizations will provide medical information and insurance for overseas travelers (see: Insurance, page 104).

Top Ten Health Tips while in Developing Countries:

10. **Avoid meat.** Refrigeration is minimal in many countries, and flies tend to land on meat in open air markets and spread germs.

9. **Maintain normal hygiene routines.** Keep your body and teeth as clean as you would at home to avoid germs and disease.

8. **Drink a lot of water.** Dehydration is common and leads to fatigue, other illness, and altitude ailments.

7. **But do not drink the tap water.** Developing countries lack the water filtration systems of the West and contain elements that can make you very sick. Also avoid ice, broken sealed bottled water, and portable filtered water which cannot remove viruses such as hepatitis.

6. **Food: Cook it, peel it, or forget it.** Local food from street vendors should be well cooked and still hot. Vegetables should not be eaten raw because they were probably washed with tap water. Eat only fruit that you peel yourself, and touch it as little as possible.

5. **Wash your hands frequently.** Most germs are transported from hands to mouth, and when you are traveling, you often shake hands and touch public objects, like doorknobs, handles, and railings.

4. **Avoid shellfish or seafood unless it is well cooked.** Foods from the ocean, rivers and lakes tend to spoil the quickest. Make sure the chef knows your concern.

3. **Stay away from food that requires a lot of handling or has been stored and re-heated.** A simple inquiry with the restaurant proprietor can tell you much about where and how your food is prepared.

2. **Learn about preventative medicines.** Consult a travel doctor and explain in detail the regions you plan to visit. Diamox is good for altitude sickness. Chloroquine for malaria-prone areas. Pepto-Bismol or Cipro for diarrhea. Scopolamine skin patches for seasickness. Antihistamine an hour before takeoff if you have ear problems at high altitudes.

1. **Visit a travel clinic or specialized physician before entering any developing country.** It cannot be stressed enough how important it is to have the proper inoculations and updated information before traveling to any non-Western nation. Your life could depend upon it.

Resources

The most up-to-date information on vaccines (and other health concerns) is the annual U.S. Public Health Service manual, *Health Information for International Travel*, produced by the Center for Disease Control (CDC). It is commonly used by travel agents and travel doctors, and is available at most libraries. It can also be purchased for $6.50 from the U.S. Government Printing Office, Superintendent of Documents, Washington, DC 20402. There is a CDC information line at (404) 639-3311 and a homepage at: www.cdc.org. Also request the document *Medical Information for Americans Traveling Abroad* by the U.S. Department of State which lists several domestic and international insurance companies.

Extensive medical information and a listing of doctors abroad are available for a few dollars (donation) from (IAMAT) International Association for Medical Assistance to Travelers, 417 Center Street, Lewiston NY 14092, (716) 754-4883. IAMAT offers an ID card to members and guarantees services at fixed rates worldwide.

Check your local bookstore or library for these titles: *Health Guide for International Travelers* by Dr. Thomas Sakmar; *Staying Healthy in Asia, Africa, and Latin America* by Dirk Schroeder; *The New Traveler's Health Guide* by Dr. Patrick J. Doyle; *Traveler's Health: How to Stay Healthy Abroad* by Dr. Richard Dawood, or the introduction to international travel guides.

EARTHLINGS

"Somba! Get that out of your mouth! You don't know where it's been!"

"An ounce of prevention is worth a pound of bandages and adhesive tape."
Groucho Marx
You Bet Your Life

Expenses Overseas

So soon as we begin to count the cost, the cost begins.
— Henry David Thoreau, 1841

There are so many ways to save money, or blow it, while traveling. Basically, it all depends on how much cash you have to start with and how well you can budget it along the way. When you've got a big stack of traveler's checks, it's easy to spend and not think much of it. And when you get down to your last few hundred bucks, you will wish you hadn't been so loose with the money before. That's why, as difficult as it may be, you should always be on the spending/savings alert.

Not spending money = Saving money

The biggest travel expenses, in order, are: <u>Food</u>, <u>Airfare</u>, <u>Party and Activities</u>, <u>Accommodations</u>, <u>Transportation Within the Circuits</u>, and <u>Insurance</u>. Each category has fixed costs that cannot be avoided, but there are also ways to save money in each category as well. Let's take them one at a time.

Food

Food, for a man, is usually his biggest expense. It can't be avoided. A man's got to eat! Women don't tend to eat as much, but should, just the same, want to save money. The amount you pay for meals and where you eat can make or break your travel budget. Here are some ways to save:

- Different countries have their different staple foods. Make it a habit to eat an inexpensive ethnic staple every day. Ramen noodles in Japan, souvlakis in Greece, humus falafel in the Middle East, dhal and chapatis in India, french bread in France, corn bread in Latin America, curry in Thailand, or rice just about anywhere.

- Avoid the *expensive* ethnic cuisine, however. Exotic seafood in Southeast Asia, new pastas in Italy, reindeer meat in Norway, or designer sushi in Japan can run up an obscene bill.

- Buy local brands, rather than expensive imports.

- Prepare your own meals whenever possible.

- Substitute one meal a day by snacking. Fruit for breakfast, peanuts for lunch, bread rolls, candy, etc.

- Take a flight on an empty stomach so you are hungry enough to ask for a second meal. They always have one.

- Look around where the local's chow down, and there you will find cheap eats. This is especially effective in expensive countries like Singapore. Under shopping malls are food courts where you will find good values and lots of locals munching away.

- When working away from home, take advantage of a company cafeteria, or live near a university. Food is subsidized, and when you get to know the staff, they will usually give you larger helpings.

Not to pay for food

One summer when Tommy P. and I lived in Lake Tahoe, we made a bet. We bet five bucks on whether he could last a whole month without spending a single cent on food. He worked as an usher for Caesar's Showroom and was allowed free meals. Security was laid back and lax, so he would munch hard before and after his shifts and smuggle out pocketfuls of fruit, yogurts, puddings, cereal, milk and fruit drinks. I would barter meals with him on his days off to give him a variety, but never any freebies. The bet was only to *pay* for food.

Well, he lost the bet a few days short of a month because he was fired from his job. He got the ax because he got up on stage and danced with Diana Ross during the encore. His boss did not believe she pointed at *him* to come on stage for a dance.

Airfare

This is when some research on your part can save you a whole lot of cash. Every destination in the world has a high season and a low season. For example, flights to Europe are the most expensive in the summer, which is their high season. And flights to warm climates are opposite. Highest fares come around in the winter months when demand is peaking. So if you want to go during high season, does that mean you're screwed? Not necessarily. Tickets for high season can be purchased in the low season time for the low season cost. You just have to be sure of your dates.

Calling different travel agents, and watching the travel section in your city's Sunday paper will give you an indication of price ranges. Try calling the airlines themselves when quoted prices are low. Some travel magazines or youth magazines will offer good advertised deals, such as *TNT*, or *Q* in London. *Best Fares Magazine* has been called "The most comprehensive source of bargain fares" by *US News and World Report*. For a copy, write to: 1301 South Bowen, Suite #490, Arlington TX 76013 or call: 800-880-1234. www.bestfares.com

"Do not buy airline tickets on a weekend," reports the *Wall Street Journal*. That is when carriers test fare increases to see if rival airlines will go along. If they don't, the fares come back down again on Monday. Likewise, fly midweek when planes are less full. The closer your departure date is to the weekend, the more demand there is for it. Therefore, for lowest cost, shoot for Tuesday afternoon through Thursday morning. The following chart illustrates the best time of year to buy airline tickets for domestic flights in the United States:

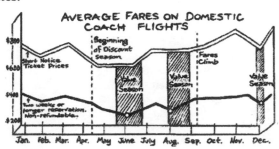

**The trick to all this is basically look everywhere.
Sniff out them deals, because they are out there.
Do not buy a ticket anywhere until you
have checked at least ten sources.**

Air Couriers exist because some companies need their time-sensitive packages to clear customs as quickly as the passenger. The task of an air courier company is to pair packages with courier travelers. This means your airfare will be subsidized by an international company using your baggage space, and thus will offer you the most discounted ticket available.

Courier flights seem like the ultra-budget way to go, and they are great for short Stomps on short notice. Prices range from 30% to 80% off regular fare prices. The bummer is most originate out of New York City, they are hard to get on, and you have to wait and then depart on short notice. The biggest disadvantage is you cannot bring a backpack because the courier is using that luggage space; you can only bring small carry-on items. On arrival at your destination, you will be met by a representative who will receive the package(s). You must also escort freight on the way back, usually within two or three weeks. To blow off your return flight means you will be blacklisted from that company for life. Courier companies require you to return. Try Now Voyager, Inc. (212) 431-1616 for courier flights to Latin America, Asia, and Europe; or World Courier (516) 354-2600, for half off tickets to Europe and other international destinations. In Sydney, Australia call Jupiter (2) 317-2230. In the UK try Bridges (1) 89 546-5065.

Ticket Consolidators are organizations that buy tickets in large quantities and pass on the savings to the individual ticket purchaser. Newspaper classifieds in Sunday Travel sections quote several of these "bucket-shops" every week, or you can call the big companies themselves. Try Unitravel (800) 325-2222, or Ticket Planet (800) 799-8888.

Discount Clubs are like ticket consolidators who also deal in cruise and tour packages (for tourist geeks). The only reason they are in here is because they offer some great airfare discounts if you join their club for a yearly membership fee of $30 to $45 bones. They specialize in selling unsold tickets and tours at the last minute for up to 60 percent off. Call for up-to-the-minute bargains on Air Tech (212) 219-7000, or airtech.com.

For a complete collection of reliable discount airfare providers, check out *The Worldwide Guide to Cheap Airfares* by Michael Wm. McColl. To order a copy, call: (800) 78 BOOKS, or send $14.95 + $3.00 (S&H) to: Insider Publications, 2124 Kittredge Street, Third Floor, Berkeley, CA 94704. Also keep an eye on: www.travelinsider.com for discounts on-line.

**In all cases of getting an el-cheapo plane ticket, how
flexible your schedule determines how many
options you will have open.**

Partying and Activities

These two things seem to be the main reason to travel in the first place, so why cut costs? Simple, to save money on more party and activities later. It takes discipline to go out and only bring enough cash for a couple drinks, but there are other ways of getting hammered without dropping a wad of bills. In Japan, it is easy for foreigners to get away with rascality because that is what they expect of us. The mischievous set smuggles in cheap bottles of vending machine beer into the clubs where they would normally cost 10 dollars in Yen.

EXPENSES OVERSEAS

**Little things, like eating native cuisine
or drinking the local brand of beer, save
good money over time.**

As far as seeing the sights, use your student card for half-off admission. Most sightseeing destinations worldwide, like the Vatican Museum in Rome, offer student discounts but they are not advertised and you have to ask for the discount to receive it.

Student cards are a Stomper "must-have."

By all means possible, get a student card, it will pay for itself many times over. If you really are a student, cards are available at issuing offices on over 400 college campuses nationwide, at all Council Travel offices, and by mail order from CIEE, ISS Department, 205 East 42nd Street, New York, NY 10017. Or call (800) 226-8624 for the location of an issuing office near you. You must show a photocopy of transcript, school declaration, or letter from the dean with the school seal affixed. Cards are $20 and require a passport photo.

If you are not a student, there are perfect look-alikes on Khao San Road in Bangkok, Thailand. Or, if you can find the issuing office at the University of Cairo, they sell cards without any questions.

Accommodations

For fear of being redundant, see the next chapter: *Crash for Little Cash.*

Transportation Within the Circuits

Getting around place to place and city to city is usually a pretty simple matter. Public transportation is universally the cheapest way to go. Public transportation is rather straightforward, easy to figure out, and designed for the not-so-educated locals to understand. If they can master it, so can you.

The problem with public transportation in developing countries is usually the lack of comfort and inherent hassles that come with it. It is not uncommon to be virtually packed in like sardines, with a rooster at your feet, and a goat in the aisle. This kind of thing is amusing for the first hundred miles, annoying the rest.

For those who prefer comfort over savings (wimps), private mini-buses and tourist coaches do most of the same routes as the public buses for twice the cost. The same applies to trains, but in different compartments. Second-class seats are half the price of second-class sleepers. On overnight trips, wimping out can sometimes preserve one's sanity. Not a high price to pay.

**The ultra-budget way to get from place to place is
public transportation in developing countries and
hitchhiking in Western countries.**

On the developed country circuits of the West, hitchhiking is a viable and practical way to get around for free. Since the cost of travel in the Western countries is more expensive, it's nice to have one option which is less than the developing nations. Hitching is rare in the developing countries because rides may be too dodgy, or public transportation is too cheap to want to bother.

Where to catch rides from? Here you will have to do some thinking. Always consider: making a sign; which roads to take; where to situate yourself on the highway so the driver can first see you and then pull off; and timing rides before it gets dark. Hitching is a classic way to meet the local cross-section of people and get into some great conversations. Some times a lift will feed you or put you up for the night.

If hitching isn't your style or you are a single woman, then public transportation on trains and buses is the way to go in the West, but are rather expensive compared to developing nations. They, too, are easy to figure out and are highly efficient.

Insurance

There are only two things to think about insuring on your World Stomp: your possessions and your health. Insurance coverage is also available for disposition of your remains in case of death. About 6,000 U.S. citizens die abroad every year, three-quarters of these from heart disease or accidents.

Many times you or your parent's homeowner policy will cover baggage loss. Otherwise travel agents offer baggage insurance at $50 for six months. If you are going on a multiple-year advoyage, this cost may be more than what your luggage is worth.

Never had it, but probably should have

When my backpack was ripped off in Scotland, I had no baggage insurance and had to take the loss. Several years later on my world tour I did not buy insurance again, but I made a vow to pay very close attention to my possessions at all times. It worked, and I had nothing insurable stolen during my whole three-year trip.

Health insurance was another one I blew off to cut costs, and luckily never got sick or injured enough to need it anyway. Again, I vowed to take care of myself by staying in shape, watching what I ate and drank, and keeping my head up for accidents.

Medical insurance considerations include accident, disability, evacuation, repatriation (ticket home), and death. Regular health insurance is usually not valid abroad, such as Blue Cross/Blue Shield or HMOs. Travel agents offer health insurance policies, as does the ISTC international student identity card. Some countries, like Japan, offer free health care to foreigners residing there.

Specialized travel insurance companies such as Travelx (POB 641070, Omaha, NB 68164; 800-228-9792) offers long-term coverage, as does Travel Guard International (1145 Clark Street, Stevens Point, WI 54481; 800-826-1300). International Underwriters Group (243 Church Street West, Vienna, VA 22180; 800-237-6615) offers good long-term insurance for people living and working abroad or extended travel. Hinchcliff International Group Services (877-237-2390; www.hthworldwide.com) specializes in student travel policies.

Annual policies are offered by Europe Assistance Worldwide Travel (9200 Keystone Crossing, Suite 300, Indianapolis, IN 46240; 800-821-2828), evacuation services by: International SOS Assistance (POB 11568, Philadelphia, PA 19116; 800-523-8930), and WorldCare Travel Assistance Association (2000 Pennsylvania Avenue NW, Suite 7600, Washington, DC 20006). The travel series Rough Guides offers insurance through a London broker; in the U.K. call 0800-015-0906 or elsewhere in the world (+44) 1243 621 046.

Crash for Little Cash

There is a time for many words, and there is also a time for sleep.
– Homer, *The Odyssey*, 8th cent. B.C.

Places to sleep around the world vary widely. From lavish five-star hotels, to mid-range motels, to family home-stays, to youth hostels, to rooftops and campgrounds, or to the commando-crash on beaches and parks for free. Since this is an ultra-budget guide, we will stick to the el cheapo options. Besides, the cheaper the accommodation, the more interesting the experience (usually).

Dorm style hostels and camping are the cheapest accommodations in the Western, more affluent countries. Single rooms in developing countries can range as low as 50 cents to $5 per night! A single room, in, say, Nepal, can be a mere fraction in cost compared to a Western campground.

Western Accommodations

Cheap youth hostels and student residence information is available for travelers touring the North American, Australian, or European circuits. You'll find the following guide books helpful for detailing room rates, food services, phone numbers, addresses, available dates, and reservations.

The International Youth Hostel (IYH) Federation publishes separate guides for each continent, encompassing nearly 5,000 hostels in about 70 countries. For Canada and the U.S., *Hosteling North America 2001* is available for free to members of American Youth Hostels. Non-members can buy copies for $5.95 plus tax, by contacting: HI AYH Metropolitan Chicago Council, 3036 N. Ashland Ave., Chicago, IL. 60657; or call 773-327-8114.

Hostels provide inexpensive dormitory accommodations for travelers of all ages. Sleeping rooms are separated for men and women, but some have separate rooms for families. Guests share the lounge, kitchen, dining room and usually bathroom facilities. Overnight fees range from $7-$20, per night. The best hosteling Internet resource is www.hostels.com.

During school holiday periods the *Campus Lodging Guide* lists over 700 campus locations in 31 countries. Nearly 400 university and college listings are in the United States and Canada, rates for single and double rooms averaging $15-$30 per night. Copies of this guide are available for $14.95 (plus $2 postage and handling) from: Campus Travel Service, PO Box 5486, Fullerton CA. 92835; or call (800) 822-6787.

IYH beds usually cost more than independent ones and have stricter rules. Independent hostels are more like young traveler's boarding houses and do not require membership cards, either.

Another listing of the hundreds of independent hostels across North America is *Hostel Handbook for USA & Canada*. This one describes just the basics like, address, telephone number and price. It is available by sending $4 to: Hostel Handbook, 722 St. Nicholas Ave., New York, NY 10031; or call (212) 926-7030. Make checks payable to Jim Williams.

On the Australia circuit, camping is quite popular. You do not even need a tent at some places – they are provided or there are bunk houses. The amenities are the same as hostels: showers, community rooms and kitchens, bus services, and outdoor firepit. They are easy to walk into and use the facilities without paying, and soft scammers have been known to crash elsewhere and do this.

There are over 100 YHA hostels in Australia, and the Volume II of *Budget Accommodations Guide* covers them all plus Asia, Africa, and the Americas ($12.95 each plus $3 postage for each book). For membership applications, book orders, and general information on hosteling, contact: Hosteling International, PO Box 37613, Washington, DC 20013-7613; (202) 783-6161 or (800) 661-0020. There are over 1000 independent backpacker hostels in Australia and New Zealand. Many of these are not advertised and offer the traveler more flexibility at a lower cost.

In most European cities you will find a hostel-hotel booking office in or near the main train station.

Budget travelers in Europe need only make a 24 hour advance reservation on hostel rooms. Travelers simply show up, locate the train station office, and determine the going room rate. To avoid a booking fee, do not use the hotel hot-lines in airports or train stations. They rarely offer discounts, and 800 reservation lines offer <u>no</u> discounts. In southern European countries and Middle Eastern countries you will find many low cost hotels with their venders awaiting you at bus or train stations. Know the price range for rooms in the area first, and then go out and talk to the vendors so they will not overcharge. Time is on your side to check around because hotel rooms are perishable items, worth nothing if they sit vacant. Leave your pack in the train station checking room and wander around until you find something suitable. The more casual your inquiry, the less desperate you'll seem, and thus be offered the cheapest rate.

Youth hostel reservations can usually be made the morning or day of, unless the location is in season or the location is highly regarded. *The Budget Accommodations Guide Volume I* available from HI/AYH covers all Europe and the Mediterranean and is available at the same contact information as above.

The cheapest way to do it is just arrive and figure it out from there. That way you can meet other travelers to split costs or haggle with the vendors and further reduce your rate.

Euro-freakout

European summers are warm and mild at night and ideal for outdoor snoozing. About half my of nights throughout Europe I just pulled out my sleeping gear and commando-crashed outside. On the beach, in a park, on the roof of car park stair well, and in the back of station wagon or van. Wherever I ended up at night, that's where I would crash.

Only once was I disturbed during the night. After a late night train ride into Arles, France, I spotted a sand pile that could suffice for a bed. I couldn't be bothered to find a room, so I just passed out on the sand pile. Sometime in the middle of the night I awoke to a Frenchman standing a few meters away, smoking a cigarette, and just looking at me. I climbed out of my blankets, jumped up, and said "What's up? What do you need?" He stared at me for a minute, said something in French, and marched off. Needless to say, I didn't sleep too well that night, and resolved it best to crash outdoors with other people from then on.

Outdoor Snoozing

Rip-offs are rampant for people commando-crashing outdoors, particularly in Europe. Backpacks are taken, money belts being used as pillows are unzipped and cleared of contents, and even shoes are swiped. If you are going to Europe on a low-budget and plan to sleep outdoors part of the time, consider a few tips. First, it is always best to sleep in a group. There is definitely safety in numbers. Second, sleep with your money belt inside your sleeping bag, but not all the way at the bottom. There have been incidents of thieves feeling the bottom of a sleeping person's sleeping bag for a money belt, then cutting the bag open with a knife and removing it. Third, chain your backpack to something, lock all the zippers, and try to use part of it as a pillow. Lastly, whenever sleeping with a group, lock all the packs together in the middle and position yourselves like spokes around a wheel hub. Detour thieves by making it hard for them to steal anything.

Asian Slumbers

Since the cost of a room is so cheap on the Asian circuits, there is really no reason to crash outdoors. In many places the dollar-a-night yardstick still applies, and finding a cheap place to sleep is hardly difficult (except in Japan and the Tiger Nations). Usually the problem is a horde of hotel operators swarming around you at the bus stand competing to have you stay at their place. A good technique is to listen for the lowest price and see if any other vendor can beat it. When you are satisfied that you have the lowest rate (they are all pretty much the same rooms but locations vary), go to check it out. Always look over the room, the bathroom, and potential breaches of security before you agree to take it.

If there are no vendors to take you to their hotel, have a walk around the train or bus station, it is usually a good place to start looking in a new town. The travel guides always list their favorites, but since they are in the book they tend to be more expensive and more crowded, so that is why *World Stompers* recommends freestyling. Sniff it out yourself, or ask other travelers where they have been.

Japan and the Tigers (South Korea, Taiwan, Hong Kong, Singapore) all have hostels for cheap. Walk around the older city sections where the low-priced guesthouses usually are. Again, locate the tourist information office when you get to the airport or train station and get a free map and accommodation price list.

Other Developing Countries

On the Middle East and the Central and South American circuits, the idea of simply showing up and finding a place is certainly the way to go. Use the same techniques as Asian Slumbers.

Address Book Lodgings

Your address book can be your greatest source of ultra-budget accommodations. Collecting addresses from other travelers is easy, and the people you have traveled with at one time or another will roll out the red carpet when you show up in their neck of the woods. Research your family tree for long lost relatives, or friends of friends living abroad. Any contact, no matter how distant, is better than no contact at all. Chances are you'll be welcomed with open arms and have someone to show you around.

Keep the lines of communication open with your host, and establish right away when you plan to leave. Remember this Italian proverb: house guests are like fish, only good for a few days. Be sensitive to your host. Helping out with household chores is always appreciated, or giving them a present. Send a postcard or call a few weeks before you expect to arrive, and send a thank-you note sometime after you leave.

Earthlings

"AHHHHHHH!! ... Randall! Stop
toying with my emotions!"

"Ours is not to reason why, ours is but to do and become
permanently deactivated."
The Robot
Lost in Space

Ask a Stomper ...
Questions and Answers

The first key to wisdom is this — constant and frequent questioning ... for by doubting we are led to questions and by questioning we arrive at the truth.
— Pierre Abelard, *Sic et Non*, 1120

General Questions

Where did you sleep? On expensive country circuits like Europe, Australia, North America, or Japan, it is wise to stay with friends, outside if it's warm, or in youth hostels. On the cheap circuits of Asia, South and Central America, the Middle East, and Africa, it is very easy to locate an inexpensive guesthouse when you arrive at your destination. Reservations are unnecessary and prices in developing countries are way too cheap to bother sleeping outside, unless you really love doing it.

I want to buy souvenirs, but I do not want to get ripped off, any tips? A few. First, the name of the game is haggling for everything — that is, outside Western countries. There is no such thing as a fixed price, so ask the merchant the price for everything you look at. Even if the price is unbelievably cheap, feign a shocked look, and offer a quarter of the price. Usually you will both meet somewhere in the middle. If the merchant will not budge, try flashing the cash amount you want to offer and see if he bites ... money talks, bullshit walks. Leave if you don't get your price, it's better than being pressured. Sometimes you will be outside the shop and the merchant will come running out and sell at your price.

How did you afford it? Good saving and spending habits before leaving the country. Always being conscious of making or spending money while working or traveling abroad. That's really all it takes.

What countries would you recommend as the best to visit? The worst? Too numerous to list all the good (see: Part Three: Stomping Grounds). The worst are also listed in Part Three.

What did you eat and drink? Wherever there are travelers and tourists (in 90% of all countries worldwide), there are restaurants and shops that cater. Not all are good, but finding food and drinks is rarely a problem. A good rule of thumb to avoid dehydration in tropical countries is to remember to drink two liters of safe water everyday.

Okay, but what *kind* of food? The ethnic, staple food of each country will always be the cheapest, but not always the best. There are loads of restaurants that cater to Westerners and serve Western food. For example, breakfast: banana pancakes, yogurt, coffee, juice. Lunch: sandwiches, stir-fry, fruit salad, soda pop. Dinner: pizza, spaghetti, meat products, beer, mixed drinks. Just like a typical menu in a diner here.

How about tipping? Tipping is only a North American and sometimes European phenomenon. Tips are not expected or required in most regions of the world because service is included in the price. Such tip sources as restaurant waiters, cab drivers, hostel staff, and airport baggage handlers do not expect to be tipped. If you hand them money, of course they will take it, but you are just throwing your money away. The best way to check whether tipping is appropriate is to ask another traveler or an objective local.

Earthlings

Static Cling Syndrome

When I get too much stuff, can I send it home? Absolutely. Package everything in several layers of newspaper, put it in a box, go to the local post office, wrap it, and send it sea-mail. Sea-mail takes three months compared to air-mail which takes three weeks, but is twice as expensive. Sending printed materials, such as books, print photos, and photo negatives should be packaged and sent separately because they are even cheaper than shipping sea-mail. Most post offices have printed material rates.

Where do you wash your clothes? Washing powder is available in little shops everywhere, or, on the cheap circuits, you can pay a dollar or so to have it washed by someone in the guesthouse. It's a good idea to pack a length of cord for a clothes line.

Developing Country Questions

What is the difference between a developing country and a Western country? A developing country refers to a "third world" country, or a nation in the course of becoming fully developed. A developing country is one in the process of building highways, power plants, mass housing, available medicine, and a move from an agrarian to an industrial society. Western, and developed regions of the world include: The United States, Canada, most all of Europe, Israel, Australia, New Zealand, Japan, and the far-east Asian Tigers (Singapore, Taiwan, Hong Kong, and South Korea). In general, Western countries have a developed infrastructure, telecommunications, efficient transportation, and a high standard of living.

Weren't you worried about parasites and diseases? Of course! That is the reason for seeing a travel doctor before leaving any Western nation. See: Staying Well, above.

What are the toilets like in developing countries? Squat method into a floor toilet; same as humans have been doing for thousands of years. Don't worry, you do get used to it.

How did you read things in foreign countries, like the train or bus schedules? They are written side by side in English, exclusively in English, or are easy enough to figure out. Rarely a problem.

How safe is it to travel on the buses and trains? Probably as safe as it is in any Western country. In both cases it would be wise to always know where your stuff is at all times. As far as physical safety, I would feel safer on public transportation in developing countries than I would on any American city system.

Did you ever need to contact the U.S. Embassy? Only one time when I had all my money stolen in India (see: Setbacks). They really helped me out when I was in a bind.

Is there reason to worry about being falsely accused of a crime? I have never heard this happening to anyone. Not to say it cannot happen, but when you travel you are usually a respected and revered person. You are perceived as supporting the local economy. Basically, it is in everyone's best interest to keep travelers happy, unless, of course you are doing something illegal.

What if I'm busted, is it possible to bribe my way out of trouble? If done tactfully, yes. In some countries like India, Brazil, and Indonesia minor extortion scams are prevalent and buying favors is common practice. Opportunistic officials who are poorly paid and unsupervised have been known to shakedown the occasional traveler. Five or ten dollars on a blank piece of paper usually does the trick.

What about bandits? Certainly, there are many scam artists and thieves out there, but that can be said about any country. As far as roaming gangs looking to bump off travelers, I have heard of that only on rare occasions.

Plane Ticket Questions

If I want to take a world tour, what kind of airline tickets should I buy? What about a package tour? I do not advocate travel tours or packages because of the incremental, added costs. The round-the-world tickets (RTW) package is probably the cheapest way to do a world tour if you shop around and find a good deal. Around $1,800 is the low-end price, best purchased from a consolidator. In London try Trailfinders, 194 Kensington High Street, London W8 7RG, UK; (071) 938-3939. In the U.S. try Ticket Planet, 50 Grant Ave., San Francisco, CA 94108; (800) 799-8888 or Air Brokers International, 150 Post Street, Suite 620, San Francisco, CA 94103; (800) 883-3273.

The big problem with round-the-world-one-way is they are only good for one year. If you happen to get caught up in one place for six months, like India, you would have to hurry through the rest. So they limit you with time. If you do not use the rest of your tickets within that year, you forfeit them – no refunds! Most times RTW tickets go only one direction. Once you have gone east, for example, you cannot backtrack west of your farthest eastern city.

The other way to do it is look for cheap tickets as you work your way around. After I finished teaching in Japan, I was already in Asia and picked up my tickets one at a time, whenever my visa expired or when I wanted to move on.

Is it easy to do it that way? Very easy. All travel agents abroad speak English and in some places the ticket prices are the lowest in the world. The best places to buy individual tickets are: Penang, Malaysia; Bangkok, Thailand; Athens, Greece; and London, England. Almost all tickets are open for one year, so it is wise to pick up your next circuit ticket(s) in these cheap locations.

I asked my travel agent and she said that was very difficult to do! Of course she did. When Stompers pick up tickets along the way, the domestic travel agent gets no commission. To be honest, I never deal with U.S. travel agents anyhow, apart from quotes on one-way ticket prices out. Travel agents here cater to tourists, getting fat commissions on car rentals, hotel reservations, lame tours, and package deals. Any travel agent will try to talk you out of the one way-ticket plan. My advice: just get over there and wing it! William Shakespeare's advice: "Let every eye negotiate for itself, and trust no agent."

What are some other ways to save money on plane tickets? Glad you asked. Check fares until the day you depart, even after purchasing a ticket. If your fare is reduced, the airline may refund the difference, but only if you ask for it. Confirm your flight a few days prior to departure to check if the flight has changed, and if it might be overbooked. If it is overbooked you might be able to receive money back. Overbooked flights pay up to the cost of a ticket for anyone willing to forfeit their seat and take another flight. It might mean waiting around several extra hours or even a week, but for a few hundred dollars it could be worth it. To position yourself on a potentially overbooked flight, get to the airport early. Put your name on the top of the overbooked list. Clear customs early to avoid the risk of losing your seat if you really have to depart. (For more tips, see: Expenses Overseas.)

Is there a best time to fly? Yes. If you are traveling eastbound, schedule your arrival for morning, destination time. Westbound, shoot for a late afternoon arrival. This will help your body's internal clock get "in sync" faster and minimize jet lag.

Money Questions

What is the best currency to travel with? U.S. dollar traveler's checks by far. If they are lost or stolen you are insured to have them replaced for free, and they are the most widely recognized, therefore, least hassle in exchanging. Get denominations of $20, $50, and $100.

It is also a good idea to bring one or two hundred dollars in small bills. Stash a twenty or a fifty in your backpack or shoe just in case your money belt, checks and check receipts are stolen. Having U.S. notes are also good for exchanging money on the black markets of Nepal and China, to name a few. U.S. dollars are the most recognized currency in the world. Rarely is there a merchant who will not accept dollars if you have not changed money yet, or run out of the local currency.

Isn't the black market illegal? Officially, yes. Enforced? Rarely. Many travelers are tempted by black market cash conversions which save from

10 to 30 percent over the official government version which the banks must follow. Chances are much better that you will get burned by the old switcheroo than a government bust. See China; Work and Money, below.

How much money should I bring? As much as possible! Just don't forget to leave some money behind for emergencies and when you return. For a general idea of travel expenses, see: "Lists of the World" in Part Three.

But for the most part, traveler's checks are the way to go, huh? Definitely. The first thing to remember is to sign all of the checks on the first signature line so they are insured. Never countersign until you are ready to make a purchase. It is very important to keep the check receipts (which include: serial numbers, denomination, issuing bank, date purchased, and lost check recovery instructions) separate from the checks themselves. Make photocopies of the check receipts and stash them in various parts of your luggage and leave a copy with parents or friends.

If I am working and earning money overseas, is it possible to save money on exchange rates? Indeed. Before converting your foreign currency into U.S. dollar traveler's checks, study the exchange rates in major city newspapers and the "trade-weighted value of the dollar." The latter is an index showing how the dollar is ranking against the currencies of the 10 major industrial nations – in other words, how it's doing against the world. The trick is to covert your foreign currency when you think the dollar is at its weakest point, or convert U.S. dollars in the country you are in when you think they are the strongest. It is sometimes a guessing game, but research and a knowledge of international exchange rates can only help your odds of exchanging at the most opportune moment.

What if my money is ripped off? The cash is unrecoverable, the traveler's checks can be replaced. Contact the check issuer's toll-free or city number as soon as possible, usually right after the police report is filled out. Replacement checks or a refund will be issued free of charge by a local bank during normal working business hours. If you have to wait some time before receiving replacement checks, contact the nearest local U.S. embassy or consulate. They are empowered to give you a small loan or cash a personal check if you have one.

Where can I change traveler's checks into the local currency? U.S. banks do not like to deal in small amounts of foreign currency so they usually charge hefty commissions. Hold off exchanging dollars until you arrive at you destination. Every international airport has 24-hour money changers, but their rates suck, so only change $20 for bus fares, a room, and a meal. When you check into a guesthouse and drop the pack, walk around town to see if anyone on the street offers you a black-market rate. If not, look at the rate boards in bank windows or special exchange shops, like American Express. Ask other travelers if they know which bank gives the best rate in town, it can sometimes be a substantial difference. If you intend on spending a fair amount of time in the country you have arrived in, exchange a large amount when you find the best rate. This will reduce the amount of exchange fees and service charges you incur when converting money on a frequent basis.

How about ATM withdrawals and credit cards? ATM and credit card cash advance machines are a pretty regular sight at most European and Asian banks nowadays. ATMs allows you to withdraw from your hometown bank, as do some credit cards. Both offer favorable exchange rates, with little or no service charges. ATM cards are quickly becoming the most common and convenient way of exchanging money in foreign countries. If using credit cards, just remember the perils of 18.5 percent interest rates (see: Money). Either pay it off in the first month, or continue accruing obscene interest rates until the entire balance is paid off.

Isn't it hard to figure out all those different currencies? Not really. Say you go to Egypt and the exchange rate is 4.1 Egyptian pounds to the U.S. dollar. You know then, that one Egyptian pound is about a quarter. Then you go to a guesthouse and they tell you it is 10 pound a night, you know it is close to $2.50 converted. It helps a whole lot if you are quick with these conversions, especially in shops or exchanging currency on the black market.

Visa Questions

What is the deal with visas? Each and every country has its own policy for admitting visitors. Some require you to have a visa, others do not. A visa is a stamp or sticker placed in your passport granting you permission to visit, or pass through a country. The stamp itself indicates how long you are allowed to stay in that country. Visas are issued by embassies and consulates. You must have a valid passport. You will not be issued a visa if your passport is due to expire within six months.

Nationality of the passport holder effects entry and length of stay. For example, Israelis are not permitted into most Muslim countries. The city where you pick up your visa is also important. For example, a two month visa for Taiwan can only be obtained in Hong Kong, and some countries are weeks slower than others in issuing visas. Ask other travelers for the best locations to renew or pick-up.

What if I overstay my visa? You will likely pay a fine (sometimes a bribe) anywhere from $5 to $20 for each day you have overstayed. Pay attention to the departure dates stamped in your passport. Extend your visa while you have the time, or leave the country on your allotted dates to avoid unnecessary fees and hassles.

Don't some countries have weird requirements to get their visa? Yes. Some governments issuing visas for several months, namely Australia and Europe, require evidence that you have enough money to support yourself. They do this because they do not want you working. So in order to get a six-month visa to Oz, you have to show about $3000 (called sufficient funds) to the embassy personnel. Another weird policy is the minimum expenditure requirement. Certain countries with weaker currencies require you to convert a certain amount of money into their currency, depending on your length of stay. This is designed to discourage black market trading. Countries in the former east bloc (Poland, Slovakia, Romania), South Yemen, Angola and Ghana have such requirements.

Is there a publication I can get on visa requirements? Yes. The U.S. government will send you a comprehensive list specifying all visa requirements worldwide, free of charge. Write to: U.S. Department of State, Passport Services Correspondence Branch, Room 386, 1425 K Street NW, Washington, DC 20524.

The U.S. government is a wealth of travel information. Two recommended free publications from the U.S. State Department will help get you started. The first is *Tips for Travelers*, which covers currency regulations, customs, and other general tips for individual countries. The second is *Background Notes*, which provides updated information on various countries' culture, history, geography, government, economy and political conditions. Contact the Superintendent of Documents, U.S. Government Printing Office, Washington, DC 20420, (202) 512-1800, or check your local library.

For complete (recorded) State Department travel information, call 202-647-5225; to access the Consular Affairs (computer) Bulletin Boards, call 202-647-3000; for information by fax, call 202-647-3000 from your fax machine.

Communication Questions

What if I want to call home? Making a long-distance phone call or fax from abroad is hardly a problem. In Western countries it is as simple as calling collect the way we do here, buying a calling-card, or dropping change into a pay-phone. Do not make calls through your hotel switchboard as the surcharges are outrageous. In developing countries, the government runs the PTT (Post, Telephone, and Telegraph) and the employees always speak English. Private phone owners sometimes have public telephone and faxs in their shops. Just look for the signs.

What if I need money sent? Western Union has thousands of locations worldwide. You can send and receive unlimited amounts within 24 hours. American Express and Thomas Cook offer an Emergency Funds Express service. This allows up to $1000 in U.S. traveler checks to be issued within hours. Expect to lose a percentage with each transaction. Western Union offers a Charge Card Money Order where up to $1000 can be sent or received abroad by phone (1-800-325-6000.) In extreme emergencies, the U.S. Embassy is empowered to loan you $50 until you can complete a transition through the State Department Citizens Emergency Center at Embassys and consulates worldwide. There is a $15 charge for this service, plus the communication expense.

Can I get letters and postcards sent to me while I am traveling? Sure can. Every Post Office, from the big cities to tiny villages has a GPO address (General Post Office) called "Poste Restante." In the Spanish-speaking regions of the world the general delivery is known as "Lista de Correos." If, for example, you wanted to send your buddy Brad a postcard next October when he is in Nepal for the trekking season, just address it; Mr. Brad <u>Olsen</u>, Poste Restante, GPO Kathmandu, Nepal. It's that simple, but do remember to underline the last name so it is put in the "O" box, not in the "B" box. Travelers should remember this and have a look in both boxes of their first and last name.

When you arrive, find the Poste Restante counter, and pull the letters out yourself. You may need to show your passport to prove your possessions. Letters, packages, and postcards are held for one or two months before they are sent back, so make sure the sender knows when you will be at that location. A more reliable way of receiving mail is to know someone in the country you are going to, and have your mail sent to their home.

Wrap Up Questions

Is it necessary to write to foreign governments for their free brochures? Nope. All those glossy pamphlets are pretty unrealistic and cater to tourists, anyhow. It is important not to get too bogged down with paperwork. For preparation, this book is all you need!

Is there anything I cannot bring back into the country? Yes. Ivory, marine-mammal products, furs, coral, tortoise shells, reptile skins, feathers, and certain other wildlife products will be confiscated by custom officials. Besides, buying these products is unethical and perpetuates the destruction of our planet. For specifics, call the public information office of the World Wildlife Fund at (202) 293-4800 and ask for the "Buyer Beware" booklet.

Okay, I want to Stomp, but what is the right trip or duration for me? That depends entirely on your time, money, and desire. Deciding which part of the world you wish to see should depend on what you know about that region beforehand, and also what interests you. If you have taken Spanish classes, maybe South or Central America would be fun. If you studied Western Civilization then Europe or the Middle East would be cool. If international business was your major, then East Asia or Europe would be particularly rewarding. If you like to party and kick back, go to Southeast Asia or Australia. For amazing jungles, go to South America. If you don't have much money then try the ultra-cheap Sub-Continent circuit. If you want it all, take a round-the-world-tour.

(Looking at a girl sucking on a phallic-like ice-pop)

"Enjoying that my little lovely? A bit cold and pointless, isn't it? What you got back home little lovely to play your fuzzy warbles on? I bet you've got say, pitiful, portable, picnic players? Come with uncle and hear all proper! Hear angel's trumpets and devil's trombones. You are invited."
Alexander DeLarge
A Clockwork Orange

Checklist Hell

*Why not seize the pleasure at once? How often is happiness
destroyed by preparation, foolish preparation!*
– Jane Austen (1775-1817)

Or maybe not so foolish.

Primary items are the most important. They should be sought and purchased before departure. *Secondary items* are items easily picked up on the Stomp, or brought along if you have them already.

What To Bring (*Primary*)

Passport. This pocket-sized booklet certifies your identity and nationality and is the property of the U.S. government. In effect, it is your license to Stomp. Apply in person at an issuing agent, usually a Post Office, and present: proof of citizenship (birth certificate or driver's license or state ID card); two identical passport photos; $55 passport fee; and $10 execution fee. The passport is valid for 10 years and the renewal cost is $40.

Backpack. The metal frame camping packs are out. Shoot for an internal frame, soft backpack with a detachable day pack. Make sure the zippers connect onto each other and allow a small padlock to fit through. Another alternative is a large duffel bag with a wide shoulder strap so it can be carried with relative ease. Again, check for padlock capabilities. Always keep an identification tag on each and every bag. Forget suitcases.

Sleeping bag. If you are following the ultra-budget guidelines, there is no cheaper way to crash than on a beach during warm summer nights. The bag not only serves to sleep in, but can double as a coat on cold days, serve as a cushion on hard seats, and a bed top-cover when guesthouses do not provide one. It is more sanitary to continuously sleep in your own bag than use provided blankets. Get a light bag that can be deflated so as to take up little space.

Money belt. This "life-support system" is the most essential item on the Stomp. Rarely should it ever leave your sight. In it are airline tickets, traveler's check receipts, wallet and cash, passport, International Certificate of Vaccination, International Driving Permit, address book and pen, keys, translator computer, and condoms. Look for a well-made leather belt with many zipper pockets, and adjustments   for comfort.

A pocket knife. You will use it more than you can ever guess. Shoot for a regular-sized knife with a key chain for your padlocks, and scissors for bandages.

Camera. A 35 mm camera is more bulky and harder to work than an instamatic camera, but much more durable. You make the call. A set of extra batteries is a good idea too, because replacements can be hard to find.

Document Pouch. Make photocopies of the following: your passport front page, drug prescriptions, ATM and credit cards, traveler's check receipts, and active plane tickets. Keep separate from the money belt. Leave the pouch in the bottom of your pack. Also leave a complete set at home.

Toiletry kit. Toothbrush, toothpaste, Chapstick, brush or comb, soap, trial-size shampoo, skin lotion, nail clipper, dental floss (many uses), liniment (e.g., Tiger Balm), razor, and back-up condoms. A soft leather travel case with multiple zippers to keep it all in works best.

Padlocks. A regular-sized bike lock and cable to secure your belongings to the luggage rack on a train. The lock also serves well on guesthouse doors. Two small locks for the zippers on the pack.

A travel journal. You are going on the adventure of a lifetime; writing down your individual experiences and observations will be a unique personal treasure. Adventure travel, because it removes you so completely from normal everyday life, invariably stimulates contemplation and triggers unaccustomed musings. "I never travel without my diary," wrote Oscar Wilde. "One should always have something sensational to read in the train." *World Stompers* started out no more than a travel journal.

Language translator/calculator. Not essential, but a useful tool especially in Latin America, France, or Japan.

Remember this: Less is more when packing.

What To Bring (*Secondary*)

Medical kit. Any prescription drugs, cold pills, Tylenol, bandages and Band-Aids, antihistamine for allergies, Pepto-Bismol, antiseptic for wounds, spare eyeglasses or contacts, insect repellent, sun screen and lotion, and water purification tablets. Most of these items can be purchased in developing countries for very cheap, so start out light.

Washing gear. Keep a bag of laundry powder double-wrapped in (two) plastic bags to prevent the inevitable spillage ... and maybe your hand soap, too.

Sunglasses. Best are UV-blocking sunglasses. Get side panels if you are going to the mountains.

Sunscreen. As the ozone becomes more and more depleted, so do the odds of getting severely sunburned. Do not take chances, pack lots of sunscreen (SPF 15 or higher).

Sewing kit. Threads and needles. Spare buttons. They come in handy.

Walkman or small portable cassette-radio. Tunes are a must. Walkmans are more portable, lightweight, and take up less space; portable cassette players are more convenient and social.

Cassette tapes. Bring along some of your favorite homemade mixes, but not too many. Bootlegs of the original $10.98 list tape - Nirvana's *Nevermind*, for example - can be had for as little as two bucks in places like Thailand and Nepal.

Books. Traveling is an ideal time to do a lot of reading. Bring a novel and a travel guide, then trade them off to other travelers or second-hand book-stores when you are finished.

Toilet paper roll(s). Doubles as a clean-up rag or tissues.

Lightweight flashlight. Better than a stubbed toe.

A sheet or sleeping bag liner. Keep it rolled up in your sleeping bag. Use it on warm nights, or extra cold nights in conjunction with the sleeping bag.

Map. A good pocket map or a handbook atlas comes in handy.

Clock or watch. There will be times you have to wake up early to catch a train or bus.

Therm-a-Rest. These inflatable air mattresses are invaluable if you plan to sleep on hard surfaces during some of your trip. They are more comfortable than foam pads, as well as inflatable, durable, and make a nice cushion on the bus or train.

Always have an emergency stash of food. The best is a trail mix of chocolate, peanuts, and raisins. This extraordinarily tasty high-carbo concoction provides instant energy and keeps for a long time.

Clothes (Primary)

Two pairs of underwear.

Two pairs of socks.

Swimsuit.

One pair of jeans.

One pair of shorts.

A few shirts and T-shirts.

One pair of sneakers or shoes. Cross-trainer gym shoes, lightweight hiking boots, or Doc Martens are recommended.

Lightweight jacket or raincoat.

A dress up set of clothes. Especially effective when going through customs.

Sweater or heavy sweatshirt.

Clothes (Secondary)

Sarong. A colorful, good-sized piece of cloth, very useful as an item of clothing, bed sheet, beach blanket, window covering, pillow, and emergency towel.

Sandals or thongs.

Beach towel. Large and light. Can sometimes serve as a light blanket.

What To Bring (Special Interest)

Guitar or musical instrument. For busking or entertaining others, musicians are most welcome.

Art kit. Colored pencils, fluorescent markers, thick and thin marker pens, bristol board or a drawing pad, tape, scissors, eraser, Exacto knife, and fine-tip pens. Keep it all in a macramé bag.

Small gift items. Wristbands, necklaces, stickers, cheap watches, pens, little trinkets or snap shots of home. Any lightweight and inexpensive items to give away. Small tokens go a long way.

Student card. Definitely get one of these. Even if you are not going where there are a lot of museums, they will still save you money where you would least expect.

International Driving Permit (IDP). Valid for one year, IDPs cost $10 and are available from any branch of the American Automobile Association, (800) 222-4357. You will need a current driver's license and two passport-size photos to apply.

European Train Pass. For those going to Europe, the most practical way of getting around this circuit is the Eurail Youthpass (for those under age 26). Good for unlimited travel on 17 countries' second-class trains, they also offer free or discounted travel on ferries and national bus lines. Consult a travel agent for details, or call Rail Europe at (800) 4-EURAIL. Passes must be purchased prior to arrival in Europe.

Frisbee, paddle ball, or hacky-sack. Great way to meet people and stay in shape.

Plastic playing cards, chess, or backgammon; whatever pulls your chain.

Extra eyeglasses (or contacts). For the visually impaired.

What To Bring (Specifically For Women)

Extra toiletry kit. Brush, mirror, good brand of skin cream, hairpins, hair gel and spray in small sizes, a pack of tissues, and extra condoms.

A conservative dress. Especially useful in Muslim countries. Women should consider making their primary travel garment a long, loose skirt.

One sport bra.

Tampons. Always carry back-ups, they can be rather difficult to find off the beaten track.

An extra sarong or local wrap. In many developing countries, the local women use beautiful multi-colored pieces of cloth as their primary dress. In addition to being useful as an extra towel or ground cloth, it serves as a cultural bridge. Local people will appreciate that you are adopting their traditional dress.

Know what climate you are going to and pack accordingly.

Conventional Stomping wisdom advises, "pack half as much as you think you will need, and then take twice as much money." There is nothing quite as annoying as having to leave behind a valuable piece of clothing or extra shoes because you over-packed. Running out of money sucks too.

The secret to successful packing is strong plastic "stuff bags" for the small items. It keeps things separate, clean, and dry. Do not pack any more clothes than is on this list; in fact, keep one-third of your pack empty when you leave. Reason is, you'll be picking up clothes and souvenirs along the way and you'll need the extra space.

Keep the pack streamlined.

Pack clothing combinations that work well with each other, or can be utilized in the "layered look." Several layers of clothing under a thin raincoat are just as effective as a heavy winter coat. Dark clothes are the best because they show the least amount of dirt, but can get warm in tropical climates. Khaki is the best color for warm places because it is light enough to reflect the sun, but dark enough not to show the dust. Also good for warm climates and hiding dirt are the natural fabrics the locals wear. Avoid white clothes.

What Not To Bring (*Total Deadweight Items*)

Cooking stove and utensils. Unless your entire trip is strictly camping, it's total deadweight.

Excessive winter clothes.

Valuable or expensive-looking jewelry. Irreplaceable family objects.

Large containers of anything.

Too many pills or medical items. One traveler's medical kit was so huge it included an IV bag and fresh needles!

Facial wipe pads.

Too many books. Encyclopedia (20 volumes).

Water filter or Thermos.

Tent and camping supplies.

All unnecessary credit cards.

Curling iron or hair dryer.

Portable coffee maker.

Immersion heater.

Umbrella.

Plastic tarp.

Silverware, plates, or cups.

Heavy jacket. If it's cold, just wear multiple layers.

Kitchen sink.

Personal Health Checklist

Call a travel doctor and tell him where you are going. Get all necessary shots and vaccinations. Pack and photocopy the International Health Certificate the doctor gives you (see: Staying Well).

Have a dental checkup. There is nothing worse than a toothache on the Stomp. However, if it does happen, dentistry is very cheap in developing countries.

Read up on potential risks where you are going. Be aware of any and all dangers in the circuits that interest you. Know before departure about any political strife and potential diseases for each country you plan to visit.

Exercise frequently. See: Staying Fit, above.

Avoid hell. Some seasoned Stompers have been known to enter a country with no more than a toothbrush and a comb; buying their clothes and gear upon arrival. Again, remember to pack light.

Top Ten Things You Can Do to Save the Earth

10. **Do not use aerosols.** Many species of frogs are becoming extinct because harmful solar radiation is frying their eggs and tadpoles. Ozone holes in the southern hemisphere are burning people severely. You could be next.

9. **Recycle.** Bottles, cans, plastics and newspapers have a second life – give it to them.

8. **Bring your own bag to market.** Just a simple action saves trees.

7. **Avoid wearing fur and recognize that animals have a right to live.** When you observe how horribly animals are mistreated worldwide, you cannot help but feel compassion. Many travelers have become vegetarians after they have seen how meat is really prepared.

6. **Separate your garbage.** Bulging landfills emit methane (CH_4) gasses and contribute to global warming. This is largely due to organic garbage going unseperated. Make a compost pile instead.

5. **Donate to conservation movements.** If time or money is not feasible, then educate yourself.

4. **Do not buy hardwood furniture or products made from trees such as rosewood, mahogany, or teak.** Hardwood trees are disappearing at an alarming rate. Never buy animal products, either. Ivory, tortoise shells, furs, feathers, and reptile skins will be confiscated by custom officials. Both perpetuate the death and destruction of this planet.

3. **Walk or ride a bike whenever possible.** Auto emissions are the leading cause of the greenhouse effect. Auto emissions are responsible for the melting ice caps and the warming of the planet. The U.S. is the number one fuel consumer; equaling one-quarter of total world annual consumption with only 4% of the worlds' population. Besides, most people do not get enough exercise.

2. **Plant a tree.** Globally, we are several million short of these at the moment. Anything green helps restore the natural environment.

1. **Travel the world.** Only by seeing for yourself the rape and destruction of Mother Earth that is going on right now, can you truly grasp the mess we are all in.

Whether you are setting out with a friend or a love mate, or if you are going solo and you hook up with someone on the road, remember these ...

Top Ten Terms For Partnership

10. **Respect each other's property.** Always ask to borrow items, and keep an eye out for their stuff as much as you would your own.

9. **Establish a solo clause.** If one wants to go solo at any time one should be able to do so without a guilt trip.

8. **Expect to pay your own way always, and never feel obliged to pay for someone else.**

7. **Help your partner in an emergency unconditionally.** But if it concerns money, make conditions.

6. **Share and share alike.** Food, toiletry items, tapes, books, stories, laughs. Good karma always comes around when it's you wanting to borrow something belonging to someone else.

5. **Do not get into the exclusive partner rut.** Both should make an effort to meet other dudes and dudettes because that is half the fun of traveling.

4. **Compromise.** It is only fair when everyone involved participates in making group decisions.

3. **Don't be a leech.** Establish mutual plans to travel with a group, but back off if others give you "the vibe."

2. **Don't be a mooch.** Bogarts get the boot.

1. **Respect each others privacy.** Being considerate is usually the make or break of partnerships.

"Someone did a study of the three most-often-heard phrases in New York City. One is, 'Hey, taxi.' Two is, 'What train do I take to get to Bloomingdale's?' And three is, 'Don't worry. It's only a flesh wound.' "
David Letterman
Late Night with David Letterman

EARTHLINES

Lao Tzu says: "A journey of a
thousand miles begins with
a single step."

Part

 **3**

Stomping Grounds

For my part, I travel not to go anywhere, but to go.
I travel for travel's sake. The great affair is to move.
— Robert Louis Stevenson

The road of excess leads to the palace of wisdom.
— William Blake

Go abroad and you'll hear news of home.
— English proverb

The proper means of increasing the love we bear to our
native country is to reside some time in a foreign one.
— Shenstone

A love affair imparts adventure, and adventure
is as needful to the soul as food is to the body ...
men and women are both taught to put
aside adventure with adolescence.
— Michael Drury

Work Around the Planet

*The Master said, "To learn and at due times to repeat what one has learned:
is that not after all a pleasure? That friends should come from afar,
is that not after all delightful?"*
– Confucius (551-478 BC)

Finding a job in another country is not as difficult as you might think. Sometimes it is as easy as showing up and calling a few places from a hostel bulletin board, or talking to other travelers. The key is finding a location that suits you and being prepared to make a commitment of several months to a year.

If you are aching to travel now and haven't saved enough to voyage abroad, consider working somewhere really cool in the U.S. You are legal to work in places like Hawaii, Alaska, and dozens of winter ski resorts. These locations will be discussed in The North America Circuit.

**Teaching English as a second language is the most
common full-time job for Americans overseas.**

Long-Term Employment: Teaching English

Teaching English abroad is a highly respected position in just about any community. A college diploma will almost certainly land you instant middle-class wages. Opportunities are growing as more and more nations open their borders to foreign trade. Currently the greatest teaching demand exists in the Far-East, specifically the People's Republic of China (PRC). Also, economic miracles, such as the Tiger Nations, continue to hire more English teachers in line with their ever-growing communication needs.

Teaching options vary widely. Private and informal tutoring allows you to set you own hours and commitments. Internships, such as a head teacher's aide, permits you to learn as you earn. After a year you can become a head teacher in a public school. Teaching conversation English is one of the most popular jobs. There are also a multitude of volunteering positions in "Third World" countries, the best known is the Peace Corps. For information and applications, contact: Peace Corps, Public Response Unit, 1111 20th Street NW, Washington, DC 20526; (800) 424-8580.

There are two requirements an employer will look for when interviewing prospective English teachers; being born in a country where English is the native language, and having a college degree. It doesn't matter what subject the degree is in, just so you have graduated and have a copy or the original diploma as proof. Finding a job is relatively easy after that.

A good online publication for teaching abroad is: www.iie.org. It discusses other teaching opportunities besides English, like music, drawing, writing, and seminars. The Institute of International Education (212) 883-8200 or (800) 445-0443 has information on teaching opportunities abroad. Contact them at: 809 United Nations Plaza, New York, NY 10017.

Also, *Work Abroad: The Complete Guide to Finding a Job Overseas*, by Clayton Hubbs, breaks down the world country-by-country and provide listings of the multitude of available positions offered overseas. Published by Transitions Abroad Publishers.

A good backroads way into teaching positions is to read the book parents use when looking into sending their children abroad. *The Schools Abroad of Interest to Americans* lists over 800 elementary and secondary schools in 130 countries. Write to; Porter Sargent Publishers, 11 Beacon Street, Boston, MA 02108 ($56.25 plus $3.20 for postage and handling).

A decent book about working in the land of the rising sun is *Jobs In Japan* by John Wharton. It describes in funny (and not so funny) prose all it takes to live and work in the enigmatic country called Japan. Copies are $14.95 and can be ordered from The Global Press, 1510 York St., Suite 204, Denver, CO 80206.

Other Long-Term Employment

Finding a long-term job, other than teaching English, depends on your qualifications, and the current demand for your skills in another country. For example, computer programming in Japan would be lucrative, but no demand exists. Fashion models, however, are in high demand. Independent income opportunities exist selling multi-level marketing products, such as Amway. Find out what's hot in U.S. products before leaving. In other words, think of jobs the native people cannot do themselves.

Apart from working for a multi-national company that will send you overseas, the next best way to work abroad is simply to go to the country first and put your "feelers" out. Pick up their local employment directory. Do some research in your local library. Check out the resource materials listed in this chapter.

Look for overseas employment agencies that do not require money up front. Be very suspicious of agencies requiring substantial and non-refundable fees. Many times they are rip-off scams because even if they locate a job, you may not be satisfied.

Jobs With Uncle Sam. The U.S. government is the largest single employer of American citizens working overseas, placing over 150,000 civilians in positions abroad. The U.S. Department(s) of State, Commerce, Agriculture, and the U.S. Information Agency all hire personnel for positions overseas. *International Jobs Directory*, by Ronald and Caryl Rae Krannich, lists 1001 employers with advice on being hired. The book also describes all the agencies who hire for overseas jobs, as well as tips on how to prepare for the Foreign Services exam. This book is available for $19.95 by Impact Publications.

Au pair. Au pair work is basically full-time baby-sitting, house cleaning, and cooking for a foreign family. It is available mostly to young women aged 18–30. It can be rather arduous living with a family for months at a time, but it is a good way to learn a language and see what family life is like in other countries. There are many organizations that arrange au pair work all over Europe, a popular one is *Au Pair/Homestay Abroad* at 161 16th Avenue, New York NY, 10013, or call (800) AU-PAIRS.

Resource materials. The following are books related to finding long-term jobs and careers overseas. *Careers in International Affairs*, compiled by the Georgetown School of Foreign Service, provides a broad overview of available opportunities in such fields as the U.S. government, banking, business, consulting, international organizations, media, educational and research organizations. This book is available for $18 by writing to: P.O. Box 4866, Hampton Station, Baltimore MD 21211; or call: (800) 246-9606.

The U.S. government publishes a realistic guide of the major considerations to finding work overseas called; *Employment Abroad: Facts and Fallacies*. It can be obtained from the U.S. Chamber of Commerce, International Division, 1615 H Street NW, Washington, DC 20062. The cost is $7.50.

A helpful guide for job-seekers interested in Europe should check out *How to Get a Job in Europe*, by Robert Sanborn and Cheryl Materly. It covers twenty countries from Greece to Germany to Portugal, listing potential employers in such industries as retail and wholesale, service, and tourism as well as American companies operating in the region. This book is available from Surrey Books, 230 East Ohio Street, Suite 120, Chicago, IL 60611; (800) 326-4430. The cost is $21.95.

Where to Set Up

The top priority to working and living in a foreign country, or another place in the U.S., is to leave showing a profit. This will build your confidence and finance your next move. This objective is difficult in developing nations because wages are much lower. Hey, if you're gonna work in the first place, you might as well make as much money as possible, right? Go to where the money is, which is North America, Europe, Australia, the Pacific Rim, and some scattered Latin American countries. Pay particular attention to high economic growth areas – they have money coming in and a demand for English teachers and foreign workers. Just be careful not to get stuck in a place that sucks. Here are some factors to help you consider what to look for in a location:

Money. Will your wages over time (three months to a few years) allow you to build a travel fund that will get you comfortably to your next destination?

Cost of living. Even if you make a high wage, but spend a lot on rent, food, transportation, and partying, can you still achieve your monetary goals? The way to beat the high cost of living in expensive countries is to establish low fixed costs on rent and transportation (share rental home, ride your bike everywhere) and moderate your food and partying expenses (eat at home often, only go out a few nights per week).

The cultural and educational experience. Getting to know the people, their language, the museums, and historical sites can be the most rewarding aspect of life abroad. These things are best understood by long stay visits. Partying all night in the clubs with a group of friends, or some genuine Stomping around the country will leave lasting memories.

Safety and prejudices. How much crime exists in the city you are considering living in? Are the men sexist towards Western women? How friendly are the local people towards foreigners? Does a person's creed or color make a difference? These are all relevant questions to consider.

Leisure and recreation. This can often be the deciding factor for a successful or unsuccessful long-term stay. What is the point if you're bored and lonely? All work and no play makes Jack a very dull boy, just look what it did to Nicholson in *The Shining*. Things to look for are: beautiful natural scenery, English libraries, foreigner hang-outs such as pubs or social clubs, and variations of sporting facilities (tennis, basketball, aerobics, field sports, mountains for skiing and hiking, workout gyms, swimming pools, and bike trails).

Approximate start-up costs. This expenditure could deplete your entire travel fund in the process of looking for a job. It is imperative to reduce your spending to the bare minimum when first starting out. Give up your addictions and soft scam whenever possible until a job is landed. Employers overseas want to see that you are established and stable before hiring you. Nobody wants to resort to desperate measures like borrowing money from friends or calling home for a loan. Scale back your spending habits now. It may spell the difference between landing a job and saving for a world tour, or heading home empty handed.

Low-Wage Stomper Employment

If a long term commitment is not appealing, there are easy, short term jobs available along the way. The most common is exchanging your services or products for money as you go. Here are some general ideas:

Service jobs. Manual labor is the most available work for travelers. Seasonal farm work such as harvesting and picking is popular and attainable almost everywhere in developed nations. In most Western countries the yellow pages list temporary job agencies. Again, listen to word of mouth or check hostel bulletin boards.

Bartending jobs are common for travelers in resort areas. The resorts like to hire foreigners in order to give the place a more cosmopolitan feel for the mixed clientele they draw. Same goes for tennis instructors, hair stylists, activity directors, waitresses, and even bell boys or room service clerks.

And, of course, there are lousy jobs everywhere.

The longer your trip lasts, especially while working along the way, the less it will cost per day. *It is cheaper to travel than it is to live on your own in America!* **Airfare is the biggest expense for short trips, while food averages out to be the biggest expenditure on multi-year advoyages.**

Street performers. Buskers are those who sing, play an instrument, or otherwise entertain outdoors for their living. Some people really clean up on good nights in wealthy nations like Japan, South Korea, Germany, and Australia. Other talented travelers have a go at juggling, pantomiming, comedy acts, puppetry, ventriloquism, fortune telling, tarot card reading, magic acts, or giant bubble making. Just throw down a hat and stop the crowd with your act and see what comes of it.

Arts and crafts. Those with a knack for drawing can make decent money doing sketch portraits or caricatures of people. Another way to capitalize on your artistic talents is to create chalk masterpieces on the pavement where people are walking by. Both require an initial investment in supplies, but that can be made up in one good day.

Hair wrapping has become a very trendy and popular way for travelers to make some quick cash. The only supplies you need are several spools of multi-colored thread, an assortment of beads and the know-how to make them. Jewelry making is also common with travelers. Collecting coral on the beach and converting it to necklaces, earrings, mobiles and ankle-bands sell pretty well in craft fairs. Other craftworks include: tie-dying, earrings, wristbands, rings, carving, beading, leatherwork, belts, brooches, and musical instruments. Some creative types draw their own postcards to sell. Arts and crafts can be sold at flea markets, festivals, street fairs, or parks. Just throw down a blanket anywhere there is a good flow of pedestrians.

Buying and selling around the world. Before you leave the U.S., look around for small things to bring with that can be sold overseas at a profit. Buy low, sell high. Look around and find something lightweight and unique. Examples include: stickers, wristbands, small toys, wristwatches, anything Disney, jewelry, and macramé change purses. Be creative; if you do not sell them they make great gifts.

The same applies when traveling through inexpensive countries where the mighty dollar goes a long way. Pick up cheap items to re-sell like: batiks, bush knives, small statues, trendy clothes, icon necklaces, silver jewelry, prints, and assorted little knickknacks.

Okay, you have arranged the time, saved the money, and are totally pumped on the desire to Stomp around the planet. Congratulations! Now, where to go? The rest of Part Three outlines the world's travel circuits, highlights of each country, and the best ways to get around. The reason each area is called a circuit is because travelers usually do a giant loop, or circuit, and end up at the place they started before moving on to the next circuit. After all, that's the goal of a world tour; see as much of each region as you can, and eventually make it back home.

**You are living in one of the ten circuits.
Now there are nine more to go.**

"Life is just a bag of tricks."
Felix the Cat

Bus Overland and Cruise Ships

Ships that pass in the night, and speak to each other in passing;
Only a signal shown and a distant voice in the darkness;
So on the ocean of life we pass and speak to one another,
Only a look and a voice; then darkness again and a silence.
— Henry Wadsworth Longfellow, 1874

Back in old Henry Longfellow's day, they had not yet invented the ultra-decadent tourist cruise ship. While *World Stompers* could never advocate paying for a cruise, it does recommend working on one. Highly experienced travelers (lifers) can make a decent living on cruise ships and bus overland journeys.

The days of the "magic bus" doing the overland route from England to Greece and Spain in the 60s is not over, it's merely expanded. The company Magic Bus (popularized by The Who song of the same name) went out of business because they grew too fast without proper management. The vacuum was filled by other bus overland companies that became much more specialized. There are also quite a few individual bus owners who pick up stray riders along the way.

The Rasta School Bus
From the travel journal (31, Jan. '94)

After a three-day non-stop techno party in the ruins of Hampi, an abandoned ancient Indian city, I needed a ride back to Goa. I thought it would be cool to catch one of many world-touring buses that came out for the party.

I talked to a few travelers and they directed me to Thomas, the owner and driver of a rasta striped school bus. He re-built an old German *schulbus* and re-made it into a techno touring bus. He said I could come along, so I hopped in with my pack and joined the crowd.

The ride back to Goa was classic; chillums roasting and techno music cranked the whole way. In the afternoon we stopped to feast in some way off-the-beaten-track village, and all of us stoners piled out Spicoli-style. Just the sight of that bus would draw a crowd, let alone 30 brightly dressed, long haired hippie freaks. Word of the UFO landing spread like wildfire in the village, and by the time we finished lunch, there was a crowd of over 400 gawking Indians assembled around the bus. We departing aliens shook hands, took pictures, and re-boarded our craft for the voyage back to the future.

Overland Bus Tours

Lately, a popular bus overland trip has been passing through continental Africa. Most trips leave directly from London and go through France and Spain and cross over the Mediterranean into Morocco. After motoring through the Sahara, some trips go to the Congo rainforest (Zaire), or the wildlife sanctuaries of Kenya, Uganda, or Tanzania. For the real intrepid traveler, you can hit all these places and carry on straight down to South Africa. Travelers pay their own visa and personal expenses on the journey.

Dragoman is the best and most expensive on the Africa circuit – $2,900 for a three month trip. Other London based companies are Kamuka, and Hann which are a couple hundred dollars less, but deliver fewer amenities. Phoenix is the cheapest, but offers no showers. Truck About is a new Kenya bus company and tours seven different countries along three separate routes.

A Canadian named John D. had this to say about his four-and-a-half month overland journey from Morocco to Tanzania: "The trip was expensive, especially the western African nations – over one grand per month. The truck ride was bumpy and a lot of time was spent in the vehicle. Some areas were quite volatile, like the army escort for 100 km in southern Morocco. Visas add up and some are rather costly. Prices here change day to day. The wildlife was unreal; elephants, giraffes, hippos, and even a tiger, which is a rare sight these days. We had to push the bus out of the mud a few times in Zaire, but all in all, real good fun and adventure."

The Latin American circuits are operated and run by different competing companies. Well-organized but expensive are Encounter Overland, Top Deck, and Exodus. These three companies also do the Asia overland, but Americans cannot get a visa for Iran, so that route is closed for us. Moderately priced Central and North America companies include Green Tortoise out of San Francisco (www.greentortoise.com) and Adventure Bus (www.adventurebus.com). Both do the western National Park circuits; Baja, Mexico in the winter; and include sports, meals and activities.

Daniel Peyrou of URU Adventures leads trips from Rome to New Delhi for $1,300 O/W, where Top Deck would charge $2,400 and stop less. "Going fast seems to exhaust the passengers," says Daniel. "I go two days on and three off to maximize the riders' experience. There's no reason to hurry from point A to point B."

Most overland companies are based in London around Earls Court. Go in person and inquire, or just pick up a *TNT Magazine* when you are there and check the travel section. This is the best way to get the lowest price for the time frame and budget you want. Savings tip; if you arrange your trip ahead of time, you pay full pop, but if you book a week or a few days before departure, you can save up to 50 percent of the advertised cost. For a travel company, selling a half-price ticket is better than an empty seat. They will ask for you not tell the other passengers what you paid.

Overland or boat travel is a great way to see remote spots and usually cheaper than flying.

Cruise Ships

In between travel, or when passing from circuit to circuit, how about a job on a cruise ship? A multitude of service oriented jobs from dishwasher to PR man exist. What is your specialty? Entertainment director, dive master, photographer, card dealer, waiter, entertainer, DJ, and shopkeeper are perhaps the best cruise ship jobs. The trick is not getting stuck with a grunt job. Any work that pays tips is ideal, because out at sea, tips and wages are tax-free. For work information on the big cruise lines, contact their reservation offices for hiring procedures, dates, and locations of departure:

Carnival	(800) 327-9501
Club Med	(800) CLUB-MED
Cunard	(800) 221-4770
Princess Cruises	(800) 421-0522
Raddison 7 Sea Cruise	(800) 333-3333
Royal Caribbean Cruise Line	(800) 327-6700
Royal Viking Sun Holiday	(800) 422-8000
Seabourn Cruise Line	(800) 929-9595

To secure a cruise ship job, call the above numbers and find out where to send your cover letter, resume, and a recent photograph. These jobs are competitive, so the more professional your presentation, the better your chances. The most important aspect of your correspondence should be the stressing of your strong social skills and how you have applied these marketable abilities in the past. Some cruise ship jobs are hired through a third party, or concessionaire, who manage their own businesses on the ships and share the profits with the cruise line corporation. The gift shop, the beauty salon, casino, and photography services are all concessions, but these jobs must be secured off ship. A great resource book is Mark London's *Cruise Ship Jobs* (www.shipjobs.com) which lists all the major cruise lines and concessionaires.

The cool thing about working on a cruise ship is the ready made social life. Crew members throw cabin parties nearly every night. Meals are free, booze is cheap, and there are few ways to spend you wages while at sea. Strong friendships are made with other crew members — but, while tempting, do not have an open affair with a passenger! It is an easy way to get fired. The drag is that shore leave is short and infrequent for employees, you must sign a 3-6 month contract on one ship (usually the same route), and the good jobs are pretty hard to get, unless you work on the ship for a while and get promoted.

Overland travel is the best way to experience a native place. The more you are in an airplane, the more you miss.

Lists of the World

And I gave my heart to know wisdom, and to know madness and folly:
I perceived that this also is vexation of spirit.
— Ecclesiastes

Top Ten Coolest cities:

10. Jerusalem, Israel.
9. Kathmandu, Nepal
8. Cape Town, South Africa.
7. Sydney, Australia.
6. Venice, Italy.
5. Rio de Janeiro, Brazil.
4. Amsterdam, Holland.
3. Kyoto, Japan.
2. Prague, Czech Republic.
1. San Francisco, CA U.S.A.

Top Ten Worst Dirty Ugly Cities:

10. Tijuana, Mexico.
9. Gary, IN U.S.A.
8. Manila, Philippines.
7. Jinjang, China.
6. Jakarta, Indonesia.
5. Belfast, Northern Ireland.
4. São Paulo, Brazil.
3. Madras, India.
2. Pusan, South Korea.
1. Lagos, Nigeria.

Top Ten Totally Rad National Parks:

10. Sibiloi Game Reserve, Kenya.
9. Santa Rosa National Park, Costa Rica.
8. Yosemite, CA U.S.A.
7. Halong Bay, Vietnam.
6. Ngorongoro National Park, Tanzania.
5. Haleakala Crater, Maui, HI U.S.A.
4. Santorini Island, Greece.
3. Kruger National Park, South Africa.
2. Toya-Shikotsuku, Hokkaido, Japan.
1. Annapurna Sanctuary, Nepal.

Country by Country Expenses

I did not keep records of each separate country on my backpack tour of the European circuit in the summer of 1988. However, the entire three-month trip cost $3,000, including R/T airfare and a two-month Eurail pass.

In Oct. 1991, I left for Japan with a R/T airline ticket and $2,250 cash. That was enough money to take a short hitchhike journey around Japan and support myself long enough to find a job. 14 months later I saved $10,110 which was my world tour fund.

After I left Japan for China on my world tour, I kept detailed records of all travel expenses. Maybe a list of them will help you prepare a budget and anticipate your own costs.

 Note: All $ signs represent U.S. dollars, and * denotes special expenses.

China. From: 28, Nov. '92, to 23, Dec. '92, —26 days.
Spent: $300 cash and $350 T/C (traveler's checks), — $650 total.
* bought one internal plane ticket for $65, and many souvenirs.

Hong Kong. From: 23, Dec. '92, to 31, Dec. '92, —8 days.
Spent: $50 FEC (Chinese currency) leftover and $600 T/C, —$650 total.
* purchased HK to Saigon, Saigon to Bangkok plane ticket for $300, and Vietnamese visa for $90.

Vietnam. From: 31, Dec. '92, to 28, Jan. '93, —28 days.
Spent: $200 cash and $250 T/C, —$450 total.

Thailand. From: 28, Jan. '93, to 11, Feb. '93, —14 days.
Spent: $120 cash and $250 T/C, —$370 total.
* partied very hard.

Malaysia. From: 11, Feb. '93, to 15, Feb. '93, —4 days.
Spent: $575 T/C, —$575 total.
* purchased airline ticket (open one year) from Perth, Australia, to KL (Kuala Lumpur), Malaysia– KL to Delhi, India, for $435. Also bought a boat ticket from Penang to Medan, Indonesia, for $33.

Indonesia. From: 15, Feb. '93, to 12, Apr. '93, —57 days.
Spent: $125 cash and $1,340 T/C, —$1,465 total.
* missed boat to Timor, had to buy expensive plane ticket in a hurry to Australia before visa ran out, Bali to Cairns, Australia, for $435. Also purchased an Australian six-month visa for $20, and many souvenirs.

Australia. From: 13, Apr. '93, to 19, Sep. '93, —5 months and 6 days.
Spent: $ 1,570 T/C, —$1,570 total.
* worked four jobs in that time and had several places to stay for free which cut expenses considerably.

Malaysia. From: 19, Sep. '93, to 26, Sep. '93, —7 days.
Spent: $155 T/C, —$155 total.
* purchased six-month Indian visa for $40.

India. From: 26, Sep. '93, to 9, Oct. '93, —14 days.
Spent: $800 T/C, —$800 total.
* made carpet investment for $300 and purchased many souvenirs.

Nepal. From: 9, Oct. '93, to 8, Nov. '93, —31 days.
Spent: 800 Indian Rupees ($24) and $500 T/C, —$524 total.
* purchased Nepalese visa at the border for $40 and many souvenirs.

India. From: 8, Nov. '93, to 19, Mar. '94, —4 months and 11 days.
Spent: $24 cash and $1,800 T/C, —$1,824 total.
* got refund on $300 investment, lost $288 in another scam. Purchased airline ticket to Egypt; Bombay to Cairo, Cairo to London, for $530. Egyptian visa and fees: $56.

Egypt. From: 20, Mar. '94, to 16, Apr. '94, —28 days.
Spent: $560 T/C, —$560 total.

Israel. From: 16, Apr. '94, to 24 Apr. '94, —8 days.
Spent: $300 T/C, —$300 total.
* could not get new Egyptian visa in time for flight out of Cairo, had to buy rip-off plane ticket from Tel Aviv to Cairo for $147. Egypt Air provided a free room at the Cairo airport during my layover.

England. From: 25, Apr. '94, to 4, May '94, —10 days.
Spent: $120 T/C, —$120 total.
* had free places to stay every day.

Holland. From: 4, May '94, to 25 May '94, —21 days.
Spent: $340 T/C, —$340 total.
* stayed with girlfriend entire time, purchased O/W airline ticket to U.S., Amsterdam to Chicago, for $260.

Returned to the U.S. on 25, May 1994 with $9 cash, $20 T/C, —$29 total.

Top Ten Most Over-Rated Places:
10. Bali, Indonesia.
9. Edinburgh, Scotland, UK
8. Los Angeles, CA U.S.A.
7. Athens, Greece.
6. Honolulu, Oahu, HI U.S.A.
5. Tel Aviv, Israel.
4. Acapulco, Mexico.
3. Daytona Beach, FL U.S.A.
2. Bangkok, Thailand.
1. The west side of peninsular Malaysia.

Top Ten Most Famous World Stompers:
10. Amelia Earhart.
9. Walter Cronkite.
8. Christopher Columbus.
7. Marco Polo.
6. Herodotus.
5. L. Ron Hubbard.
4. Homo Erectus.
3. The Vikings.
2. Mark Twain.
1. Charles Darwin.

Top Ten Killer Surf Spots (and best months to go):

10. Both coasts, Costa Rica. (Seasons vary)
9. Puerto Escondido, Mexico. (Year round)
8. Jeffrey's Bay, South Africa. (May – Oct.)
7. Burleigh Head, Queensland, Australia. (Feb. – May)
6. Grajagan (G-land), Java Island, Indonesia. (April – Oct.)
5. Sri Lanka's west coast. (Winter)
4. Nias Island, Indonesia. (April – Oct.)
3. Todos Santos Island, Baja peninsula, Mexico. (Winter)
2. North shore Oahu, HI U.S.A. (Oct. – March)
1. Margaret River, Western Australia. (March – Oct.)

Another Stomper's Budget

To further illustrate expenses, here is Canadian Trevor Zimmer's budget(s) for one day in:

Kas Turkey (on the Mediterranean Sea)

* Sleep on a rooftop	$2.00
* One bottle of water	.70
* Repair broken sandal	.50
* Two toasted cheese sandwiches	2.00
* Three tomatoes	.40
* Brick of cheese	1.50
* Loaf of bread	.20
Total	$7.30

Pushkar India

* Bootleg Hudu Guru tape	$1.20
* All-you-can-eat breakfast	.80
* Four hour bike rental	.40
* Made to order vest	1.20
* Three lime sodas	.60
* Photo of a holy man donation	.15
* Fresh pineapple juice	.20
* Train ticket to Agra (300 km)	3.30
Total	$9.60

Trevor also kept records of his ultra-budget days when he was trying to spend the bare minimum (and still have a great time). An example of one such day in India: Orange juice – $.20; vegetable, rice, and sauce lunch – .33; bike parking fee – .03; all-you-can-eat supper – .80; chocolate bar – .20; bungalow on the beach – 50 cents. Total expenses for the day – $2.06.

Top Ten Coolest Places to Snorkel and Scuba Dive:

10. São Tomé and Principe, Africa.

9. Sipadan Island, Malaysia, (tie) Moorea, French Polynesia.

8. Maldives island chain.

7. Truk island, Micronesia.

6. Belize and Honduras outer reef.

5. Vanua Levu Island, Fiji.

4. Cayman Islands, Caribbean Sea.

3. Dahab, Egypt.

2. Molokini, Maui, HI U.S.A.

1. Great Barrier Reef, Australia.

Top Ten Places Known for Rip-Offs:

10. Bangkok, Thailand.

9. All of Morocco, (tie) all of Egypt.

8. Amsterdam, Holland.

7. The beaches of the French Riviera.

6. Lima, Peru.

5. Housebreaking in Goa, India.

4. Saigon, Vietnam.

3. Rio de Janeiro, Brazil.

2. Night trains worldwide.

1. Kuta Beach, Bali, Indonesia.

Top Ten Best Ski Resorts:

10. Las Lenas, Chile.

9. Squaw Valley, CA U.S.A.

8. Banff, Alberta, Canada.

7. Iwappara Mountain, Japan.

6. Jackson Hole, WO U.S.A.

5. Coronet Peak, New Zealand.

4. Chamonix, France.

3. Aspen Mountain, CO U.S.A.

2. Verbier, Switzerland

1. Whistler-Blackcomb, British Colombia, Canada.

Top Ten Nationalities of World Stompers:

10. South Africans.

9. French.

8. Swedes.

7. Canadians.

6. Dutch.

5. New Zealanders.

4. Israelis.

3. Germans.

2. British.

1. Australians.

(Note – Americans rank 13th)

Top Ten Most Wicked Ruins:

10. Zanzibar Island, Tanzania.

9. Hampi, India.

8. The Forum and Coliseum, Rome, (tie) Pompeii, Italy.

7. The Great Wall of China.

6. Borobudur, Java, Indonesia.

5. Petra, Jordan, (tie) Masada, Israel.

4. The Acropolis, Athens, Greece.

3. Stonehenge, England.

2. Machu Picchu, Peru, (tie) Tikal, Guatemala.

1. Angkor Wat, Cambodia.

Note – Egypt is in a class by itself – *see* page 223

On The Stoner's Trail

A friend in Silicon Valley told me there is one ton of grass smoked in that area EVERY DAY ... Most of the companies in Silicon Valley are unwilling to institute Piss Wars. They know if they did, they would lose their most talented, diligent and inspired software experts immediately.
– Robert Anton Wilson, How Green Was My Valley

The ganja connoisseur, the traveler who enjoys sampling the crops of local farmers, or just the inquisitive type searching the world over for that perfect joint – rejoice! A growing number of countries worldwide have legalized or decriminalized the smoking of Planet Earth's most controversial plant. The cool countries look the other way and allow it to be smoked openly – the un-cool ones still prosecute the user. Oh, a world of contradictions!

Let's clear things up with some top 10 listage:

Buzzkills. They will bust you hard.

10. Japan.

9. Southern European countries (especially Greece and Italy).

8. Certain states in the U.S. (Nevada, Michigan, Alabama).

7. All Middle East, Muslim countries.

6. Post-Cold War Eastern European countries.

5. Leeward Islands, or on any boat in the Caribbean Sea.

4. Singapore.

3. China.

2. Israel.

1. Malaysia.

In fact, most countries will bust you for just a doobie, but the severity differs from as little as a fine (bribe), to time in jail. The buzzkill list is the jail-term countries. Stay sober here, wasteoids!

Some of the Spliff Zone stoner towns will have a rare crackdown, but it's mostly because the cops are short of cash. The shakedown can be particularly unpleasant because they will physically search you and take you for as much money as they can. Often dealers work hand in hand with the police, selling it to users then getting a cut for turning them in. That is why you should only buy from other Western travelers, or get to know a local very well. Discretion, as true everywhere, is key.

The World's Top Ten Best Stoner Meccas:

10. The whole country of Laos. (page 185)

9. Dahab, Egypt. (page 222)

8. Nimben, Australia. (page 179)

7. The ski mountains of Lake Tahoe, CA U.S.A. (page 151)

6. Tuk Tuk peninsula, Lake Toba, Indonesia. (page 190)

5. Pokhara, Nepal. (page 243)

4. San Pedro, Guatemala. (page 158)

3. The whole country of India (excluding cities). (page 246)

2. The state of Alaska, U.S.A. (page 153)

1. The whole country of The Netherlands. (page 208)

So join us, won't you? Look for this chillum master and follow his icon all the way through the circuits **On The Stoner's Trail.**

Happy Trails!

"What are you people – on dope?"
Mr. Hand
Fast Times at Ridgemont High

On The Partyer's Trail

The whole world is about three drinks behind.
— Humphrey Bogart

Awise man in a cave once said there is a partyer in all of us. Whether it's the social drinker who shows up to hang out and watch the madness (and may not even drink alcohol), or the totally full-on rager who can never get enough, the wise man knows – traveling and partying are synonymous.

All around the planet, right now, humans are partying hard. From small and mellow beach shindigs, to the out of control street ragers during national holidays. The trick is knowing the who, what, when, where, and why. Whatever your tastes in partying may be, *World Stompers* has documented the best of the best for your bashing and chilling out pleasures.

Top Ten Best Bashes:

10. Hong Kong, Kowloon – **Christmas Eve.** (page 194)

9. The whole island of Jamaica – **Reggae Sumfest and Sunfeast.** (page 159)

8. Trinidad and Tobago (tie) the whole country of Brazil – **Carnival.** (page 160, 171)

7. Key West, Florida (tie) Lahaina, Maui, U.S.A. – **Halloween.** (page 152)

6. Ios island, Greece (tie) Glastonbury, UK – **All summer.** (page 204, 212)

5. Saigon, Vietnam – **Tet (Chinese New Years).** (page 183)

4. British Virgin Islands – **Full Moon at Bomba's Shack.** (page 159)

3. Vagator Beach, Goa, India – **Christmas and New Years.** (page 245)

2. Munich, Germany – **Oktoberfest.** (page 209)

1. Haad Rin Beach, Kho Phangan Island – **Every Full Moon.** (page 183)

Run, don't walk, and follow this icon through the circuits to discover these wild scenes in the **Top Ten Best Bashes:**

Top Ten Best Mellow Party Scenes:

10. Hanelea, Kauai, Hawaii U.S.A. (page 152)
9. Magnetic Island, Australia. (page 180)
8. Varkala Beach, Kerala, India. (page 244)
7. Jeffrey's Bay, South Africa. (page 239)
6. Butterfly Valley, Turkey. (page 221)
5. The whole Costa Brava, Spain. (page 209)
4. Vilcabamba, Ecuador. (page 167)
3. Krabi, Thailand. (page 186)
2. Yangshuo, Guangxi province, China. (page 197)
1. Santorini Island, Greece. (page 206)

Everybody needs some time to chill out for a while before the next big bash. Others prefer the mellow party scene altogether, leaving the huge street parties to the drunken masses (who are usually asses).

Follow this icon through the circuits
and shoot over to these
Top Ten Mellow Party Scenes:

LET'S TAKE
A STOMP
AROUND
THE WORLD!

http://www.stompers.com

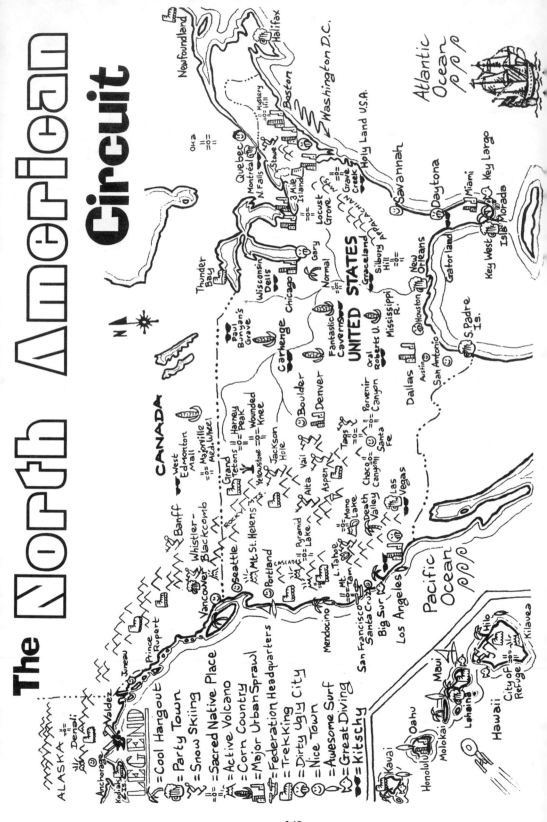

The North American Circuit

The North American Circuit

With all beings and all things we shall be as relatives.
— Sioux Indian

Only two countries exist on this circuit, the United States and Canada. While these two giant countries have much in common, like both being former British colonies, they differ in several major ways too. Both were, in part, French colonies at different times. When the French called it quits in North America (Louisiana Purchase), the U.S. gave up nearly all of its French identity. Not the case in Canada, however. The province of Quebec, where French is the primary language and rumors abound that it will secede from the rest of Canada, proves the French *joie de vivre* remains alive and well.

The natural scenery in Canada is similar to that of the northern states in the United States From Pacific fjords leading up to Rocky Mountain peaks, all the way out to craggy Atlantic bays with a whole lot of farms, lakes, small towns, and disgruntled postal workers in between. Both countries offer a high standard of living, stable governments, and equal rights to its citizens. But ask your average Canadian how the two differ and you will likely receive a lengthy dissertation that could go on all night. Unfortunately, most Americans would just consider "The Great White North" as little more than our 51st state.

While the two share a lot, including a border where mutual citizens need only show a driver's license for stays up to 180 days, an awareness of Canada's uniqueness and work possibilities might make this your first destination before setting off on a world tour.

Canada

Canada is proud of its French heritage and the many years as a British Crown Colony. The country is still a commonwealth of the U.K. and the Queen of England continues to grace its coins and currency. Canada is officially bilingual, speaking French as well as English.

Canada is larger than the U.S. in total area, yet only a tenth in population size — making it one of the world's largest but least populated nations. Another marked contrast is how clean, uncrowded, and well-organized Canadian cities are. Year after year they rank among the highest and most livable places in the world. The Canadian public education and transportation systems are excellent. Social benefits are generous, and little of the poverty and homelessness that plague American cities can be found on Canada's clean streets.

Traveling in Canada will acquaint you with wondrous wilderness expanses, from arctic tundra to soaring mountains to the great plains. You will see some of the most workable and hassle-free cities in the world. Meet a culture that is different, yet very similar to our own. And best of all, it's just right over the border.

Work and Money

While locating a legitimate job requires obtaining a work permit outside the country first (and will only be granted if it is determined no permanent resident is qualified for the job), students seeking summer employment and under-the-table jobs are much easier to come by. Full-time students over 18 enrolled in college or universities may apply for CIEE's Work Exchange Department, 633 3rd Avenue, New York, NY 10017, or call (888) COUNCIL. Past participants have done hospitality work, various hotel jobs, conservation work, and housekeeping.

The most common under-the-table job in Canada is tree planting during the summer months. Reforesting the planet is good karma work for anyone, especially those conscious of the widespread destruction happening to forest ecosystems worldwide. Reforesting jobs are found all over the country, especially in the western province of British Colombia. Jobs can be located at university job centers in the spring. Basically, you are paid by the amount of trees you plant, so wages vary. Quick workers net $200 a day, slow workers as low as $50 per day. The companies provide housing and meals for about $30 a week. The potential to save a lot of money is great because they work you six days a week and there is nowhere to spend your money. Look into smaller companies. They are more apt to hire foreign laborers than the big ones who must pay taxes and stay legit. Do it for the experience as much as for the money.

The U.S. dollar is currently very strong against the Canadian currency, so travel and the cost of living is quite cheap in the Great White North. Many Americans living near the border of Canada cross over on a regular basis to go shopping or stock up on supplies. The exception are cigarettes and liquor, which are both heavily taxed by the Canadian Government.

The United States

*I have a dream that one day this nation will rise up, live out the true meaning
of its creed: we hold these truths to be self-evident,
that all men are created equal.*

– Rev. Martin Luther King, speech, 1963

Tired of the same old routine in the same old town with the same old
people? Go west, young person, and grow up with the country! I'm sorry,
but for a few exceptions, the East Coast, the Midwest and the South are all
pretty damn boring. The fun starts at the Rocky Mountains and keeps on
getting better once you leave the "Lesser 48" and check out Hawaii and
Alaska.

**Yes, it's true: the west *is* the best . . .
Get here and we'll do the rest.**

Living on a Ski Mountain

Every ski resort in every state needs a vast supply of seasonal workers
before the snow begins to fall. Hiring for lift and cat operators, sales and
concession staff, bus drivers, ticket punchers, hostesses, resort staff, ski
instructors and many other town jobs that depend on the ski season traffic,
begin mass hiring in late October and November. Free ski-passes and ski
rentals, subsidized housing, meals, and lessons are only some of the perks
of living and working in a ski-town. Just pick a resort, any resort in the
Rocky Mountains or Sierra Nevada Range, and show up in the fall. Jobs
come about, contacts are made, and housing is found when you get out
there and start looking.

On The Stoner's Trail (#7)

The motto at Lake Tahoe, CA in the wintertime is "Eat
pasta, smoke rasta, ski fasta." Basically the mountains are a
white haze of snow and smoke, attracting a fine group of
freaks on snowboards and dudes with dreads leaping from
precarious boulders.

To score the KGB (killer green bud), you have to have a
connection up here. Living on the mountain is the best way
to meet the ski-bum, stoner crowd. After making a few
friends, it's as easy as showing up on the mountain, skiing a
few runs, and seeing someone you know with pot.

Hawaii

The "Aloha State" offers many job opportunities within this adventurous tropical paradise. The multitudes of resorts on the five main islands (Hawaii, Maui, Molokai, Oahu, and Kauai) are hiring all the time. Such positions are regularly available: room service; tour guides; bellhops; porters; waiters; sport instructors; lifeguards; security personnel; bartenders; and activity sales people. Jobs can also be found in banks, law offices, hospitals, or just about any other trade job or profession people do on the mainland.

Keep costs down by bringing your own bike (as a piece of luggage) to get around with initially. Look in the local newspaper for job listings and a place to live. Chances are you will find both within a week. It's a whole lot easier than most people think, just beware of island fever after about six months.

Top Ten Mellow Party Scenes (#10)

The little hippie enclave on the north shore of Kauai Island called Hanelea is famous for its unbelievable natural beauty and the laid back attitudes of its residents. Excellent surfing, scuba diving, trekking, and boating along the amazing Na Pali coastline become regular activities for the locals living here. Reside in a tree house, work at the resort, and party and play the rest of the time. Hang loose, brah!

Top Ten Best Bashes (#7)

Many towns try to host big Halloween bashes, but few succeed. The first ingredient, of course, is costumes. The more the better. Second is lax drinking laws and mellow cops. Third is to keep main street open all night without a rude break-up until the people feel like going home. Right? Toss in tropical weather and the only places that live up to muster are Key West, Florida, and Lahaina town on Maui, Hawaii. Shaka, brah!

Alaska

Just getting up here is half the fun, and once you do you will find yourself in one of the last great wilderness regions left on the planet. Summer is the best time to travel here when the salmon are running and the northern lights (aurora borealis) are going off.

Hard work, but well paying jobs are found tree planting, in cannery factories, and on fishing boats during the summer. There are seasonal jobs (Memorial Day to Labor Day) in many of the resorts that cater to tourism. This work includes; dish washing, housekeeping, and various other hotel jobs. Another option is to wait for another oil spill and get on the clean-up crew for $30 an hour.

On The Stoner's Trail (#2)

Every true stoner has heard of the legendary Northern Lights Bud and Matnuska Thunderfuck (MTF). It grows like mad during the 20-hour days of summer. Perhaps the connoisseur's choice for best fat, it's aroma alone can seemingly get you high. Take a couple of rips off the bong and don't bother doing anything for the next few hours. Although Alaska has the most lax laws for possession under an ounce, they will bust you hard for growing. It's still the United States of Amorika.

Earthlings

Neanderthal Man rides the New York City subway.

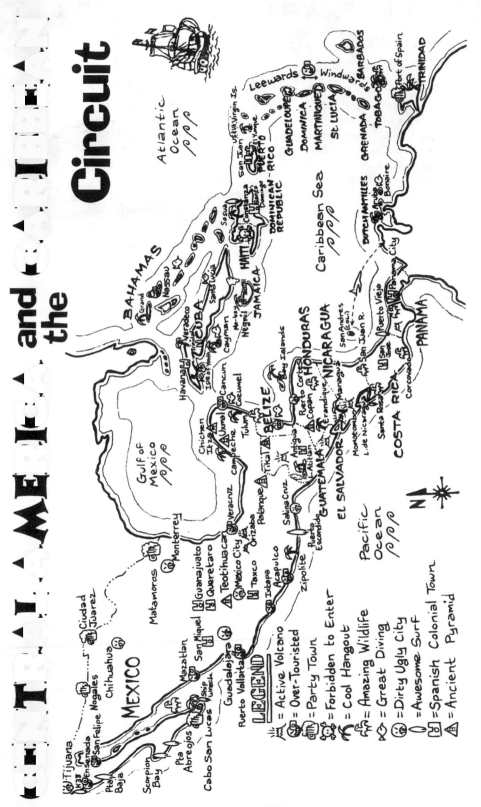

CENTRAL AMERICA and the CARIBBEAN Circuit

LEGEND

- = Active Volcano
- = Over-Touristed
- = Party Town
- = Forbidden to Enter
- = Cool Hangout
- = Amazing Wildlife
- = Great Diving
- = Dirty Ugly City
- = Awesome Surf
- = Spanish Colonial Town
- = Ancient Pyramid

Central America and the Caribbean Circuit

They are our brothers, these freedom fighters. ...
They are the moral equal of our Founding Fathers and
the brave men and women of the French Resistance.
We cannot turn away from them, for the struggle here
is not right versus left; it is right versus wrong.
– Ronald Reagan, speech (1985)

The Central American land mass connecting the two continents and the hundreds of islands in the Caribbean have been attracting Europeans and Americans for centuries. First as discoverers and military conquerors, then as colonizers and plantation operators. Until finally, today, it is simply one of the most popular places to go for a tropical vacation.

Most of the countries in Central America are easy to traverse overland, and the ultra-budget way to do it is by bus. In the Caribbean it is necessary to fly from destination to destination, unless you are lucky enough to be on a boat. Like the southern Mediterranean coast in Europe, there are many yacht-havens throughout the Caribbean where crewing work is sometimes available. Jobs are usually found on the spot, and if located, you could be setting out the next day for wages, passage, and meals. But life on a yacht can be trying at times. Living close to the boat owner will really test your patience, the work can be hard, and you will obviously need some sailing experience.

Having a working knowledge of Spanish is a must in most Latin American countries. Without knowing a few niceties and basic speaking skills, you'll be labeled 100% *gringo* and certainly run into more than one big *problemo*. Review old school books or notes if you have studied Spanish before. Purchase a phrase-book, learn by flashcards, and build up your vocabulary. There are many cheap Spanish conversation schools in Central America, and the most popular ones are in Guatemala. Live with a family or bear down in a course for three weeks and you'll be all set to converse.

The Bahamas

The Bahamas are a coral archipelago consisting of some 700 low-lying islands and over 2000 cays. Some 3 million tourists arrive every year, and the tourism industry provides 70% of the country's gross national product. While the diving and beaches are incredible, the main islands are over-touristed and expensive. U.S. citizens do not need a visa for stays up to 8 months. Departure tax of $15 paid at the airport.

155

Belize

Since it was formerly known as British Honduras, English is widely spoken, but with a heavy "Creole" accent. Most of the citizens are black or of mixed ancestry; leftover slaves from the British colonial days. Belize derives its novelty from the extensive coral reef gracing its shores – it's the longest reef in the western hemisphere and the diving is excellent. Stompers also enjoy hiking, canoeing, spelunking Chiquibul Cave, and abundant wildlife in the rainforests.

Keep your alert up while traveling in Belize, as theft and petty crimes are on the increase. The capital Belize City is getting pretty rough and dangerous these days, as well as the border towns to Mexico and Guatemala. Extreme caution should be taken here, and women are advised not to travel alone. Visa not required for stay up to 30 days.

Cayman Islands

The British Crown colony of the Cayman Islands consists of three small islands lying south of Havana, Cuba. The beaches and diving rank among the best in the world. English is widely spoken, the prices are reasonable and the seafood exceptional. Proof of U.S. citizenship, onward ticket and sufficient funds required for a tourist stay up to 6 months.

Costa Rica

Perhaps Costa Rica's most famous property is the numerous national parks which protect the extraordinary ecosystems and teeming wildlife of this varied region. About the size of Vermont, it has more species of birds than the whole of the United States. Most Costa Ricans are from European descent and the country is largely free from racial tensions and political problems – issues that continue to plague its less affluent neighbors. It is home to the highest standard of living and greatest degree of economic and social advancement in Central America. This makes it safe and easy to travel through, but is also relatively expensive.

Extreme adventures abound in Costa Rica, including whitewater rafting, volcano excursions, scuba diving off Cocos Island, jungle treks, and the famous canopy tour. The cool party scenes are Cahuita on the Caribbean side and Moctezuma on the Pacific. The surf on both sides is fantastic. Another unique aspect of Costa Rica is that it has no army. Abolished in 1949, the army is now a khaki-clad Civil Guard. John Lennon could imagine that. Passports required for stays up to 90 days; $10 tourist card fee payable upon arrival.

Cuba

When the United States House of Representatives lifted its embargo policy in July 2000, Cuba officially became open to U.S. tourism for the first time in 40 years. It's a good sign that Fidel Castro didn't need to take a fall from power for us to enjoy this beautiful country full of colonial architecture and smiling people once again. Accommodation can be expensive and transport is primitive. American dollars and traveler's checks can be used, but not credit cards. Passport and visa required, 90 day tourist visas cost $26.

Dominican Republic

While trying to build up its tourist trade, the Dominican Republic has much to offer in the way of natural beauty and old colonial architecture. The climate is tropical, with the rainy season coming September to November and also May and June. This is the prevailing rain pattern for most of the northern Caribbean.

The Dominican Republic is one of the cheapest countries on this circuit to travel in, and the spoken language is Spanish. The palm fringed beaches around the island are wonderful, prices are very affordable, and the people are open and friendly. A tourist card (like a visa) can be obtained on the airplane serving the Dominican Republic for $10 and is valid for a 2 month stay. There is a $10 airport departure fee as well.

Dutch Antilles

The three main islands which make up a part of the Kingdom of Netherlands are Aruba, Bonaire, and Curacao (popularly known as the ABCs). There are three other obscure islands subject to the Dutch crown as well, but they are rather small and remote compared to the ABCs. Aruba was granted separate status from the rest and has been fully independent since January, 1996.

Bonaire has one of the best preserved coral reefs in the Caribbean. On days off from diving, check out the old fort in Kralendijk and a famous pink beach. Curacao is the largest island only 60 km off the Venezuelan coast. It's a pretty dry and barren island, which means lots o' sunshine on the beaches. Oil is big business on the ABCs and everything needs to be imported, so expect to pay a lot for your stay here. Visa not required for 14 days; extendible to 90 days after arrival. The same visa requirements apply to Aruba. Departure tax is $10 from all islands.

El Salvador

El Salvador is the smallest, most industrialized, and most densely populated of the Central American republics. Since the political unrest and violence has let up in recent years, El Salvador is once again welcoming visitors – but be forewarned: terrorism still takes place and Americans are sometimes the target. Travel with extreme caution. There are several volcanoes that can be climbed and most of the highlands are covered in a deep layer of lava and ash. Passport and visa are required, and length of stay will be determined by immigration authorities upon arrival.

Guatemala

Guatemala is the most populous of the Central American republics next to Mexico, and the only one that is largely native Indian in culture and language. The scenery of the indigenous regions around the capital, Guatemala City, is full of life and color. Excellent sites of Mayan ruins and culture can be found amidst the jungle. In the towns and villages are colonial churches, yet the local religion is a compound of image-worshipping paganism combined with outward forms of Catholicism.

The popular backpacker Mecca is around or near Lake Atitlan, a beautiful lake that changes colors throughout the day. Panajachel is the hippie hang-out with quite a bit of amazing wildlife nearby. A day trip away is the active volcano of Santa Maria which wiped out the town of Quezaltenango in 1902.

Since Spanish is the spoken language for most of Central and South America, many travelers opt for an inexpensive language course before setting out. The best way to learn Spanish is to stay with a family for ten dollars a day (including meals) and immerse yourself in the language. Classes are advertised extensively around major towns and cities (mostly Antigua) and homestays range from one week to three weeks. Passports are required for entry and a visa for stays up to 30 days are free.

On The Stoner's Trail (#4)

On the amazing Lake Atitlan is a trippy village called San Pedro where doobage is sold and smoked openly. Just walk into any shop and the pot is sold on the shelves with the cookies and candy bars. The town voted out the existence of police a few years ago so the whole area is a total Spliff Zone. Smoke a fat one and go climb a volcano. The towering San Pedro volcano can be climbed in three hours, four if you're really baked.

Haiti

As the poorest country in the Western hemisphere, Haiti is a basketcase of troubles. If the U.S. military is not occupying it, chances are some dictator will be. Bad scene, don't go. If you do go, visas are not required for 90 days.

Honduras

Almost all of the country is mountainous and covered with dense tropical jungles. Honduras is a pretty backward country (Banana Republic) and has a smaller population than most of its Latin American neighbors. The highlight of any visit is the magnificent Mayan ruins of Copan. Low pyramids, passageways, tunnels, ball courts, The Hieroglyphic Stairway, and a wide assortment of intricate steles grace the site. Other attractions are the outlying Bay Islands, and the many villages and towns that bear reminders of the Spanish settlers who came in the 16th century. No visa required for 60 day stays, departure tax of $10.

Jamaica

As a former British colony, English is the spoken language of Jamaica and the government closely resembles that of England. As a former slave island, descendants of Africa comprise 96 percent of the population. The resulting mix is a hilarious sounding pidgin English (Patois).

Reggae music, the sound of the Rastafarians, can be heard on the streets and beaches everywhere. The whole island is a virtual Spliff Zone, so don't expect things to move too quickly. Beware: police look to shake down travelers smoking pot and crime is pretty bad all over Jamaica. Passport or birth certificate required for entry, but not a visa for stays up to 6 months. Departure tax of $22 paid at the airport.

Top Ten Best Bashes (#9)

Jamaica is known as the World Reggae Headquarters, but the fun and dancing really kick in during the Reggae Sumfest and Reggae Sunfeast. Both music festivals are held each summer and attract participants and audiences from all over the world. The beaches at Montego Bay and Negril are good places to chill out *and* party hard if the madness of Kingston becomes too much. Gotta love talkin' to *Jah*, mon!

The Leeward and Windward Islands

This eastern Caribbean archipelago of islands called the Leewards (The U.S. & British Virgin Islands, Anguilla, St. Martin, Antigua & Barbuda, Montserrat, St. Kitts & Nevis, Guadeloupe, and others) and the Windwards (Dominica, Martinique, St. Lucia, St. Vincent & the Grenadines, Barbados, Grenada and others) are named after the predominating wind patterns in the region. Previously colonized by the French, Dutch, British, Danish and Americans, these islands today have gained much of their independence back.

Top Ten Best Bashes (#4)

The British Virgin Islands (BVI) is an archipelago of over forty emerald islands and cays set in the crystal clear waters of the Caribbean, just east of Puerto Rico. Though internationally renowned as a sailing and scuba paradise, the islands have preserved their relaxed West Indian charm and festive attitude. On the largest island Tortola in the BVIs is the famous Bomba's Shack on the beach of Apple Bay. Every full moon for almost two decades Bomba and his staff go out and collect indigenous "magic mushrooms" for their special tea served after midnight. Reggae bands rock the night away as the psilocybin-induced crowd spills into the street and down the beach for psychedelic fun under a fat tropical moon!

The economies of the Leeward and Winward Islands are heavily dependent on holiday makers and are thus rather expensive to get around and stay. The ultra-budget way to visit these tropical beauties is to crew on a yacht, work on a cruise ship, or work in a hotel and make day trips out. Otherwise, leave these islands to the tourist set. None of the islands require a visa and stays are granted for 3 to 6 months. Most require a departure tax of $10 paid at the airport.

Mexico

Many treasures await "south of the border" for the hordes of Americans who head that way every year. Because so much of U.S. culture has assimilated into Mexican culture and vice versa, the two are becoming more and more alike by the minute. Yet, many dissimilarities exist between the two, and only a visit there will reveal this world of differences (see: Mexico, below). No passport or visa is required for stays up to 90 days. Tourist cards are given upon entry and required at departure. Departure tax $10 paid at the airport.

Nicaragua

Some of the most famous volcanoes in Central America stretch along the Pacific coast here. Several tower over 1,500 meters in height and are accessible within a day. Around the city of Managua are gorgeous crater lakes for swimming, boating, and fishing. Nicaragua is a rather poor country so the price of travel is cheap. The town of Bluesfields on the Caribbean coast has a groovy Reggae scene and interesting people. There may still be outbreaks of civil unrest so travel with a fair degree of caution. Passports are required for entry and 30 day tourist visas are $5 at the border. Airport departure tax is $18.

Panama

Home to the most famous of canals, it also boasts tropical forests, cool highlands, volcanoes, wildlife, and a multitude of pristine beaches and offshore islands. There are many thieves (Noriega like) in Panama City and muggings are frequent. It is not recommended to walk any city street at night, and never take a cab with two or more people in it because they might gang up and rob you.

The natives in the hills are very friendly and the cost of travel is less than urban areas. Do not forget to take Malaria pills! Note: The overland route from Panama to South America is impossible to traverse. There are no roads through the swampy expanse called the Darien Gap. Passport, onward ticket, and visa required for entry. A 30 day visa can be obtained on the airline serving Panama or at the border for a $5 fee.

Puerto Rico

The old-world charm of Puerto Rico's colonial plantations and towns, mixed together with a relaxed concept of time, makes this tropical gem a rather popular tourist destination. The level of development is advanced, the roads are well paved, English proficiency is good, and many National Forests are protected. Puerto Rico is closely akin to the U.S., but also uniquely different. Hop over and discover the contrast. As a U.S. commonwealth, U.S. citizens can travel to and from Puerto Rico without documentation, just as they would to any of the other 50 states.

Trinidad and Tobago

These two islands traded hands with colonizing Europeans for a long while before Britain finally won them over in the late 19th century. Today they are still commonwealth republics of the UK, and English is widely spoken. The fun-loving people of Trinidad and Tobago are rather cosmopolitan and quite religious.

The economy is prosperous and based mainly on the petroleum industry. This makes travel expensive, but at the same time it's a great stopover for South America – which is only 10 km away from Trinidad. Visa not required for stays up to 3 months.

Top Ten Best Bashes (#8)

The time of year to go are the two wild days of Mardi Gras proceeding Ash Wednesday. As its bashing cousins up in New Orleans, USA, and down in the big cities of Brazil, Trinidad and Tobago celebrate Carnival in style. The people flock to the streets in extravagant costumes dancing to the music of calypso and the beat of steel drums. Gotta love them beads!

Mexico

Xata zac xata amac. "Only may there be peace in your presence."
– Ancient Mayan Saying

The 2,400 km frontier with the U.S. – sometimes a shallow river called the Rio Grande, but more often an imaginary line in the desert – separates one of the most affluent nations with a poor and developing nation, often reluctantly. While the political border is crossed by thousands of legal and illegal people every day, the real division is historical, cultural, economic, and linguistic. This is usually the hardest border of all to cross.

Mexico is the most populous nation on this circuit, and the largest Spanish-speaking country in the world. The geography ranges from swamp to desert, from tropical rainforest to high alpine shrubs, and the soil ranges from nonexistent to so fertile it can grow three crops a year. Much of the country sits at an altitude over 1000 meters up which include several different mountain ranges, volcanoes, and high mountain plateaus.

Contrasts

Perhaps the most striking contrast of Mexico is its relationship between new and old. Good examples are glitzy tourist resorts not too far from deserted beaches. Poverty ridden slums contrast to ancient pyramids, from 20 million people packed into Mexico City, to a few dozen rural families in a picturesque colonial village. Dirty ugly industrial cities are near some of the coolest hangouts anywhere.

Mexico veritably offers all the best and worst traveling can be. Friendly locals, beautiful scenery, wicked ruins with loads of activities, juxtaposed next to thieves, poverty, rip-off scams, and pollution. But the good aspects definitely outweigh the bad, especially on the Yucatan peninsula where some of the finest beaches are close to some of the best Mayan ruins on this circuit. Proceed with caution and you should have a blast.

Work and Money

Since the value of the peso plummeted in 1995, the currency remains volatile, but the cost of travel is el cheapo. This is a real good time to Stomp in Mexico. It is a wise idea to bring small denominations of U.S. dollar bills. No Mexican merchant will turn down dollars and you can actually pay a lower price than the peso's exchange rate if you bargain correctly.

Wages paid in pesos are a joke, but since the advent of NAFTA, jobs with multi-national companies paying in U.S. dollars are no laughing matter. There are many big companies in Mexico City and other large towns that regularly need workers with American business experience. Speaking fluent Spanish is required in most jobs, and once hired, the company will assist in getting you a work visa.

Getting Around

Traveling around Mexico is best done by bus. The main roads are well-developed and extensive, and going by bus allows you to immerse yourself in Mexican culture and save quite a bit of money. The train system is pretty well developed in Mexico, but less expansive in range and less frequent in running compared with the bus system.

Renting a car or driving your own car down allows maximum independence and comfort. U.S. driver's licenses are accepted, but drivers should realize that rural Mexican roads can be quite hazardous with frequent stops avoiding oxcarts, people, farm animals, and potholes in the road. To drive legally in Mexico a driver must obtain Mexican car insurance.

For those wishing to drive through Central America to South America, guess again. You can only get as far as Panama where the road ends at the swampy and impassable Darien Gap. The shipping cost to get your car from Panama to Colombia is $2000+ and takes about a week. Hitchhiking in Mexico is a viable option, and is done by both Mexicans and foreigners alike.

Earthlings

Early Mayan amusement rides.

The South American Circuit

COLOMBIA · Santa Marta · Maracaibo · Margarita Is. · Caracas · Mérida · **VENEZUELA** · **GUYANA** · Angel Falls · Kaieteur · **SURINAME** · **FRENCH GUIANA** · Bogota · Cali · Esmeraldas · Pasto · Galápagos Is. (EC.) · **ECUADOR** · Quito · Iquitos · Manaus · Amazon R. · Belem · São Luis · Vilcabamba · Pucallpa · **BRAZIL** · Recife · **PERU** · Machu Picchu · Salvador · Lima · Cusco · Morro De Sao Paulo · Nazca · Lake Titicaca · La Paz · Tiahuanaco · Corumba · Brasilia · Porto Seguro · **BOLIVIA** · Pedro Juan Caballero · Petropolis · San Pedro · **PARAGUAY** · São Paulo · Rio de Janeiro · Rapa Nui · Easter Is. (Chile) · **CHILE** · Salta · Iguazu Falls · Asunción · **Atlantic Ocean** · Las Lenas · Cordoba · Colonia · **URUGUAY** · Farellones · Buenos Aires · Punta del Este · Santiago · **ARGENTINA** · Montevideo · Bariloche · Lake Nahuel Huapi · **South Pacific Ocean** · Patagonia · Falkland Is. · Punta Arenas · Tierra del Fuego · Chilean Navy Route · U.S. Palmer Station · **ANTARCTICA**

LEGEND

- ☺ = Nice City
- ☹ = Dirty Ugly City
- = Dangerous City
- = Colonial Town
- = Wicked Ruins
- = Halucinogenic Cactus (San Pedro)
- = Alien Markers
- = Jungle Boat Trips
- = Amazing Wildlife
- = Primitive Tribes
- = Snow Skiing
- = Sheep Country
- = Party Town
- = Active Volcanoes
- = Cool Hangout

The South American Circuit

This Latin American continent is an exciting destination for travelers seeking indigenous people with roots in mysterious antiquity, multifaceted geography, and a European colonial legacy of the Spanish and Portuguese. Ask your average American on the street what they think of their southern cousins and what you will probably hear is something about the endangered Amazon rainforests, cocaine barons in Colombia, or the ancient ruins of the Inca high up in the majestic Andes Mountains. While these descriptions stand out on the forefront of the South American Circuit, dig deeper and ye shall find the subtle aspects are equally, if not more, fascinating and educational.

Hang out with a Stone Age tribe, shake hands with a *gaucho*, or encounter practitioners of Afro-Caribbean voodoo and santeria. Soak in the European atmospheres of the cities or explore remote mountain villages. Go powder skiing in July, trek along the rocky coastline of Patagonia, or get shit-faced during Brazilian Carnival. Focus on one country or do the whole circuit, it's all up for you to decide.

Argentina

Once the envy of the developing world, Argentina fell on hard times in the 70s and 80s with debilitating rates of inflation and a series of brutal military dictatorships. Down, but not out, the proud people of Argentina have bounced back with a decade of democracy and a stable economy.

Many visitors comment on the European flavor of Argentina, especially the capital Buenos Aires with its wide boulevards, outdoor cafes and cosmopolitan architecture. In fact, most Argentineans are of European descent. They were drawn to this "land of opportunity" in the same way immigrants left the Old Country for the United States.

The country is enormously varied both in types of land and climate. The north is warm and forested, the west is mountainous, and the southeast, called Patagonia, is stark, flat, and dry. All over the countryside are the flamboyant *gaucho* cowboys who work the many Argentinean cattle ranches. Proud in heritage, natural beauty, and distinctively different from its neighbors and ancestors, this land and its people offer many opportunities for travel and discovery. Visa not required for stays up to 3 months.

Bolivia

Often reported as the Stompers favorite country on this circuit, Bolivia offers much in the way of geographical diversity, and friendly people with a colorful culture. Most of the people live up on a bleak, cold, and treeless plain called the *Altiplano* (high plateau), which comprises about 30 percent of the nation's land area. Rich in minerals and studded with snowcapped peaks, the *Altiplano* is a hostile environment of rare beauty.

The population is poor and prices are cheap in Bolivia. In fact, the cost of travel is the lowest in all of South America, but getting around is time consuming and sometimes difficult. The cool hangouts are Copacobana on Lake Titicaca and Uyuni. Don't miss the pre Inca ceremonial center Tiahuanaco near La Paz on the southern shore of Lake Titicaca. No visa required for 30 days to Stomp.

Brazil

The land of rainforests, wild parties, and pristine beaches is more accessible today than it has ever been. But get there quick, the Amazonian habitats are disappearing at an alarming rate, as well as the indigenous people who inhabit them (see: Brazil, below). A visa must be obtained before departure. Visas are $45 when applying in person at an Embassy or Consulate; an additional $10 service fee is added if you apply by mail.

Chile

Perhaps one of the most diversified climactic countries in the world, Chile is a ribbon of land 4,200 km long wedged between the lofty Andes Mountains and the Pacific Ocean. The Northern frontier is a rainless hot desert of brown hills and dry plains devoid of vegetation. The Second Zone is semi-desert, leading to the Middle Zone which is the heartland and home to most of the population. Farther south is the Forest Zone filled with lakes, rivers, heavy rainfall, and primeval forests. The extreme south is right back into the nasty weather. This area is sparsely populated and features spectacular glaciers, fjords, islands, mountains, and channels.

To get on a Chilean Navy boat to Antarctica in the summer, one must inquire in person at Tercera Zonal Naval Base, Lautaro Navarro 1150 in Punta Arenas. The cost will run you about $1500, and the round trip journey takes 4 weeks or so.

Another popular sidetrip from Chile is out to the mysterious Easter Island, or *Rapa Nui* as it is known to the Polynesian natives. The tall and gaunt *Moai* with elongated faces and ears are scattered all over the island and some stand as tall as 9 meters in height. Flights from Santiago go over once a week. To enter Chile, Antarctica, or Easter Island, a passport is all that is needed for a 90-day stay. $45 arrival tax for U.S. citizens.

Colombia

Most people perceive Colombia as being totally out of control, with drug barons bombing each other and assassinating political leaders in an endless series of violent power struggles. While this is partially true and most cities can be quite dangerous by night, the countryside offers Andean tranquillity and friendly people as few others can. From tropical swamps to snow-dusted volcanoes, the scenery in Colombia is awesome. Many of the roads are unpaved and rough going, so getting around overland can sometimes be quite a chore. Overcome the obstacles and you will be rewarded with warm hospitality and exuberant Colombian pride.

The cool hangouts for wicked ruins are the Valley of the Statues near San Agustin and the Lost City near Santa Marta town, also an intense stoner's mecca. The cheapest way to enter South America via the overland route from Central America is a domestic flight from Colombia's Caribbean island, San Andres. A passport is all that is required for stays up to 30 days.

Ecuador

The land of contrasts. Unending scenery. Mountain and tropical adventure. Unusual people and ancient folklore. The name of this country is derived from the equator, which bisects the nation. Crossing it the other way, from north to south, are the Andes Mountains that form a backbone to the country. In between are a wide variety of climates, from the hot and humid Amazon rainforest to snowcapped volcanoes, many still active.

If the geography is widely diverse, so then is the culture. Dozens of Indian tribes exist today as they have for centuries, retaining their own clothing, way of life, and language. In other regions, the Spaniards left their indelible mark after 300 years of colonial domination. Left behind are their architecture, language, and religion.

Top Ten Mellow Party Scenes (#4)

The best mellow party hangout on this circuit is Vilacabamba, a quaint little village in a beautiful valley. Towering over the valley are the snowcapped Andes and a special Sacred Mountain. Most backpackers flock here to try the hallucinogenic San Pedro cactus with native shaman. Many report a vision quest state of mind, but  only after throwing up. Other attractions are horseback riding, steam baths, mud treatment, and private sun bathing in an agreeable climate.

Pry yourself away from this fascinating country and make a visit to the Galapagos Islands. Like Darwin, visitors are amazed by the unique plant and animal life found in these remote islands. Flights go daily from Quito, but there is an $100 entry fee into the national park and must be paid in cash upon arrival (U.S. dollars or Ecuadorian sucres). No visa required, but passport and onward ticket are required for stays up to 3 months.

The Guianas

These three former colonies of Britain (Guyana), Holland (Suriname), and France (French Guiana), are sparsely populated and have much the same surface. The coast is flat and marshy and is where almost all crops are grown and people live. Behind lies a belt of gorged uplands leading further to the mountainous Guiana Highlands. The basic population consists of Creoles, the descendants of non-indigenous blacks and East-Indians who were both imported here to work the land. There are few whites or tribal natives anymore, but English is widely understood, especially in Guyana. A visa is required for Suriname but not for Guyana or French Guiana. Suriname requires currency conversion upon arrival. Stays from 3 weeks to 3 months granted in all 3 countries.

Paraguay

This tiny landlocked country can be divided into two geographic zones. The *Chaco* to the northwest is a flat and infertile area that is sparsely populated. The Parana Plateau to the southwest is of rolling hills, forests, farms, and home to most of Paraguay's inhabitants. Almost everyone in Paraguay is either a farmer or a rancher. Spanish is the official language, as well as Guarani, the language of the indigenous Indians who mostly live in the *Chaco*. No visa required for stays up to 90 days, extendible. Exit tax $20 paid at the airport.

Peru

A patchwork of cultures from the ancient Incas to the Spanish Conquistadors, amidst towering Andean mountains and exotic Amazonian wildlife make up this amazing country. The fabled Inca city of Machu Picchu is not to be missed, nor the mysterious Nazca Lines, both of which elude experts as to their function and date of construction. Another highlight is the river port city of Iquitos that links the Amazon River and provides boat access all the way out to the Atlantic Ocean.

Many colonial churches and mansions of the Spanish legacy can be seen in almost every village or city of Peru. The missionaries did one heck of a job stamping out Inca culture, but they never could quite erase it. This is evident in the colorful costumes, handicraft, music, and festivals still alive in Peru today. Try to arrange your visit around the time of the summer or winter solstice to observe the ancient *Inti Raimi* celebration in Cuzco. Shamans from all over South America come to pay Inca tribute to the departing and returning phases of the sun.

Petty theft is common in cities and touristed areas and travel here should be undertaken with caution. Terrorist violence has diminished over the past years and is not targeted at tourists any longer, but there still may be roaming bands of thieves in the mountains. A passport is the only requirement for stays up to 90 days.

Uruguay

One of South America's smallest nations, Uruguay, and its capital Montevideo, are often called "a big city with a large ranch." There is not a whole lot going on here apart from cattle ranching and long grassy plains and hills. A notable mention is the world-famous beach resort of Punta del Este and the Portuguese colonial town of Colonia. Visa not required for stays up to 3 months.

Venezuela

The discovery of oil has radically transformed Venezuela from a poor, agrarian country into South America's most prosperous nation. There is an affluent middle class and a stable democratic system, and getting around is quite easy. There are many natural splendors to attract the visitor: beaches on the Caribbean Sea, the Andes mountains where snowcapped peaks and waterfalls inspire awe, and dense tropical jungles where Stone Age tribes and a plethora of wildlife make their home. A passport is all that's required for a (non-extendible) 90 day stay. $12 departure tax required.

Earthlings

The Dalai Llama

Brazil

"I'm Charley's aunt from Brazil — Where the nuts come from."
— Brandon Thomas, *Charley's Aunt*, 1892

A few images of this huge country shape most people's overall impression of it. The gorgeous g-string babes on a Rio beach. Miners and ranchers slashing and burning their way through the delicate Amazon rainforest. Nazis hiding out after WWII. Megacities like Brasilia and São Paulo just bursting at the seams with people. Presidents being booed out of office. Expansive, untouched beaches and the Mosquito Coast. While all of these images are real, one should really travel there for the best perception of all. With so much to see and do, on so much land, and so many people to meet, one needs at least a few weeks before scratching the surface.

Except for the United States and Russia, Brazil is the largest country in the world to have essentially one language, and that is Portuguese. Brazil is the fifth largest country in size and home to the eighth largest population on the planet. It comprises nearly half of all of South America. Every country on the continent borders it except Chile and Ecuador. The distances to get around Brazil are enormous: 4,320 km from north to south, 4,328 km from east to west, a land frontier of 15,719 km and an Atlantic coast line of 7,408 km.

Brazil's population is exploding. Today it hovers at 140 million people and half of those are under the age of 25. In 30 years the population is projected to grow to 245 million. Yet out of these millions of people, only 100,000 or so indigenous inhabitants remain, and that number continues to drop.

The Amazon

This is the largest intact rainforest in the world and comprises more than a third of the whole country. The basin is broadly based on the Andes mountains, and the river funnels its way narrowly out to the Atlantic Ocean. The rainfall is heavy and the flooding frequent, especially now that so much forest has been destroyed. The climate is hot and humid throughout the year.

The best way to see the Amazon River is by boat. Riverboats provide most of the transportation in this vast area. They access nearly every city and village from the Atlantic coast all the way up to Peru and Colombia. Travel tip: for the best scenery, take boats that are going upstream. Downstream boats go down the middle of the river where the current is the strongest and it becomes difficult to see anything. Upstream boats travel near the banks where the current is less severe and everything of interest can be seen up close. Birds flying about, natives running out to greet the boat, and wild animals drinking from the river are some highlights from any trip.

THE SOUTH AMERICAN CIRCUIT

The Culture

Brazil had been the premiere colony of Portugal for 300 years. It was an integral nation in the Latin American independence movement, achieving its freedom not through wars, but reason. The people of Brazil take great pride in this fact. Travelers are usually greeted with a warm welcome and a hearty laugh, especially if attempting to speak Portuguese. Rooms can be hard to find during Carnival, but if you even remotely know someone, chances are they will insist you stay with them.

Top Ten Best Bashes (#8)

The most popular and colorful time of year to go to Brazil is during Carnival. The Brazilians start partying seven weeks before Easter, but the wild times really kick in the last few days before Ash Wednesday. The whole country goes nuts and cities like Salvador, Rio, and Recife transform into giant street parades of mass drinking, lavish costumes, music, and dancing. The festive atmosphere and rowdy alcohol consumption are the calls of the wild. They call – we get wild.

It has been said that the Brazilian people are among the friendliest in the world. Even in the congested cities where people are usually stressed out, the locals will find great interest in a foreigner. If you like attention, make this fact well known by wearing a button or a patch. You will be greeted warmly and chances are your newly found friends will buy you a drink or offer you a place to sleep in their home. The farther out into the country you go, the nicer the people seem to become. Get to know a *gaucho* and maybe he'll offer a ride on his horse or llama.

The party scene along the coast is big on booze, but there are psychedelic techno parties starting to pop up on the beaches. Most notable are the all-night raves near Porto Seguro. Tango to techno?

Travel

Most overland travel is done by bus, but due to the vast distances, travel by road can be slow going. Many travelers intent on seeing different regions of the country generally resort to air transportation for at least one leg of their journey. The domestic airline Varig Brazilian Air offers several multiple flight deals, but the time frame allowed is sometimes too short. Check fares and schedules by calling (212) 682-3100.

A word of caution: credit card fraud is rife in Brazil, as it is elsewhere in South America. Beware of the scam where the merchant runs off several extra vouchers when a transaction is being processed. If you bring a credit card on your trip, and this is true everywhere, never let it out of your sight.

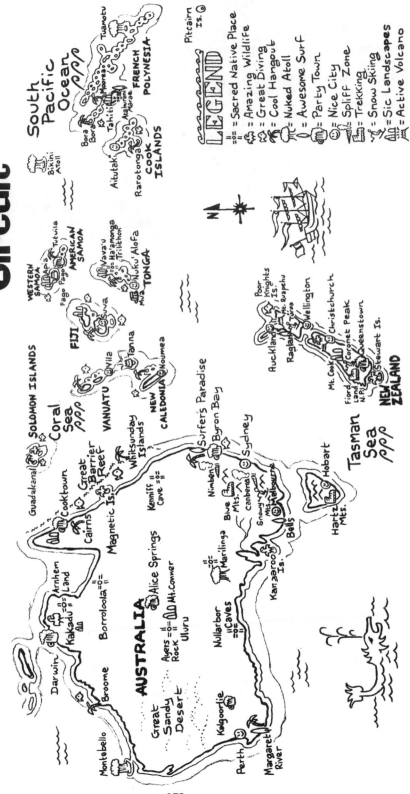

Australia and the South Pacific Circuit

Australia and the South Pacific Circuit

All the time our visits to the islands have been more like dreams than realities: the people, the life, the beachcombers, the old stories and songs I have picked up, so interesting; the climate, the scenery, and (in some places) the women, so beautiful.

— Robert Louis Stevenson, 1889

Scattered across the vast South Pacific Ocean are tens of thousands of small islands collectively known as Polynesia. This triangle of culture stretches from New Zealand to Easter Island to Hawaii. Similar islands in the Coral Sea and Papua New Guinea are known as Melanesia. Nearby is the continent and nation, Australia. Nearly all of these nations have a long history of being dominated by their colonial masters; France, the U.S., and especially Great Britain. The influence of these imperialist nations is very evident today in the form of language, religion, politics, economics, territorial status, and old colonial architecture.

The only circuit devoid of dirty ugly cities, Australia and the South Pacific is the adventurer and beach lover's wet dream. Generalizing this vast area it can be said to contain some of the most amazing landscapes and mellowest people — not without a hitch, however. Unfortunately, it is one of the most expensive circuits in both moving from place to place and cost of living. But, as with every other place, there are ways to work around costs, like crewing on someone's yacht or working in Australia and New Zealand.

Australia

The land down under has long been a fascination of discoverers and explorers alike. Entrenched in the American psyche with images of outback excursions, the Great Barrier Reef, aboriginals, kangaroos, and *Crocodile Dundee*. Australian culture today is much like a cross between Britain and the U.S., yet uniquely different. Travel is easy, costs are reasonable and the Aussies are a great lot of sarcastic cobbers (see: Australia, below). Visas must be obtained prior to arrival. Multiple-entry 3 month visas are free, anything longer, up to 1 year, cost $24. Departure tax of $20 paid at the airport. Australian customs now requires an Electronic Travel Authority (ETA) letter for entry. ETA letters are issued from the travel agency or from the airline issuing Australia tickets.

Cook Islands

Much the same as their French Polynesian neighbors by the way of scenery and native friendliness, the Cook Islands differ in two major ways. The first is colonial masters. The Cook Islands were discovered by the eminent British explorer Captain Cook and claimed as a colony for the U.K. They reverted to New Zealand for a long while until becoming an independent republic in 1965. All those years under the thumb of British masters have made the Cook Islanders fluent in English. The second major difference is the money used here. They continue to use the New Zealand dollar, which happens to be weak against the U.S. dollar, so travel here is affordable. Good value combined with loads of attractions. Visa not needed for stays up to 31 days.

Fiji

Of all the South Pacific island countries, Fiji is the best equipped to offer an ultra-budget experience. Suva is a busy airport for stopovers across the South Pacific, and there are many guesthouses on the popular islands. Fiji is renowned because it is relatively cheap and filled with other World Stompers. Scuba diving is no-frills and inexpensive. The reefs and lagoons scattered about the islands are amazing for diving, and the Rainbow Reef off Vanua Levu island is considered one of the best dive sites in the world. When not in the bright blue sea or combing a remote beach on one of the more than 300 islands, have a chat with an extremely friendly local in one of their tribal-style villages. Hard to believe their ancestors were cannibals only a century ago.

Most of all, Fiji is just an awesome spectacle of nature – above and below the water. This is, after all, the place where *The Blue Lagoon* was filmed. Visa issued on arrival for stay up to 30 days and may be extended up to 6 months. A brief government coup in June, 2000 did not concern tourism, and now the country is back to "business as usual."

French Polynesia

The spectacular physical beauty of glorious tropical settings, back set by soaring ridged mountains, are most people's first impression upon arrival in this enchanted wonderland. And then the sun sets over an outlying jagged island, and you will wonder if it's not some kind of primordial dinosaur resting out on the horizon. This is Tahiti, Bora Bora, and Moorea, whose names alone impart tropical tranquillity. Toss in a few thousand more remote islands, ancient monuments, pristine lagoons, reefs for diving and surfing, charming port towns and villages, and there you have French Polynesia in a nutshell.

Still a territory of France, these islands are both blessed and cursed by their colonial masters. Blessed with fine food, wine, and good cheer that are sure to follow the French wherever they go, they are cursed by a far-away government that insists on continued nuclear testing when there is absolutely no reason to do so. The currency is tied into the French currency so travel here is pretty expensive. The scenery and people of French Polynesia will live up to anyone's idea of a paradise on earth, just so long as you're not hanging out on a radioactive atoll. Passports required, but not visas for stays up to one month.

New Caledonia

Another French South Pacific territory, this group of islands is a precarious mix of French and Melanesian cultures. There is a boisterous independence movement by the natives against their French masters. The conflict is set to be resolved in a few years when New Caledonia may or may not become an independent nation. In the meantime, travelers enjoy deserted beaches, the French Riviera at Noumea, colorful people, and a vast aquatic playground along the world's third-longest barrier reef. Passport required but not a visa for stays up to 30 days.

New Zealand

New Zealand is the adventure and adrenaline capital of the world. The birthplace of bungy jumping is also home to the latest craze – rap jumping – which is like rappelling face first. Hosting numerous other activities such as powder and heli-skiing, bike touring, scuba diving, mountain climbing, hunting, fishing, sailing, surfing, whitewater rafting, and trekking; this is *the* country to visit if you are into the great outdoors.

The reason all these thrills happen is because of the three amazing islands that make up the land mass of New Zealand. Smoldering volcanoes, raging rivers, towering glacial mountains, grand fjords, exotic temperate rainforests, pristine beaches, and plunging waterfalls are enough to entice any traveler to fall in love with this place. Basically, spectacular scenery lies around every bend, and action-packed adventures can be had from top to bottom. Over one third of New Zealand is preserved land in the form of a national park or wilderness area.

Getting around the two main islands is easy. Trains and buses will get you to almost any part of the country, and are pretty cheap. Another option is renting a car, or the ultra-budget choice of hitchhiking. Helpful New Zealanders are probably the coolest in the world for giving rides. Since New Zealand is so sparsely populated (more sheep than people), the friendly Kiwis usually enjoy meeting overseas visitors. People of British descent and other Europeans make up the majority of the population, but the indigenous Maori people and Pacific Islanders are over half a million strong. All these races co-exist in relative harmony. Besides, who wants to be stressed in paradise?

The work situation in New Zealand is much the same as Australia, and will be covered in the Australia section, below. A passport is required for entry, but a visa is not. Three months are given, and travelers must show sufficient funds, an onward plane ticket, and a visa for their next destination to pass customs.

The Samoas

Smack dab in the heart of Polynesia, independent Western Samoa is like a cultural museum, especially when compared to its little brother, American Samoa. There are many relations between the two, including family, politics, landscapes, and age-old traditions. Yet, there are many differences. Western Samoa is *Fa'a Samoa*, or The Samoan Way, and is proudly Polynesia's oldest culture and remains relatively unchanged by modern materialism. Continuing its ancient ways of producing food, celebration, dress, and beach communities of grass huts, Western Samoa is like venturing back in time.

So strange that just a few kilometers away is an entirely different society. When the U.S. military moved into American Samoa in 1890 for the finest South Pacific harbor at Pago Pago, things changed forever. The emphasis is away from grass skirts and communal living for business and progress. A fish and root diet submit to hamburgers and french fries, and unspoiled lagoons are lost to cannery factories that smell and pollute. But some things cannot change so drastically. Both offer fantastic beaches, dramatic beauty, and arguably the friendliest people in the world.

All this paradise has a price, however. Costs are relatively high, especially in American Samoa where the U.S. dollar is the currency and everything needs to be imported. Avoid the traffic jams and fast food joints on the American isles and go hang out with a tribal chieftain on the Western islands. Extreme hospitality and Polynesian paralysis will be your greatest challenge. Passports are required for entry into Western Samoa, but no visa for stays up to 30 days. U.S. proof of citizenship for entry into American Samoa.

The Solomon Islands

For WWII war buffs there is perhaps no greater place to visit for relics than the Solomon Islands. Home to the famous Guadalcanal Island, this is where the U.S. Marines effectively halted the Japanese Imperial Army's relentless advance through the Pacific. Over ten thousand men perished on this tropical paradise in some of the bloodiest fighting of the war. Today the rusting or coral-encrusted wreckages of those battles a half century ago are a highlight of any visit. Scuba dive down to hundreds of sunken planes and ships lying in shallow, crystal-clear lagoons. Hike the islands in search of old tanks and battle memorials. Check out Gizo in the Western Province where a young U.S. Navy lieutenant named John F. Kennedy was stranded after his PT boat was shot out from under him. "Kennedy Island" is a popular day trip and picnic site.

Another thing the Solomon Island is known for are the friendly people and multitudes of smiling faces, well deserved of the nickname "the Happy Isles." This country is also one of the least touristy destinations in the South Pacific. Passports required, but not a visa for stays up to 2 months.

Tonga

There are many special things about these tiny islands right in the heart of Polynesia. First off, it's just east of the international date line and the first nation to see the light of every new day. After a beautiful sunrise, have a walk around the last surviving South Pacific kingdom, home to a 350 pound monarch named King Taufa'ahau Tupou IV who cruises around on his bike. Over a fresh fruit shake, have a chat with a friendly local about what to see and do. He will likely talk in length about where to dive, which are the best beaches to comb, ancient monuments and tombs to explore, and maybe a grumble about the king too. But he will be extremely happy to see you and show you the way, after all, these are the people Captain Cook named "The Friendly Isles" after. The Visitors Center gives a good description, "The kingdom still remains far away from it all; still different, still alone, and to the joy of those who find their way to her – essentially unspoiled." Passport and onward ticket required for entry, but no visa for stays up to 30 days.

Vanuatu

Apart from Port Vila on Efate Island, this chain-o-islands nation is very primitive. Most of the people live in bamboo huts and wear grass skirts. Basically, you will be on your own to round up transportation, lodging, and meals from the locals — who may or may not wish to help you. Perhaps the biggest single attraction is the roaring volcano called Mount Yasur that is easily accessible. Nearby the volcano is a village where the natives reject anything Western, and the men wear nothing but penis sheaths. Maybe they could identify with The Red Hot Chili Peppers. Visa not required for stays up to 30 days.

Earthlings

Babushkas in Paradise

Australia

> *"If the madmen triumph and the button is pressed and this earth is reduced to a smoldering radio-active cinder, maybe, out on the old Barcoo or somewhere out west, there will be a survivor, a lone battler to emerge from his timber-and-corrugated shack, look out across the ruined planet, roll himself a smoke, and say, 'she'll be right, mate.' "*
> – Henry Williams, *Australia-What is it.*

The indigenous people of Australia, the Aboriginals, are said by anthropologists to be the oldest variety of Homo sapiens on earth. Migrating to Australia some 40,000 years ago, their Stone Age culture remained intact until the white man showed up in the late 16th century. Their numbers then became drastically reduced through disease and genocide, much like the American Indians. The island-state of Tasmania was ethnically cleansed by early settlers on an extermination campaign that hunted down every single Aboriginal from top to bottom.

Today, the Aboriginal people of mainland Australia are having a hard time adjusting to the modern world of the White Fellows, and alcoholism is rampant. Out on the reservations, especially in the remote Northern Territory, the ancient culture of the Aborigines can still be found. Venture far into the bush to find the hunters of spears and boomerangs, and players of the didgeridoo, for the true Australian experience.

The white people of Australia represent the vast majority of the population, yet thousands of Asians and South Pacific Islanders continue to immigrate here every year. Ethnically diverse, egalitarianism runs deep and the social programs are some of the most generous in the world. The stereotypical image of the 21-year-old blond and tanned surfer is pretty much true, as Australians are big into sports. They also have one of the mellowest and laid back attitudes to be found anywhere.

The Land of Oz

A common sight in gift shops and book stores all over Australia are maps depicting the Southern Hemisphere at the top of the world. "Up Over Down Under" they declare, and it's correct; just because something is familiar and etched into our brains a certain way, does not mean it's the *only* way of perceiving it. An Aussie bloke will be quick to point out the many differences with the U.S. or Great Britain, such as a lack of crime, low population, and an easier way of life. Another popular one is how water empties out of a bath in a counter-clockwise direction down under, whereas it drains clockwise in the Northern Hemisphere. No one knows why, but it's true.

As a member of the British Commonwealth, Australia recognizes Queen Elizabeth II as its officious head of state, but there is a strong movement to become an autonomous republic. Like Canada and New Zealand, the Queen graces Australian coins and notes. The prime minister and parliament are seated in Canberra, a planned city designed to serve as the nation's capital.

Australia's population is rather small for a country so huge. The 17 million people of the whole continent are about the size of Greater New York City, or the amount of new people added to India's population every year. Sixty percent of Australia's population live in the five largest cities and all are located on the coast. The rest of Australia is very sparsely populated, and the fact that more than 50 percent of the country receives less than 12 inches of rain a year may be the reason why.

On The Stoner's Trail (#8)

Near an old volcanic crater that is now a verdant playground of rolling hills and forests is a little hippie enclave called Nimben. A stroll through town past the vegetarian restaurants and head shops will bring you in touch with more than one dealer of the Kind Green Cones. Cops are known to occasionally crack down, so be discreet whom you buy from and where you smoke.

Scattered around Nimben are several communes where hippies live in harmony with nature and smoke copious amounts of pot. Most communes will welcome you to stay with them, just remember to bring along some supplies and help with everyday chores. As stoner nations go, Australia must have the highest per-capita number of baked citizenry; it's a way of life down-under.

Good on ya' mates!

The Great Barrier Reef

Up in the northern state of Queensland lies the longest and most diverse coral reef in the world. Sheer size and a wide variety of sea life make the Great Barrier Reef (GBR) one of the most popular diving sites in the world. The GBR contains 350 species of coral and 1,200 species of fish along a series of reefs extending over 2,000 km, from Papau New Guinea to halfway down the eastern coast of Australia. In places it extends over 300 km out to sea.

Most towns on the coast across from the GBR will offer boat excursions out to the reef, or a trip to an outlying island where diving is accessible. The most popular diving town is Cairns, the self-proclaimed "Gateway to the Great Barrier Reef." Inexpensive diving courses are offered here, as well as a multitude of reef trips ranging from the tip of the Cape York Peninsula and way out to the Coral Sea. The close proximity of the reef from town (24 km), off-shore islands, a multitude of adventures inland, and the party atmosphere of Cairns makes it a very popular destination for visiting Stompers.

Top Ten Mellow Party Scenes (#9)

Magnetic Island is synonymous with mellowness. Perhaps in all of Australia there is no better place to hang out with a babe on some pristine beaches, just off the Great Barrier Reef. The excellent hiking trails take you to abandon hidden fortresses that once protected nearby Townsville from Japanese attack in WWII. Living all around the fort area are tribes of wild Koala bears. After sunset, head into town for a piss-up with some new found mates.

Work and Money

A country remarkably similar to the U.S. in size, culture, racial makeup, age, small towns and modern cities, and of course, language. Unfortunately, like America, it can be expensive to live and travel in, if done the conventional way. The unconventional way, the World Stomping way, is to work here illegally and supplement the travel budget. Americans cannot work here legally unless they establish residency or have a special arrangement with the government and a sponsoring company. Wages are generally good, but jobs in the way of career work are hard to find. The only exception is for teachers of Chinese or Japanese language, mathematics, or science, which Australian public schools have a shortage of these days.

If lacking the proper credentials, the thing to do is come here on a tourist visa and travel to where work can be found. Some employers require you to have a proper visa, such as a working holiday visa the Brits and commonwealth countries can get, others do not. Some employers require a tax-file (social security) number, (which can be made up and gotten away with for about three months), others do not. But the most important thing an Aussie employer will look for is a good attitude.

The most popular backpacker job in Oz is fruit picking, which is happening somewhere in the country year 'round. Depending on where you are at, ask a local or fellow traveler where and when and what crop. These jobs are found by being in the right place at the right time, usually out of a hostel or very early Monday morning in the town square. Whoever shows up, works. The hours are long and the work is mundane, but by doing the joppi task you can make from $60 to $100 per day, cash in hand. Similar work is on a produce-processing assembly line. These jobs are boring and indoors, so employee turnover is high and jobs are easy to get on short notice. The best picking jobs are on the "friendly farms" which provide rides to and from the hostels and allow you to wear a Walkman on the job.

Other possibilities are basically all the jobs the Aussies do not want to do themselves. Under-the-table work includes: farm hands, leaflet delivery, brick-laying, odd jobs, busking, waitering, street selling, construction, baby-sitting, or just knowing someone who can recommend you somewhere or put you to work for himself. Always check the hostel bulletin board and ask around when you arrive somewhere new. Work is not too hard to find in Australia, and the creative ones position themselves as hosts on diving boats or bartending beach side. Seek and ye shall find.

Travel

There is no sea passage between Indonesia and Australia, so most overland travelers fly cheap from Kupang on Timor island to Darwin. Once in Australia, keep in mind the vast distances between cities. Food, gas, water and other travel essentials can be difficult to find in the bleak interior. In the sparsely populated outback areas it is realistic to travel 300 miles (500 km) per day between settlements, but much less than that on the more populated eastern coast. Hitchhiking is relatively easy in Australia, but can result in long, hot periods of waiting in between rides. Renting or buying a car, or bus transportation, is the popular way to go.

New Evolutionary Message: Stay Clear of Driftnets.

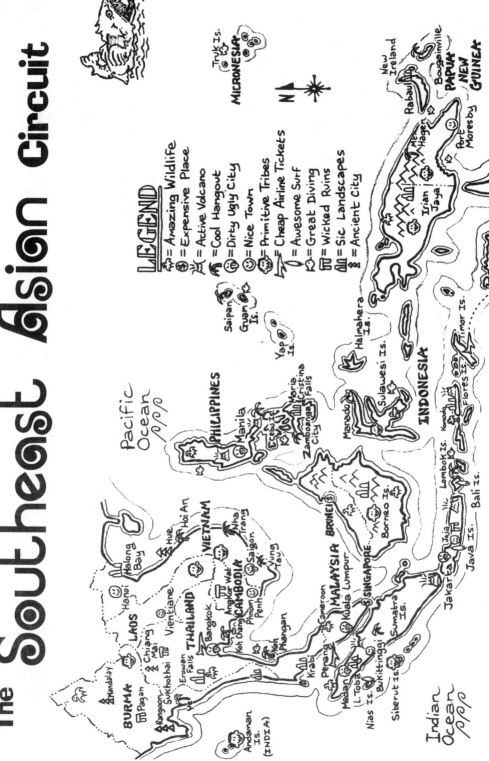

The Southeast Asian Circuit

LEGEND

- 🐾 = Amazing Wildlife
- 💲 = Expensive Place
- 🌋 = Active Volcano
- 🏙 = Cool Hangout
- 🏚 = Dirty Ugly City
- 🙂 = Nice Town
- 👥 = Primitive Tribes
- ✈ = Cheap Airline Tickets
- 🏄 = Awesome Surf
- 🤿 = Great Diving
- 🏛 = Wicked Ruins
- 🏔 = Sic Landscapes
- 🏯 = Ancient City

Pacific Ocean

Indian Ocean

MICRONESIA
Truk Is.
Saipan
Guam Is.
Yap Is.

PHILIPPINES
Manila
Cebu
Moria
Cristina Falls
Zamboanga City

BURMA
Mandalay
Pagan
Rangoon
Sukhothai
Erawan Falls

LAOS
Chiang Mai
Vientiane
THAILAND
Bangkok
Koh Chang
Koh Phangan
Krabi

VIETNAM
Hanoi
Halong Bay
Hue
Hoi An
Nha Trang
Vung Tau
Saigon
Phnom Penh
CAMBODIA
Angkor Wat

Andaman Is. (INDIA)

MALAYSIA
Cameron
Penang
Kuala Lumpur
SINGAPORE
Medan
Bukittinggi
Sumatra Is.
L. Toba
Nias Is.
Siberut Is.

BRUNEI
Borneo Is.

Manado
Sulawesi Is.
Halmahera Is.

INDONESIA
Jakarta
Java Is.
Ujung
Lombok Is.
Bali Is.
Komodo
Flores Is.
Timor Is.
Darwin

Irian Jaya
Mt. Hagen
Port Moresby
Rabaul
New Ireland
Bougainville
PAPUA NEW GUINEA

182

The Southeast Asian Circuit

*In the river there is the crocodile. On the riverbank,
there is the tiger. If you go to the forest, there are
the thorns. If you go to the market,
there is the policeman.*

— Cambodian Proverb

The mere mention of Southeast Asia conjures up images of things exotic. Lush tropical greenery, exquisite art forms, timeless traditions, ancient architectural wonders, happy people, thriving urban centers, quiet hamlets, and a multi-cultured population that never ceases to intrigue the visitor. Whether you go for pristine beaches or rainforest treks, amazing wildlife or primitive tribes, parties in Thailand, or the fantastic variation of ethnic groups, this circuit will dazzle you with a multitude of fascinating travel experiences.

Southeast Asia was originally inhabited some 500,000 years ago by the now extinct humanoid *Homo Erectus* from Africa. Other migrating aboriginal tribes followed, eventually inhabiting Australia and thousands of remote islands. Many of these primitive tribes, but not all, were wiped out when the Malay people migrated south from mainland Asia. As time progressed, the shores of Southeast Asia served as harbors for many water borne traders and missionaries. Each new wave of visitors brought fresh concepts that aided and modified the region's development. The most important influences came from India, whose merchants and priests introduced Southeast Asia to its three major religions – Hinduism, Buddhism, and Islam. The Chinese made their way down and contributed with their culture and vast amounts of immigrants relocating. Next came the European powers who set up colonies and created empires. Cities emerged from colonial trading centers, and most large cities today are located along the major shipping routes of old.

Rural living continues to be the mainstay for most of the population of Southeast Asia. Out in the country you will observe the way people have lived since antiquity. Rice growing is the primary occupation for traditional farmers, and religion is pervasive. As the population grows rapidly in Southeast Asian cities every year, so does the poverty. While most cities are relatively safe and an interesting melting pot of people, it is the countryside where this circuit shines the brightest.

Brunei

This tiny Islamic Sultanate is the second wealthiest per capita nation on earth entirely due to the vast reserves of oil found underneath it. Traveling here is very expensive and only recommended if the Stomper has a line on a job. It is a high wage-earning location to live for a while, only if you can arrange a work visa beforehand. Otherwise, tourist visas are free for 90 days. Apart from working in the Petro-chemical industry or teaching English, there is not a whole lot to see or do. The magnificent Sultan's palace is closed, and the museums, mosques, and tombs are nothing special. Outside the city it's all jungle and rubber plantations, apart from the famed Headhunter's Trail from Limbang to Mulu, which involves longboat travel on the river, a bus ride, and trekking in the N.P.

Burma

Burma, now officially called Myanmar, is a country with hardly any traces of the West. This country lives in a virtual time-warp socially, politically, and economically. Formerly sealed off from the outside world with few travel amenities it is worth a trip because the people, ruins at Pagan, and landscapes are truly amazing. Rebel fighting continues in pockets around the country, and human atrocities continue. Many human right groups call for a full travel boycott of Burma, yet tourism helps educate the world as to what's really going on in the country. If you do go, try not to support any government-owned businesses or transportation. Instead, pay a local to take you around and buy souvenirs from the people directly. Foreign independent travelers must change a minimum of U.S. $300 upon arrival. Single entry visas for 28 days cost $14 and are best obtained in Bangkok, Thailand.

Cambodia

Another time-warp country, Cambodia is only now emerging from a three-decades long civil war. Brutalized by the ultra-communist Khmer Rouge under leader Pol Pot, well over a million people perished during their 1975-1979 reign of terror. Today, Cambodia is just starting to heal its wounds and open up for Stomping. And a good thing too, the ruins at Angkor are some of humanity's most magnificent architectural achievements. Phnom Penh is an enchanting French-influenced city, and the people are arguably the friendliest on this circuit. Take note of any and all travel advisories *before* entering Cambodia. Several foreigners are killed every year by Khmer Rouge guerrillas. A one month visa is issued upon arrival, and requires a $20 fee.

Indonesia

A country steeped in history and tradition, the 13,000+ tropical islands that make up Indonesia are enough to fill any travel itinerary for years to come. See: Indonesia, below. Apart from environmental degradation which resulted in massive burnings a few years ago and the occasional riot in Jakarta, the only bummer is that visas are valid only two months (but are free), and are non-extendible. Just when you begin to scratch the surface, it's time to bail. But that's what return visits are for.

THE SOUTHEAST ASIAN CIRCUIT

Laos

Laos has been known since antiquity as the "Land of a Million Elephants." Today it's more like the land of a thousand elephants after widespread hunting and poaching has decimated the once vast pachyderm population. Still a wonder of nature, Laos is a beautiful, friendly, and slow-moving country that never ceases to charm its infrequent visitors. Transit visas cost $10 for 5 days and no travel outside the capital Vientiane is permitted. Tourist visas valid for are 30 days cost $35 and is your license to freely Stomp around the country. The best place to arrange a tourist visa is on Khao San Road in Bangkok, Thailand. 15-day visas are issued on the spot for $50 in the airport or on the International Friendship Bridge at Nong Khai near the capital Vientiane. A better option is to secure your visa ahead of time at a Lao embassy in Vietnam or Burma.

On The Stoner's Trail (#10)

The most often ignored country in Southeast Asia, Laos, is also the biggest stoner country and ganja cultivator. An article appeared recently in a Bangkok newspaper about Thailand's request to the Laotian government to make growing marijuana illegal. The Laotian government's official response was "Our populace has been consuming marijuana for many generations, therefore it is not practical, now or in the foreseeable future, to make growing or consumption of marijuana illegal in Laos."

Most farmer markets in Laos sell pot right alongside the vegetables and spices – by the bushel, or by the spliff. Bags of weed are just that; seedy and stemmy. Don't pay more than a dollar for half a baggy full. The same situation applies in Cambodia and parts of Vietnam.

Malaysia

Malaysia is home to one of the largest Chinese populations outside of China, comprising 35 percent of the overall population. It also has a large Indian population, but it is the Malay people who make up the majority and control the government. The laws are extremely harsh on drug smugglers and several are executed every year, including the occasional Westerner to set an example. No sparkin' up here, wasteoids.

Malaysia is a land of many contrasts, from sun-drenched beaches and cool mountain highlands to noisy cities and quiet villages. Chinese temples juxtapose next to Moorish mosques and Hindu shrines, while modern shopping arcades outpace the colorful country markets. The nation consists of the heavily populated peninsular West Malaysia and the remote Sabah and Sarawak states on Borneo Island. Several foreign tourists were kidnapped from scuba mecca Sipadan Island in April, 2000 by Islamic separatists from the southern region of the Philippines. Precautions should be taken in the remote Muslim islands scattered around the South China Sea. No visa required for stays up to 3 months.

Micronesia

The Federated States of Micronesia consists of the mega-tiny-island groups of; Marianas, Palau, Caroline, Marshall, Gilbert, and Ellice. Massive in geographical size, the inhabited islands are only a few dozen. The only real towns are on Kosrae, Yap, Ponape, and Truk islands.

Truk is perhaps the most famous destination in Micronesia for the lagoon of the same name. Truk lagoon is an underwater tomb of an entire Japanese fleet. The huge WWII battle took place on 17 February, 1944, and is remembered as the United States answer to Pearl Harbor. Complete with sake cups, skeletons, fighter planes, submarines, and cargo ships with jeeps and tanks in the hold, the wrecks have been declared an underwater sanctuary. Scuba diving into a sunk Japanese destroyer has to rank one of the most eerie experiences of any world tour. No visa required for stays up to 30 days; $5 departure fee.

Papua New Guinea

Until the recent discovery of vast natural resources, Papua New Guinea (PNG) had been a very primitive and poor country. Today copper, gold, oil-palm, fish, and timber are being extracted from the vast wilderness and sold to the highest bidder. All fair in a capitalistic world, but it's certainly watering down this once magnificent Pacific culture. There are still some amazing primitive tribes up in the hills, especially around the Crater Mountain Wildlife Management Area in Simbu Provence, but like so many other rural people around the world, these tribes too are being sucked into the vortex of the cities. Expensive as it has become, PNG is still a very cool destination, especially the towering mountains, coral reefs, the Bismark Archipelago, and ample white sand beaches. Tourist visa are granted free at the airport or port of entry for stays up to 60 days.

Philippines

Despite political instability and horrendous shanty towns around Manila, the Philippines remain an attractive bargain and favorite Stomper destination. If island hopping sounds like fun, there are 7,100 tropical beauties to discover along this archipelago. Cheap flights and boats go everywhere quite regularly, and communication is easy because the friendly Filipinos speak English. The steeply tiered rice terraces are some of the most picturesque in the world. In May, 2000 several foreign tourists were killed after being kidnapped from a Malaysian resort and taken to the far southern Philippine islands of Jolo and Basilan. The rebels are fighting for a separate Islamic state in the impoverished Mindanao region, home of the country's Muslim minority. Visa not required for 21 day stay, otherwise a $25 visa must be obtained for a 59 day stay.

Singapore

This small country is modern Asia in a nutshell. The city-state republic of Singapore consists of a main, tropical isle and about 54 tiny islets. Originally established in 1819 as a trading station for the British,

Singapore grew rapidly because of its strategic location. It was briefly occupied by the Japanese during WWII, then for a short time became a part of Malaysia, then in 1965 it separated and became an independent sovereign state. Today it is a mess of skyscrapers with an anal sense of cleanliness. Chewing gum is prohibited, smoking is forbidden, and strict penalties exist for antisocial behavior. Stray from the norm and risk four whacks from a batten cane. Visa not required for stays up to 30 days; extendible to 3 months maximum.

Thailand

Get the hell out of smoggy Bangers (Bangkok) A.S.A.P. The exotic islands down south and the jungle country up north is where this country really gets good. Some of the best ruins, deserted cities, and Buddha statues in Southeast Asia are scattered about near Chiang Mai, as well as thousands of spired buildings called wats. Quite amazing as this old culture is, most people come to Thailand simply to laze in a hammock or explore the wilderness.

Top Ten Mellow Party Scenes (#3)

The small town of Krabi is nothing exciting, but an off-shore excursion into the melting rocks on the Indian Ocean side will take you to Phra Nang Beach. The natural cliff formations, the lagoon, and the multitude of caves are enough to impress even the pickiest tourist, except it's mostly freaky travelers who rule the place. There are no roads in, boat traffic only, so only the intrepid traveler discovers this hidden gem.

As Thailand becomes more Westernized by the minute, the tourists pour in and the jungles disappear. Easy travel, moderate prices, excellent food and service, great beaches and a wide variety of Stompers have made Thailand a very popular travel destination as of late. So popular, you might begin to wonder if you are not really on a Western beach somewhere. A 30 day travel visa is free at the airport, and a 60 day visa costs $15.

Top Ten Best Bashes (#1)

Full Moon Tan. One beach on one island has all night rave parties like none other on this circuit. Haad Rin Beach on Koh Phagan is synonymous with full moon fever. The lunatics show up in force and howl at the moon all night under the influence of their favorite intoxicant, which is readily available from shopkeepers or traveler-freaks. Choose your poison and trance-dance until the sun pops up over the Gulf of Thailand. And then keep going.

Vietnam

Still a thorn in the American psyche, Vietnam has recovered from its wartime wounds much faster than the superpower who invaded it. The only vestiges of war seen today are old military bases, rusting tanks, a tattered infrastructure, and widespread poverty after the 17 year U.S. trade embargo. President Clinton made the right move for lifting the embargo and establish diplomatic relations with Hanoi. No POWs here anymore, unless it's a returning vet playing a joke on some gullible young backpackers in a Saigon bar.

The natural Vietnam of lush jungle scenery, towering verdant mountains, and pristine tropical beaches on the South China Sea never fail to enchant those who visit. Equally enticing is the unique and rich civilization, the French designed cities, and a highly cultured people who welcome visitors from the West, arriving this time with money instead of guns. The war is long over in Vietnam and there is nothing to fear from Stomping here, apart from pickpockets and hustlers. The 'Nam is very much the wild, wild west of Southeast Asia. Chin, chin, Ho Chi Minh! A single-entry tourist visa costs $25 and is valid for 6 months.

Top Ten Best Bashes (#5)

Tet is not a celebration for skittish people who have an aversion for loud and constant firecrackers. This festivity goes on non-stop for three days straight. No rest for the wary, but that's what it's all about. That is how the Viet Cong briefly took Saigon during the Tet offensive in 1968 – no soldier could discern the crackers from gunshots. The bashing over those three days is the most insane, no-holds-barred, freak-show party scene in all of Asia; perhaps the world. Come prepared to be shocked and have ringing ears for a week afterwards.

Earthlings

**Gilligan's Island gone
commercial.**

Indonesia

There is Malaya. Everything takes a long, a very long time, in Malaya.
Things get done, occasionally, but more often they don't, and the
more in a hurry you are, the quicker you break down.
— Han Suyin, 1956

Indonesia is such a vast expanse of tropical islands it would take years of solid traveling to see all there is to see. The islands range in size from tiny atolls and volcanic mounds emerging from the sea, to the second, third, and fifth largest islands in the world (New Guinea, Borneo, and Sumatra respectively). Where Java Island is one of the most densely populated on earth, others remain completely uninhabited. Indonesia's necklace like archipelago stretches across 4,828 km of ocean parallel to the equator. At last count, the tally was said to encompass 13,677 islands.

As the fourth most populous nation in the world, Indonesia is a complicated racial mixture representing hundreds of ethnic groups, each with its own dialects, customs, and traditions. Although there are more than 250 distinctive languages, the government actively promotes the one national language, Bahasa Indonesia, which is very easy to learn. But even for the lazy linguistic, English is widely spoken, especially in those areas where tourists venture.

Critters

Some of the most varied and bizarre animals of Asia live in Indonesia. On Irian Jaya there are tree kangaroos and wallabies, marsupial critters common to Australia. Long-nosed tapirs and orangutans cruise around on Sumatra and Borneo, while Java is home to the one-horned rhinoceros and the wild "banteng" ox. Still other animals include scaly anteaters, tigers, panthers, elephants, apes, monkeys, wild boars, and a number of species of deer.

On Komodo Island are the 3-meter long carnivorous Komodo dragons that roam wild and eat a lot of goats. These giant monitor lizards are believed to be the only living genus left of the prehistoric *Varanus kmod - oensis*. Other reptiles co-existing on Komodo Island are crocodiles and pythons.

Cup o' Java

Almost all the history of Indonesia lies on the long and narrow island of Java. The first to settle here a half-million years ago was *Pithecanthropus Erectus*, a primitive humanoid also known as Java Man. The Indian and Chinese traders arrived around the century of Christ and brought with them their own religions: Hinduism and Buddhism. The Buddhist sanctuary of Borobudur and the Hindu complex of Prambanan stand as proud testaments of architectural glory from the 8th and 9th centuries. Later the Muslims came and defaced them both.

When the Europeans figured out how to sail around the southern tip of Africa and circumvent Arab land trade routes, one of the first places they went to colonize was Java, also known as the Spice Islands. The Portuguese were the first to set up shop, soon to be booted out by the Dutch who held onto the colony for the next 300 years. The spice trade made European empires fabulously wealthy. Their legacy can be seen in old fortresses and colonial buildings scattered about the island. It was the Dutch colonists who coined the region *Malayo*; referring to the Malay Archipelago and Peninsula.

On The Stoner's Trail (#6)

Lake Toba, the largest crater lake in the world on the island of Sumatra, grows some real fruity buds. They might be cutting down all the rainforests in the region, but they sure are planting some killer pot seeds. Also nice are the magic mushrooms the boys bring around every morning. Have your guesthouse mamma-san cook you up an omelet, and off you go!

Be discrete about whom you buy from, ask any freaky traveler first for the going rate and a connection. The rainforest trek on Samisir island offers many opportunities to smoke the fine local's yield. You might just need to be stoned out of your head to get over the widespread ecological destruction going on here.

Work and Money

While not too lucrative wage-wise on the English teaching route, Indonesia is home to thousands of expatriates who work for a host of international firms. Foreigners need an employment visa to work, and a job must be secured before a company can sponsor a work visa. Getting a permit for casual work is impossible. For long-term employment, the applicant must have a skill not available locally.

The cost of travel is pretty cheap and most people are content just seeing the sights and hanging out. Indonesia is an excellent place to purchase handicraft treasures. Buyers from around the world shop the Indonesian islands for export. Batik art, silver jewelry, wood carvings, puppets, leatherwork, statues and bush knives are often sold by the people who crafted them, and the prices can be ridiculously low. The hardest part is often finding room in the backpack to carry them away.

Overland travelers on their way to to Australia make the jump-over from either Maluku or Timor islands. Flights from Ambon, Maluku or Kupang, Timor to Darwin, Australia depart two and three times per week.

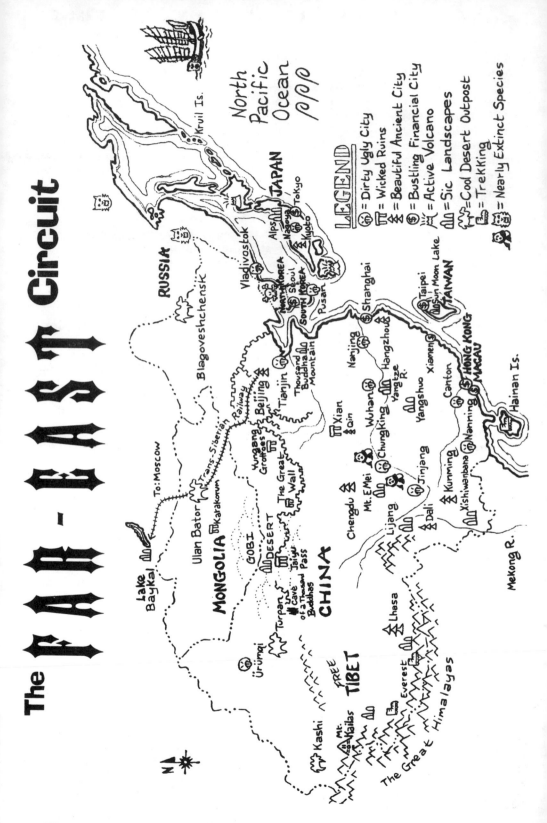

The FAR-EAST Circuit

The Far-East Circuit

In a word, we desire to throw no one into the shade [in East Asia], but we also demand our own place in the sun.
– Count Von Bulow, Reichstag, 1897

Since Marco Polo went overland to the Far-East in the 13th century and returned to Europe with tales of riches and grandeur, the countries of Europe have long sought out its mystique and fortunes. In fact, it was to find a short-cut to Japan that Columbus sailed west from Spain in 1492. Of course what he found were the Americas, but that didn't stop other seafarers from overcoming obstacles to reach the shores of the Far-East.

Nearly all the powers of Europe set up a colony somewhere in the Far-East, and many of the huge cities today are a result of old trading outposts, most notably Hong Kong and Macao. You can visit grand colonial buildings along the Bund in Shanghai, the Dutch village amusement park in Japan, old forts in South Korea, or travel along the former Silk Road in Tibet. Wherever you go, you are certain to be overwhelmed by a diverse culture and swarms of people. The Far-East Asian Circuit is home to nearly a third of the world's population and continues to grow at breakneck speed, not only with people but also with powerful national economies.

The extraordinary ascent of the Pacific Rim signals great opportunity for Westerners willing to do business and learn about Asia. For the balance of this century and into the next, the great new commercial opportunities will be in Asia. Today the Pacific Rim is undergoing the fastest period of economic expansion in history. This region is expanding at five times the growth rate of the Industrial Revolution. Opportunity for work and fun abound, and rarely is the traveler disappointed with all there is to discover on this amazing circuit.

China

This sleeping giant is finally awakening from its 50-year communist slumber. China's economy continues to grow at double digit rates annually and shows no signs of letting up, despite a continued repressive government in Beijing. Filled to the brim with history and humans, the Middle Kingdom is wide open for your Stomping pleasures. See: China, below.

Obtaining a visa for China involves dealing with a fair bit of government bureaucracy. Getting a visa from Hong Kong is the easiest, and a one month visa ranges in price from $30 to $150, depending on how quickly you want it and where you get it. Arranging a visa from overseas requires a "letter of confirmation" from the China International Travel Services (CITS) or an invitation from an individual or institution in China. CITS tours may be booked through travel agents or airlines around the world. A one month visa will cost $30, plus fees to obtain your "letter of confirmation." These letters can be expensive.

Hong Kong

While no longer a British colony, Hong Kong (HK) remains to be the New York of Asia, with all it's trappings. Brash, colorful, vibrant, bustling, noisy, expensive, and loaded with obnoxious merchants. It is also home to some fine museums, parks, and an insane nightlife.

Top Ten Best Bashes (#10)

 A half million people flood onto the streets at Tsimshatsui in Kowloon on Christmas Eve, even though the population is only 9% Christian. Open liquor is allowed and the crowd gets pretty wild. The cops break up the bash around 1:30 a.m., but until then it's wackiness with the rambunctious Hong Kong youth. Beware of silly-string shots to the back of the head.

Hong Kong is a Special Administrative Region of China now, and the saying "one country, two systems" seems to hold true. Despite the changeover, Hong Kong remains one of the biggest financial cities and economic powerhouses in Asia. The Beijing government would be extremely foolish to mess with such a well-oiled machine. Besides, according to the 1984 Joint Declaration between Britain and Beijing, Hong Kong is guaranteed to remain an "open and free plural society" for 50 years after the handover.

In addition to a number of attractions around the former colony, Hong Kong is a transportation hub for the world and jumping-off point for surrounding countries. Many jobs exist for foreigners teaching English and working for international companies, but British and Commonwealth citizens have first crack at the best jobs. Visa not required for tourist stay up to up to 90 days, departure tax $13.

Japan

The Land of the Rising Sun is more like the land of the rising yen. Japan is the most expensive country in the world. But with high prices also come high wages, which makes Japan a popular destination for teaching English and other well-paying opportunities. Some advice on how to get a job and save money follows, as well as a few unique aspects of this highly misunderstood nation. See: Japan, below. Passport and onward ticket required, but not a visa for 90 day stays. Departure tax of $26 paid at the airport.

Macau

Macau is no longer designated a Chinese territory under Portuguese administration, and was handed back to China in 1999. The territory is only 16 square km, consisting of a small peninsula and two islands. Big hotel casinos are the main attraction, and Macau is called the Las Vegas of the Orient. A good day trip from Hong Kong is all it takes to see this place and do some gambling – if you have the money to blow. Visa not required for stays up to 60 days.

Mongolia

Hungry for hard currency and just opening its doors to tourism after long decades of communism, Mongolia represents one of the last unexplored Stomping Grounds in the world. A brutally harsh climate of vast deserts, high mountains, and rolling grasslands, Mongolia is beautifully unspoiled and pristine. Getting around can be quite difficult, no English is spoken, and accommodations are primitive here. The Mongols are a friendly, yet tough race of people to exist in such frigid and extreme conditions. It's little wonder they conquered half the known world in the 13th century. 48 hour transit visas cost $35, and 6 month multiple-entry visas cost $65 and require confirmation from Mongolian Travel Agency (Zhuulchin). This confirmation costs $25.

North Korea

The only Americans visiting this devoted Marxist country are downed helicopter pilots. The U.S. government highly discourages travel here and so does the North Korean government. Only a few select tour groups are permitted to enter annually, and those who venture behind the Iron Curtain are treated to the last true communist society. Propaganda is rife, and so are the secret police. Visas and tours are best arranged in Beijing.

Siberian Russia

With the advent of *glasnost* and the breakup of the former Soviet Union, Siberian Russia is now experiencing something brand new — tourism. Still only a trickle compared to the rest of the Far-East, this area has the distinction of being one of the world's last great wildernesses. Unfortunately, some of the tourists are big game hunters who are intent on shooting the last remaining Siberian tigers into extinction.

The highlight of Siberia is the immensely deep and large Lake Baykal and the cultural city Irkutsk. Both are on the Trans-Siberian Railway route from Moscow to Beijing and worth getting off the train for a look. The cost of the full route is around $300 and remains one of the greatest travel bargains around, just be sure to convert your currency into roubles at the border first or you'll go hungry. The visa situation is the same as Russia. *See:* Russia, European Circuit.

South Korea

Brutally cold in the winter and scorchingly hot in the summer, the political situation is equally volatile. The DMZ with North Korea is a sobering sight and remains the last vestige of the Cold War. Students continue to riot in the streets every year over a number of issues, and the country is constantly on red alert against attack from its northern brothers.

Yet, despite all this turmoil, South Korea's economy continues to kick ass. Rising from the ashes of a bitter three year war in the 1950s, this Asian Tiger has emerged as a vibrant force not only in Asia, but the world. Once-drab Seoul has become an exciting and cosmopolitan metropolis, filled with multi-national companies and many opportunities for English teachers. Visa not required for 15 days, longer stays must be applied for at an Embassy or Consulate for a $20 fee.

Taiwan

This mountainous island off the coast of China is one of the most densely populated countries in the world. The government of China officially regards the island as nothing more than a renegade province, and the Taiwan government has never declared its independence from the main-land. Taipei's National Palace Museum is considered one of the finest in the world. It contains all the looted treasures of mainland China that the Nationalists took with them when they fled the communists in 1949.

Subtropical in climate, the heat and humidity can be brutal in the summer. Explore the island and you will find unsurpassed gorges, beaches, forests, temples, and aboriginal tribes on small offshore islands. Another economically thriving Asian Tiger nation, Taiwan offers many opportunities for teaching English. The bulletin board in the Taipei Hostel lists new jobs coming in every day. Getting a job, an apartment, a motorbike, and girlfriend can usually be arranged within a week. Americans are very popular and you will have to get used to being the center of attention all the time. The best place to arrive from is Hong Kong where you will be given a 2 month visa (extendible up to 6 months). Otherwise, 14 days are given (without a special visa) when arriving from elsewhere. AIDS tests are mandatory for anyone staying over 3 months.

Earthlings

**Circa 1275: Marco Polo
reaches the Far-East *without*
his American Express card.**

China

None are as blind as those who don't want to see.
– Chinese proverb

China has a long history of opening and shutting its doors to the world. The Great Wall was erected to keep the louts out, and more recently, the Communists expelled all the "foreign devils" when they swept into power 50 years ago. Today, the doors are wide open for travel and business due to China's effort to catch up and modernize with the West. So rapid is Chinese development, *The Economist* recently reported that there are more cranes at work in Shanghai alone than in the whole of North America.

Although most of the country is now accessible, China is not always an easy country to travel within. Government bureaucracy and absurd restrictions can be maddening, as well as bumpy roads, apathetic clerks, and the tendency of Chinese people to spit everywhere. A little patience will get you far in China, and the reward is a rare opportunity to see an amazing country long shut off from outside influences.

Bizarre Evolution

 Twenty years ago the Chinese government imposed the strict "one child per family" law to curb the burgeoning population. Since then the numbers have begun to level off, but China still remains the world's most populous nation – clocking in at a whopping 1.3 billion people.

It is a widespread belief that the first newborn child in every Chinese family should be a son. This son will bring the family wealth and prestige. But now with the new laws, many families are aborting daughters for want of a boy. Schools are reporting abnormally high percentages of boys over girls as of late. Talk about frustrated men when they all grow up!

Lay of the Land

China is a huge country, surpassed only by Russia and Canada in size. It is also quite varied; from the high plateaus of Tibet to the subtropical jungles of the southern coastal regions. From fertile river valleys along the coast where most of the population resides, to the desolate and windswept Gobi Desert where hardly anyone lives. The temperatures can range from scorching hot in the summer to bitterly cold up north. Then there are the soaring Himalayan Mountains in Tibet which taper off like a descending staircase down to the sea.

Top Ten Mellow Party Scenes (#2)

The mountain and rock formations around the little hamlet village of Yangshuo are right out of *The Hobbit*. Limestone pinnacles towering up from the flat rice patty fields evoke a fantastical quality found in very few places on earth. The dreamlike scenery attracts many Western travelers who marvel at the sights by day and relax over cheap beer at the many outdoor cafes by night.

The land and climate represent as much variation as the emerging economical situation between "haves" and "have-nots." The helter-skelter industrial growth along the well-placed coastal regions is sprinting far ahead of the less developed inland provinces. The inland provinces attract little foreign investment because the communist system is strong and suspicions of capitalism still abound. Migrating peasants are placing enormous stress on already over-crowded cities, and the environment is feeling the growing pains as well. Chimneys belching out thick, black smoke are not an uncommon sight and most cities are blurred in a perpetual haze of smog.

1989 was a good year to understand the true colors of the present communist government. That was the year the tanks rolled into Tiananmen Square and literally squashed the democracy movement, leaving hundreds of unarmed students murdered in their wake. Today, the student voice is quelled, but there is a brewing freedom movement growing in Tibet, where 98 percent of the population represent a majority in this supposed minority group. The government is cracking down in a similar fashion; locking up dissidents, unseen executions, and mass arrests. The region may or may not be open for travel, including the road between Nepal and Tibet, depending on the current level of turbulence. If you do get into Tibet, DO NOT engage in a political discussion with anyone. You will find yourself deported from China and the person you were talking to arrested. As it is, there is no foreseeable way to remove the communist thugs from office and ensure everyone their freedom. One thing *is* certain about suppressive government officials – their karma will catch up to them someday.

Work and Money

The discrepancy between the Chinese currency and the true market value has created a thriving black market in China. "Change money, change money?" is about the only conversation you'll receive from your average Chinaman, but exchanging a large U.S. dollar bill will allow you to tap into substantial black market savings. But beware! The old money switcheroo is alive and well. They count out the money in front of you, then distract your attention for a second by saying, "Lookout, police!" and give you a wad of small bills back with a big bill on top. If you exchange money on the black market, and this is true anywhere, always take the money first and count it yourself *before* handing over your traveler's checks or U.S. dollars.

As China emerges as an economic powerhouse on the world stage, so do the opportunities to work and ride this building tidal wave. Wages for teaching English are still lower than the Tiger Nations or Japan, but they are bound to catch up as the demand for teachers increases every year. The trick to teaching English in China is to be hired at the wages offered in Hong Kong or Taiwan, *then* have your school transfer you out to a mainland branch. Multi-national companies are moving into China rapidly and anyone fluent in Mandarin or Cantonese will have no trouble landing a decent job.

> "I can't eat that Chink food; those people do their cooking and their laundry in the same pot."
> **Fred Sanford**

Japan

For the building of a new Japan
Let's put our mind and strength together,
Doing our best to promote production,
Sending our goods to the peoples of the world,
Endlessly and continuously,
Like water gushing from a fountain.
Grow, industry, grow, grow, grow,
Harmony and Sincerity.
– Matsushita Electrical company anthem

Japan is such a complex nation with so many layers of activity and social customs, it is not surprising that most travelers feel overwhelmed when they first arrive. In a nutshell Japan appears; perfect, orderly, brash, expensive, tedious, subtle, mountainous, varied, wet, ancient, and ultra-modern. Despite the initial confusion and culture shock, it won't take long before the visitor befriends the honest and amiable Japanese people. It is the people, after all, who represent Japan's greatest natural resource.

Outside the busy and crowded cities it is much easier to get a good idea of the real Japanese way of life. Out here the visual beauty of the land becomes apparent, and the country begins to charm and grace the visitor in its own unique way. The rural areas are fascinating to visit, but the majority of jobs and places foreigners want to live revert back to the cities. Unless you want to be totally immersed in the culture and language, it is a good idea to look for work in the big towns. Teachers stuck out in the sticks don't seem to enjoy their stay as much as city dwellers.

Bizarre Love Hotels

Every Westerner who comes to Japan hears about the famous Love Hotels. Metered by the hour, you drive into a hidden entrance, pay for your room via an intercom, and receive a key through a sliding tray. Total discretion allows no interaction with any other person, apart from the one(s) you are with. Some Love Hotels have theme rooms; the bridge on the Starship Enterprise, a simulated moving train, or the *donjon* of a *Shogun's* castle. These cost extra of course.

My experience in a Love Hotel with a *yellow cab* girlfriend was just a regular room with mirrors on the ceiling and a heart shaped bed that vibrated when fed coins. On the night stand was a radio that featured over a hundred musical selections from cable stations. Flipping the dials I heard all the standard radio stations, and others, such as continuous sound tracks of water flowing or birds chirping. Scanning further, I came across some odd sounds of background office chatter and train station commotion, complete with trains pulling in and letting commuters off every so often. Confused, I asked my girl who would possibly want to listen to these kinds of stations.

"Oh those," she replied, "they are for unfaithful husbands calling home to tell wife he will not be home until late." *Yarooka!*

Conspicuous Consumers

Nothing short of a miracle happened after Japan rose from the ashes of WWII to become what it is today – the second largest economy in the world. Japan had to completely re-design its industrial base, infrastructure, its government, and old way of life. Quick to learn, the Japanese decided to emulate the U.S. model of capitalism and democratic government. A country with no natural resources to speak of, Japan's sheer survival became dependent on importing raw materials and exporting finished products. This method paid off tremendously and the Japanese love to flaunt their new-found wealth. Today in the Russian owned Kruil Islands, a strange barter is taking place. Twelve king crabs are being traded to Tokyo for one used Toyota in return.

Funny story, but Japanese psycho-consumption habits are having far greater environmental impacts, those which reverberate loudly among long-distrusting neighbors. Industrial pollution is catching up with everyone in East Asia and Japan is an easy target to blame because of all their off-shore operations. Entire forests from Southeast Asia await market prices to rise in Japanese harbors and warehouses. One of the most outward forms of Japanese consumption are the thousands of trees consumed every day in the form of throw-away chopsticks.

To illustrate the amazing amount of disposable income the Japanese people possess, and the visible side to their throw-away society, it's interesting to have a look at *gomi* piles (trash dumps). The Japanese conventional wisdom goes like this: when a new version of a stereo system comes out, discard the old in a *gomi* pile and buy the new one. When a bicycle gets a flat, toss it in a *gomi* pile and buy another one. When a TV or VCR becomes out of date, chuck them in a *gomi* pile and upgrade.

There is little poverty in Japan and thus no demand for second-hand things, no matter if they are in perfect working order. Basically, you can furnish an entire apartment with stuff found in the *gomi* piles, and have a bike to go looking for new stuff. Happy hunting!

Work and Money

Few people come to Japan just to travel and see the sights. The exchange rates will break any tight budget and vacations are ruinously expensive. To put it in perspective, a weeks travel in Japan is about the same price as two months in Thailand or three months in India. So the trick is to come here and find a job, *then* go out and explore the country.

A long-term working stay allows you to save up a sizable travel fund and take the time to meet some friendly locals and observe the subtle aspects of Japan. The most popular means of employment for foreigners is *teaching the English*. There is a large demand for native English speakers, something the Japanese people cannot do themselves. The Japanese are very particular about education and require all teacher applicants to have a college degree, but not necessarily in English or in teaching.

Teaching can be an interesting experience and quite lucrative at the same time. You do not need to have any Japanese speaking skills nor prior experience to walk into a $30-35k teaching position at a public or private school. Check local newspapers for job listings and talk to other teachers to find out who's hiring. Private lessons are another way to supplement your income. Privates are acquired through word of mouth or fliers posted at community houses, universities or other public post boards. Women do the best with privates because wealthy salarymen pay more and take their tutors out to eat and on trips. Some call it puppy love, but the salarymen are really quite harmless.

Another popular means of work for pretty young ladies is hostessing — which is often as lucrative as teaching. Hostesses work in fancy lounges pouring drinks, lighting cigarettes, and chatting with the wealthy clientele. Men have been known to do this at older women's clubs, but it is rare. Hostesses have to dress up and be *genki* every night, and work late hours. The perks are nice for hostessing — free drinks, tips, a chance to meet some nice people and practice your Japanese. To find a job, just go and inquire at the nightclub district in every Japanese city, or listen to word of mouth.

Other jobs include bartending, golf caddying or ski instructing, where the novelty of being around a foreigner is enough to create a demand. Neither pay that well nor produce great tips, and you must have a work or work-holiday visa to get hired. Modeling is still popular and pays very well.

Under-the-table jobs include: street selling wares from around the world, and busking. Both can get you in trouble with the police, but most times they will just tell you to pack up and move on. Street musicians claim to receive the best tips in the world here. One guy got $120 to play "Hey Jude" for a drunken salaryman. Musicians usually set up other gigs in bars, restaurants, lounges, parties, and festivals from offers gotten while playing on the streets. The big street pleasers and money makers have the full set-up: electric guitar, microphone, and amplifier. *Gombate*!

"ATTENTION! Up Your Head."
Japanese record store sign for a low-hanging object

The Curopean Circuit

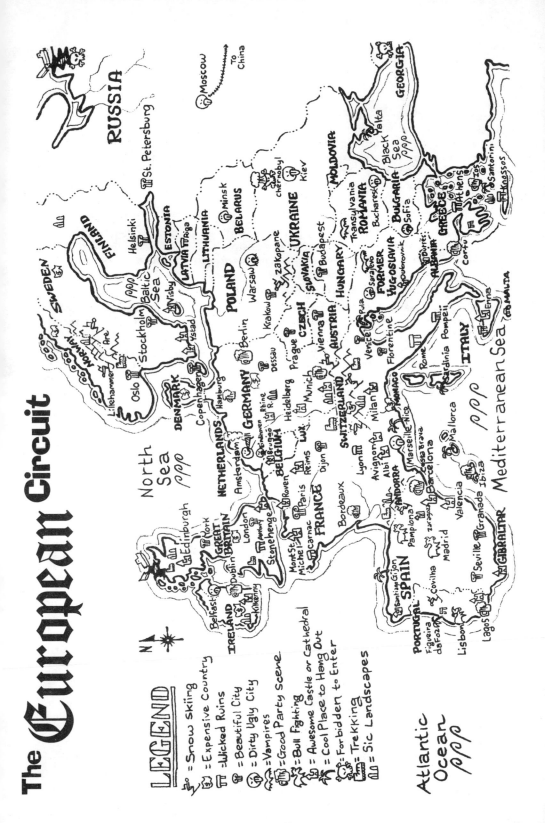

The European Circuit

The Sun himself cannot forget
His fellow traveler.

– European proverb

Europe has something for everyone. The roots of Western civilization lie in its centuries-old castles, cathedrals, museums, mountains, and winding rivers. The bustle of modern life hums in its busy cities, while the past lives on in its diversified and distinctive languages and cultures.

Where the World Stomper is concerned, Europe is user-friendly. English is recognized throughout, but attempting to speak the native language is always appreciated. Europe can be quite expensive depending on what country you are visiting and how you spend your money. But some of the best things in Europe, as in life, are free or nearly so, such as its parks and plazas, many of its museums, and the sense of history which is so prevalent on its streets and architecture. With so much to see and do in every country on this circuit, Europe offers one of the best values of all, a wealth of culture and heritage.

With the emergence of the new European Community (EC) and the end of the Cold War in the late 1980s, Europe has ushered in a new age of unrestricted travel. Gone are the days in Eastern Europe where border guards would hassle you, and the visa situation was a bundle of red tape. Today, almost no countries in Europe require a visa, and transit over EC borders is as easy as traveling from state to state in the United States.

Albania

Known by the people as the "Land of the Eagle," Albania offers up majestic landscapes of mountains, forests, lakes, and the sea. It also has a colorful culture and enchanting classical ruins at Durres, juxtaposed next to rusting cars alongside pot-holed roads and long-abandoned industrial plants. English will get you by, but a knowledge of Italian and Greek is useful. Tourism is minimal and this country represents perhaps the best old world view of Europe that still remains. No visa required for 3 months and there is a $40 entrance fee and a $10 departure tax.

Austria

"There are no kangaroos in Austria," declares a popular T-shirt, indicative of the geographic confusion many tourists have regarding this historical country in the heart of Europe. Austria is primarily known for two widely contrasting attractions; the fading imperial glories of its capital Vienna and the diversity of its alpine hinterland. The Alps mountain range, spanning the north and west of the country, lures fun-seekers in the winter and summer alike. Trekking, skiing, spa resorts and quaint little

Bavarian villages set among a panorama of peaks which continue to attract thousands of visitors per year. Most especially pleasing to the senses is Salzburg, a picturesque medieval city where Mozart was born. German is the spoken language of the Austrians, yet the dialect is different. As a member of the EC, no visa is required for stays up to 3 months.

The Baltic Countries

The Baltic nations (Estonia, Latvia, and Lithuania) re-emerged on the world map when they gained independence from the former Soviet Union in 1991. Having been colonies of Scandinavian and Russian conquerors on and off since the 12th century, the Baltic nations assimilated a culture largely similar to their dominating neighbors. Perhaps the best resemblance comes from its cousin across the gulf, Finland, whose wealthy citizens love to take the ferry over for cheap weekends of merrymaking. There are dozens of beautiful old medieval towns and cities scattered throughout, yet, in general, most places are utilitarian and drab from the long decades of Russification. Estonia, Latvia, and Lithuania require no visa for stays up to 90 days.

Belgium and Luxembourg

As two of the "low countries" in Europe, Belgium and Luxembourg have been a hotly disputed middle ground where the forces of Eastern and Western Europe have fought for centuries. In Belgium is Waterloo, site of Napoleon's crushing defeat in 1815. In Luxembourg is the Ardennes Forest where the World War II Battle of the Bulge was fought. The capital, Luxembourg City, had to be liberated by the Allies twice.

Today both are independent, a mix of cultures, distinctively different, and very much into the idea of greater European unity. Such a stand is not surprising because both have much to gain as large financial centers and crossroads for the EC. Visa not required for either and stays are allowed up to 90 days.

Bulgaria

When the "Soviet Bloc" collapsed in the late 1980s, the countries in Eastern Europe suddenly found themselves free to govern their own countries as they saw fit. Nearly all embraced democracy and free market economies. No longer intimidating to visit, the Bulgaria of today (and its Eastern neighbors) is home to some of the best travel bargains in Europe. As Bulgaria and others struggle to control inflation, stock their shelves, and cater to new found tourism, the Stomper is delighted to encounter people with a fresh interest in visitors. Bulgaria has largely been spared the onslaught of Western tourism. Transitionary times are fun times and cheap times. No visa required for stays up to 30 days, but a $20 border tax payable upon entry.

The Czech Republic and Slovakia

The Czechs and Slovaks were both culturally independent in language and tradition until the 1918 Treaty of Versailles grouped them together as a new state. In 1992 they separated peacefully, showing the world that national divorce can be achieved without bloodshed. The Czech Republic came out much better than the poor, agrarian Slovakia, but both suffer from debilitating rates of inflation not being matched by wages. Perhaps the highlight of any visit to this region is the beautiful Bohemian city of Prague in the Czech Republic. Untouched by either World Wars, it is graced with charming plazas, squares, palaces, cathedrals, and a fairy-tale castle. Prague is a city not to be missed. And to top it off, the very cool Czech president Vaclav Havel lives there. Beware of Prague's cab drivers, however, because they notoriously overcharge. Both countries require no visas for stays up to 30 days, but the Czech Republic requires showing proof of sufficient funds.

Denmark

Denmark is the smallest and most densely populated of the five Scandinavian countries. This flat and green nation consists of 500 islands and the Jutland peninsula which connects to Germany. Known for its very high standard of living, constitutional monarchy, and generous social welfare programs, it is also infamous for the high cost of travel. But if you go in the summer to camp out, hitchhike, or bike around on the cheap, it will not take long until you make some new found Danish friends. Who knows, maybe they'll be kind enough take you into their home and buy you a $7 beer. No visa required for stays up to 3 months, and this also applies to their colonies Greenland, and the Faroe Islands.

Finland

Remote, sparsely populated, and geographically isolated, Finland has been independent only since 1917. Having rid themselves of the imperial powers, the Finns still show cultural signs of the Swedes and Tsarist Russians who dominated them for hundreds of years. But the most unique cultural group in Finland has to be the nomadic Laplanders of the north who still follow and hunt the migrating reindeer. Their culture and way of life are quickly assimilating into normal Finnish, but many vestiges still exist. The natural beauty of Finland is another big attraction for visitors. Visa not required for stays up to 90 days.

France

Straddling the heart of the continent between the Iberian peninsula and the nations of central and southern Europe, France is a core country on any European Stomp. Diverse in culture and geography and different by regions in architecture, dialect, and food, France serves up some of the best Europe has to offer. It would take years of travel to exhaust all the things there are to see and do in this magnificent country.

Since the French are justifiably very proud of their heritage, they can also be arrogant about their language. Incidents of being ignored outright for speaking English and even refusal of service is characteristic of the French. Learning the language will get you far here, or even a few key phrases to shed that "Ugly American" stereotype. No visa required for stays up to 3 months and this also includes Andorra, Monaco, and Corsica.

Germany

Just the mention of this country causes derision and apprehension among most Europeans. Resented for wars it caused in the past, and feared today because of the economic giant it has become, Germany is a greatly misunderstood country that has much to offer in the way of Stomping *See:* Germany, below. No visa required for stays up to 3 months.

Greece

With loads of archeological wonders spanning four millennia of civilization, and 166 inhabited islands in the Aegean Sea to choose from, Greece delivers the double treat of impressive history and fun in the sun. The popular islands are packed every summer with party hungry travelers who come for the great mix of people and cheap prices of beer. Secluded tranquil islands and remote mainland spots, which gave birth to many seminal Western philosophers, are excellent places for a quiet retreat. It is the simple hedonistic pleasures of the landscapes, climate, food, and culture that make Greece a very special destination for almost any visitor. No visa required for stays up to 3 months.

Top Ten Best Bashes (#6)

Ios Island: The Perfect Party Lifestyle. Wake up with a hangover; figure out who you went home with the night before; take a shower; head to the beach (multiple option: A. snorkeling, B. let it all hang out on the nude beach, C. start drinking, D. all of the above); head back to the room to change; roam into town for dinner with new found friends; start barhopping; get hammered and dance on the tables; pick up babe and head back to the room for good lovin'; crash. Wake up with a hangover ...

Top Ten Mellow Party Scenes (#1)

No island on earth has what Santorini has: black, red, and white sand beaches; an active, smoldering volcano a mile out to sea; superb coral reefs for diving; and ruins from the ancient Minoan civilization. No wonder many historians regard this magical island as the leading candidate for the lost city of Atlantis. Rent a motor scooter and explore this beautiful crescent shaped island from end to end. Top marks if you come from Ios with a babe.

Hungary

Another emerging democracy in the former Eastern Bloc of communist countries, Hungary is leading the pack in terms of modernization and privatization. As a progressive society, Hungary continues ahead in its economic and political transformation geared toward full integration into the EC in the year 2000. High unemployment and an influx of Yugoslavian refugees has sparked instances of racism and the emergence of a right-wing national polity. Nonetheless, Stompers enjoy their time in the old imperial city of Budapest, the historical monuments of the Danube Bend, and the charm of rural life in the collection of traditional villages dotting the countryside. No visa required for stays up to 90 days.

Iceland

Often called "the land of fire and ice" because of the multitude of active volcanoes and mountain glaciers, Iceland is a natural and cultural phenomenon. For many centuries Iceland was the furthest outpost of Scandinavian Viking culture, and the quarter of a million inhabitants who live there today are almost all descendants of the original settlers who landed over 1000 years ago. Many of the old values and customs remain, including the Icelandic language, which is essentially old Norse. Visitors come to experience the abundance of invigorating hot springs, which may be why Icelanders have the longest average life span in the world for women, and second longest for men. No visa required for stays up to 3 months.

Ireland

As one of Europe's least densely populated, least industrialized, and least spoiled countries, Ireland is green, pleasant and relaxed. But behind those smiling faces and noisy pubs in the north, lies one of the longest and most tragic conflicts in Europe. "The Troubles" between Catholics and Protestants over the fate of Northern Ireland seems to continue ad infinitum, despite truces and peace talks. Political strife aside, landscape and people are what continue to bring droves of travelers to the Emerald Isle. No visa required for stays up to 90 days.

Italy and Malta

Italy is a treasure-trove of Western historic monuments, from ancient Etruscan forts and Roman arches, to Renaissance palaces and Gothic cathedrals. This is the land of vibrant and expressive people, whether it be the poor farmers in the south or the wealthy industrialists in the north, everyone has something to say. The Italians place a strong emphasis on living life to the fullest and this includes numerous festivals, excellent food, tasty wine, and *siestas* in the middle of the day.

The small island nation of Malta has been influenced by many of the Mediterranean forces over the centuries, but today the influence is predominately Italian because of its proximity. The British were the last to colonize Malta and many relics remain from that era, including many English speakers. Neither country requires a visa for stays up to 3 months.

The Netherlands

In the Netherlands, also commonly called Holland, tolerance is not the exception but the rule. The Dutch people hold very liberal views on gays and abortion. Prostitution is "legal and regulated" by the government, whereby each Dutch city has its own Red Light district. The capital Amsterdam is a beautiful city full of canals and old buildings and is one of the most scenic in the world. It is also a total party town by night, but watch out for the junkies who want to steal your backpack or moneybelt. No visa required for stays up to 90 days.

On The Stoner's Trail (#1)

Holland is the coolest stoner's nation in Europe for its (in effect) legalization of cannabis. Pot and hash are sold in special coffee shops all over the country. Prices are standardized and are listed up on the wall or are featured in cafe menus. Open the menu and discover six to ten choices of hash or pot on either side of the page. Make your selection of any of the worlds finest for dine in or take out.

Waiter. "Menu, Please!"

Norway

The inhabitants of the sparsely populated Kingdom of Norway are among the best educated and financially well-off citizens in Europe. Oil revenues brought sudden wealth to the people who enjoy one of the highest standards of living in the world. As a result of its affluence, Norway is an expensive country to travel within. Overcoming costs, the natural beauty of the inland mountains and fjords on the coast are a fine sight not to be forgotten. The people are hospitable and friendly and eager to meet travelers, especially those from North America and Australia. No visa required for stays up to 3 months.

Poland

The tumultuous past of Poland's history is a good example of what the nation is experiencing today. Long a battleground and colony of Eastern and Western invaders, Poland has stubbornly retained its character in the mist of many a foe. Poland was the first country to say 'no' to Hitler's expansion, and it was here where WWII began. Poland was also the first country to break free from communism in the late 1980s. The Polish economy is having a rough time changing over to a free market, and the currency is undervalued. Cheap, cheap, cheap to Stomp, Stomp, Stomp. Most Poles speak little or no English. Do not miss the medieval walled city of Krakow or the Jasna Gora Monastery. No visa required for stays up to 90 days.

Portugal

Long the seafaring kingdom of the world and home to the eminent explorers Magellan and Vasco da Gama who ventured far to discover new land and oceans. The Portugal of today is merely a reminder of that great empire past. In fact, Portugal is one of western Europe's poorest countries. Throughout Portugal you will find landmarks from the country's glorious past, such as old forts, ancient monuments, and royal castles. The coast is more built up, especially Algarve in the south, where swarms of tourists come to soak up the sun and drink cheap beer every summer. Visa not required for stays up to 60 days, which include the Azores islands.

Romania

Transylvania and Count Dracula may be Romania's most recognized entities, but there is more to discover beyond their legend. While the region of Transylvania continues to draw many travelers for the sight of imposing feudal castles, fortified towns, and rolling green hills, the Black Sea has fine beaches and the Carpathian Mountains offers towering alpine peaks. Romania has only been open to tourism for a few years, so don't expect too much, apart from cheap prices. No visas required for stays up to 30 days.

Russia and the former Soviet Union

When the Soviet Union came tumbling down like a house of cards in 1991, several independent states (Belarus, Georgia, Moldovia, Ukraine, etc.) suddenly found themselves free from the wrath of communism to form their own nations. Even Mother Russia, the pillar of socialism, switched over to a free market economy and supposed democratic government. Growing pains can be heard all over the former empire, some of them rather ugly, such as skyrocketing inflation, crime rates, and a powerful Mafia.

What does all this mean for Stomping? Well, first of all, most of these nations are now open for travel, but there are a lot of hitches. No one can predict the outcome of all these changes so any given area may be open or closed at the spur of the moment. The best travel advice comes from others who have been there recently. There are very few English speakers, so a basic knowledge of the Russian language is a must. Most cities of the former Soviet Union are pretty dirty and ugly, the environment is in shambles, and it's damn cold all the time! So why go? Well, for one, the Trans-Siberian express from Moscow to Beijing is one of the greatest travel bargains on earth and the best way to observe this vast expanse of land. But perhaps the biggest lure for young travelers is to go there and observe the West's old foe transform from a strictly ordered society to an anything-goes-frontier. Adventure always attracts the daring, and this combined with Russia's rich culture and history is enough to entice those with a curious spirit. Visa situations and fees differ drastically; from a $65 processing fee and a 2 week wait time to get into Russia, to processing fees ranging $30-$170 for the Commonwealth States. Some States require you to go through the Russian Embassy or Consulate. Contact the Russian Embassy at: www.russianembassy.org for more details regarding visas and travel restrictions. Beware of large crowds and traveling in Moscow, Chechen terrorism will continue as long as the conflict goes unresolved.

Spain

Looking at a tourist brochure, Spain may appear to be a stereotypical whirl of crowded beaches, quaint villages, castles, and Moorish palaces. Travel for any length of time and the sheer variety of Spain comes to light. Rich heritage, outrageous nightlife, exuberant Spaniards, modern and classical art and architecture, and a varied climate. Whatever you are looking for, it is hard for Spain not to impress, except for the high prices around Madrid. A popular sidetrip (along with 8 million visitors) is down to the Canary Islands off the coast of Morocco. As a colony, the Canary Islands are part of Spain and cheap flights are available from most Spanish cities. No visa required for stays up to 3 months.

Top Ten Mellow Party Scenes (#5)

The Costa Brava, stretching along the Mediterranean Sea, is home to some fantastic old beach villages and the resurgent Catalan culture and language. This separate state of Spain offers the best of Spain; Gaudi architecture, topless beaches, a wonderful mix of Europeans, and for offbeat tastes – the bizarre sport of bullfighting. Barcelona has some great clubs, nightlife, and oh! such beautiful people!

Sweden

Highly praised as the model social welfare state, Sweden is the largest, most populous, and most industrialized of the five Scandinavian nations. It is also a land of mountains, farms, forests and lakes dotted with charming villages right out of a Mother Goose tale. It is governed by a constitutional monarchy whose citizens enjoy one of the highest standards of living in the world. This makes travel rather costly, but cutting expenses and getting to know some happy Swedes can make this country one of the most rewarding on the circuit. Visa not required for stays up to 3 months.

Switzerland

The renowned Swiss Alps, charming villages, and impeccable cleanliness impress most people who visit Switzerland, as well as problem-free travel and stunning landscapes. The large financial institutions, watchmaking, and tourist industries make the Swiss people proud to have one of the highest standards of living in the world. This makes travel expensive and may prompt you to rush through faster than you'd like. The snow skiing is top notch as well as the trekking in the mighty Alps, and just about anywhere you go in the country seems like a picture postcard view. Tiny neighbor Liechtenstein is exactly the same. Visa not required for stays up to 3 months.

United Kingdom

At one point in history the mighty British empire ruled half the world's population and influenced most of the rest. Today this tiny island Kingdom is a mere glimmer of what it had once been, but don't be fooled – there is much to see and do in the country whose native language is sweeping the globe (see: United Kingdom, below). Visa not required for stays up to 6 months.

Former Yugoslavia

Only a few years ago this country was wracked by a seemingly endless civil war, but now travel has come back and it's quite cheap. The former Yugoslavia as a travel destination is appealing because of the peace now settling into the region, and to see such incredible monuments as Diocletian's Palace, the Dubrovnik old city or the Studenica Monastery. Entry permission is usually obtained at the new republic border points. Croatia was the first country to open up to tourism and offers free 3 month visas. There is a $20 processing fee for Serbia and Montenegro. Bosnia and Herzegovina visas are still granted case by case at the local hotel or police station.

Germany

If it's not mandatory, it's forbidden.
— German proverb

Germany continues to be on the forefront of history in the making — both past and present. European conquerors from Charlemagne to Hitler have made a go at ruling the continent. Religious innovations from the Gutenberg Bible to Martin Luther's reformation of the Church changed the way Europeans pray. And most recently, the felling of the Berlin wall and subsequent reunification of a divided nation in 1990 spelled the end of communism and the Cold War in Europe.

Since unification, the German government has injected huge amounts of public spending into the East to help it catch up. Many factories had to be shut down and workers retrained, but despite these and other problems, eastern Germany's long-term future looks promising. All this change has brought fourth an economic stagnation throughout Germany, which has given neo-Nazi organizations a platform for immigrant bashing. Attacks on asylum-seekers have captured national headlines and one can only wonder if history will once again repeat itself.

Lay of the Land

Diversity seems to be the best way to describe the German landscape, from flat grasslands on the northern coast to the picturesque valleys of the Rhine and Elbe Rivers, to the Black Forest in the west and the Bavarian Alps in the south. Germany is a highly industrialized country with many unsightly factories and strip mines, yet interspersed with some of the finest castles and charming villages in all of Europe. A boat trip down the Rhine River is the most popular way of seeing some of this old country.

The German language is diversified into several regional groupings, and someone from the north can have a hard time understanding the dialect of someone from the south. The German people are highly educated and learn several languages in school, including English, so being understood is rarely a problem. Once viewed as domineering and overly disciplined, the Germans of today are mellowing out and are interested in enjoying life. Germans love to Stomp and it's a good chance you'll get to know quite a few on your trip, inside *and* outside the Fatherland.

Top Ten Best Bashes (#2)

If the whole silliness of ohm-pah-pah bands, dancing on the long tables (*schunkeln*), flirting with *Fräuleins*, and downing huge steins of fresh beer sounds like fun, get to Munich for this one and it will be ten times better! The outrageous Oktoberfest celebrations (which all happen in September by the way) are perhaps the boozer's favorite trail because the festivities go on all month long and you don't get a hangover from the beer. *Prost!*

Work and Money

The Deutschmark (DM) is the strongest currency in Europe and the cornerstone for the new EC economy. Exchange rates can be disheartening, but on the other hand, wages can be very good. Most casual earning jobs are typical for all of Europe, such as grape-picking from August to October, au pair for young women, busking on the streets, bartending, or "runners" who recruit travelers on the trains to stay in the hotels they represent.

Typical German jobs would be teaching English (experience, certificate, and college degree are usually required), or working on a U.S military base. Usual base jobs for civilians include: bar backing, bussing, dish washing, or ski instructing in places that cater to U.S. service men. A nice perk for working on a base is that you are issued an ID card that gets you into the recreation facilities, discounts on local activities such as skiing, and access into the PX (a military K-Mart where everything is priced just above cost.) Those whose spouse or family is working on a base may apply to the U.S. government's school system entitled the Department of Defense Dependent Schools. Applications may be picked up at any U.S. government Civilian Personnel Office.

Check the CPO (Civilian Employment Office) near the base for job listings, or go into the local employment office located in every city for recent openings and an application for a work permit. Having a working knowledge of the German language is helpful in landing a job, but not always required. Some people arrange jobs stateside through CIEE or CDS International, or just wing it when they get there.

EARTHLINGS

"What the ... ! We're here *again?* Why is it that all roads lead to Rome?"

United Kingdom

A smooth sea never made a skillful mariner.
– English proverb

The United Kingdom comprises Britain (England, Wales, and Scotland) and Northern Ireland. In terms of area it is a small country, but the more you travel around, the larger it seems. Take your time with Britain because there is so much to see, and many travelers think they can do it in a few short weeks. While this might give a nice orientation, certainly it would take many months or years to really soak up all that Britain has to offer.

On the surface, the autonomy of the UK is not obvious – until you get there. Northern Ireland is a thorn in the nation's side that cannot be removed and continues to fester. Wales, long a separate nation in its own right, has a strong independent culture. So does the equally historic Scotland, whose people are famously at odds with the stiff upper-lipped Englishmen in London. Within England itself, regional differences are more pronounced than one might expect from a country of such modest size.

Only 60 years ago, the U.K. was at the forefront of the planet's economy and politics. As the largest empire the world has ever known began to erode, so did its influence as a superpower. Today it has politically isolated itself so much, it seems to be tucked into its own little corner of Europe. But in their day, the Brits did a great job of spreading their culture and language around the globe. Reminders of their presence seem to pop up almost everywhere, as well as the English language emerging as the universal tongue.

Getting to know Britain

With the new Channel Tunnel open for passage, Britain is closer to Europe than ever before, yet few Britons would consider themselves true Europeans. The British people are more independent culture-of-the-world types. Perhaps something to do with their centuries as colonial masters. Any conversation with a POM (Prisoner of Mother England) will reveal a very broad world view. And the British love to travel, which is evident in their ubiquitous presence around the planet today.

European history, especially British history, permeates the globe. To know it, is to know much about where the world stands today.

To examine all there is to see and know about the U.K., it is necessary to provide a brief historical perspective.

The first people to settle in Briton around 4000 BC were small bands of hunters from Europe. The next arrival of immigrants came around 3000 BC. These new people brought with them stone tools and a mysterious religion; the likes of which produced numerous monolithic stone circles, including the awesome Stonehenge.

The next great influx was the Celts who brought with them the skill to use bronze, and later iron. Their lasting legacy are the languages they

213

spoke, and can still be heard today in Wales (Brythonic), and Ireland and Scotland (Gaelic). In 43 AD, the Romans showed up in force and stuck around for 370 years. The Roman legacy can still be found with some of their old roads, Hadrian's Wall, and numerous ruins such as the city of Bath, named after the Roman baths established there. Christianity arrived in the 3rd century just as the Romans were packing up and a new Germanic people were coming in to fill the vacuum. These Germanic tribes called themselves the English.

The next wave of invaders were the ambitious Vikings from Denmark and Norway who briefly ruled various parts of the country. Several Viking ships were buried with their king on British beaches, and the relics excavated are some of the finest that survive today. The Northmen of France (descendants of the Vikings) conquered England in 1066 and established the feudal system. This divided Britain up into small territories, and imposing castles were constructed all over the country for protection as a result.

During the middle ages numerous power struggles took place between English kings, overseas nations, small dynasties, and finally the first Tudor king, Henry VII. Great cathedrals were constructed, and the Bible was translated into English. The 16th century was a golden age, as Shakespeare wrote his plays, Francis Bacon laid the foundations for modern science, and the European powers explored the world and became fabulously rich through trade. The foundation of an empire began in 1649 when Oliver Cromwell assumed dictatorial powers and modernized the army and navy.

The Empire was at its height in 1770 when France ceded all of Canada and all but two trading stations in India to Britain, while Captain Cook had claimed Australia and several other new colonies for the Crown. A decade later, the Industrial Revolution began in Britain, and soon Midland country towns became industrial cities. When Queen Victoria took the throne in 1837, the U.K. was the greatest power in all the world. Factories were set up around the globe, all linked by its dominating fleet of ships. This virtual monopoly on world trade made Britain enormously wealthy, and literally thousands of monuments, palaces, and stately buildings were constructed worldwide as a testament to this period.

The two European World Wars of the 20th century drastically shook up Britain's status quo. Well over a million British men died in the two conflicts, huge amounts of the nation's accumulated capital had been spent, and most of the colonies began gaining their independence. To top off this decline, most of Britain's industries became obsolete and subsequently collapsed. Still a very wealthy nation by world standards, the boarded up look of old factories, particularly evident in the north, are a good analogy as to where the country stands today.

Top Ten Best Bashes (#6)

Out in a remote valley in England is a sleepy little village known as Glastonbury. Nothing much going on here until 400,000 people show up for the annual festival on the summer solstice (June 21st). Officially scheduled as a three-day event, the Glastonbury "crustys" have been known to hang around for the rest of the summer. Several virtual villages emerge, as well as all kinds of musical stages and dance parties. Bring your own supplies if you go. Food, beer, and camping supplies are inflated and scarce after a few days.

Work and Money

Due to a favorable business climate in Britain, foreign laborers are finding a greater ease in the job search compared to a few years ago. The easiest jobs to find are the under-the-table types that the Brits do not want to do themselves. These are mostly labor-intensive jobs such as: farm hands, pub and restaurant workers, nannies, labor at construction sites and various odd jobs. Basically, be prepared to work long hours for lousy pay. Chances are you will just break even by the time your visa runs out. Check out *TNT Magazine* and the *Evening Standard* for jobs and agencies aimed at travelers. The government-operated job centers are scattered around London, and it's a good idea to register your name with several temporary agencies (best are the ones that ask few questions) as soon as you have an address and telephone number.

Having a work permit increases your chances greatly for finding a better paying job. It is possible to get a six month work visa through BUNAC (*British Universities North America Club*). This is an exchange program for college students that locates positions and place workers. You must be an enrolled college student, at least 18 years old and residing in the U.S. at the time of application. The cost is $160 for the service.

In good economic times, it is possible to get teaching, accounting, nursing, and clerical work (computer knowledge is a big plus) which are all well-paying jobs. An American, named Doug D., got a good job with American Express in London through his college placement office. He said, "European firms like to hire Americans when there are added-value benefits. Such are: knowledge of recent technology, a sense for business, computer literacy skills, and a good attitude. There is a definite advantage for being American and getting hired abroad. The hard part is just landing that first job."

Druid Solstice

> *"In ancient times, hundreds of years before the dawn of history,*
> *Lived a strange race of people ... The Druids.*
> *No one knows who they were, or, what they were doing.*
> *But their legacy remains here into the little rock of Stonehenge.*
> *Stonehenge!*
> *Where dew drops cry and the cats meow.*
> *I will take you there, I will show you how."*
>
> **Spinal Tap**

North Africa and the Middle East Circuit

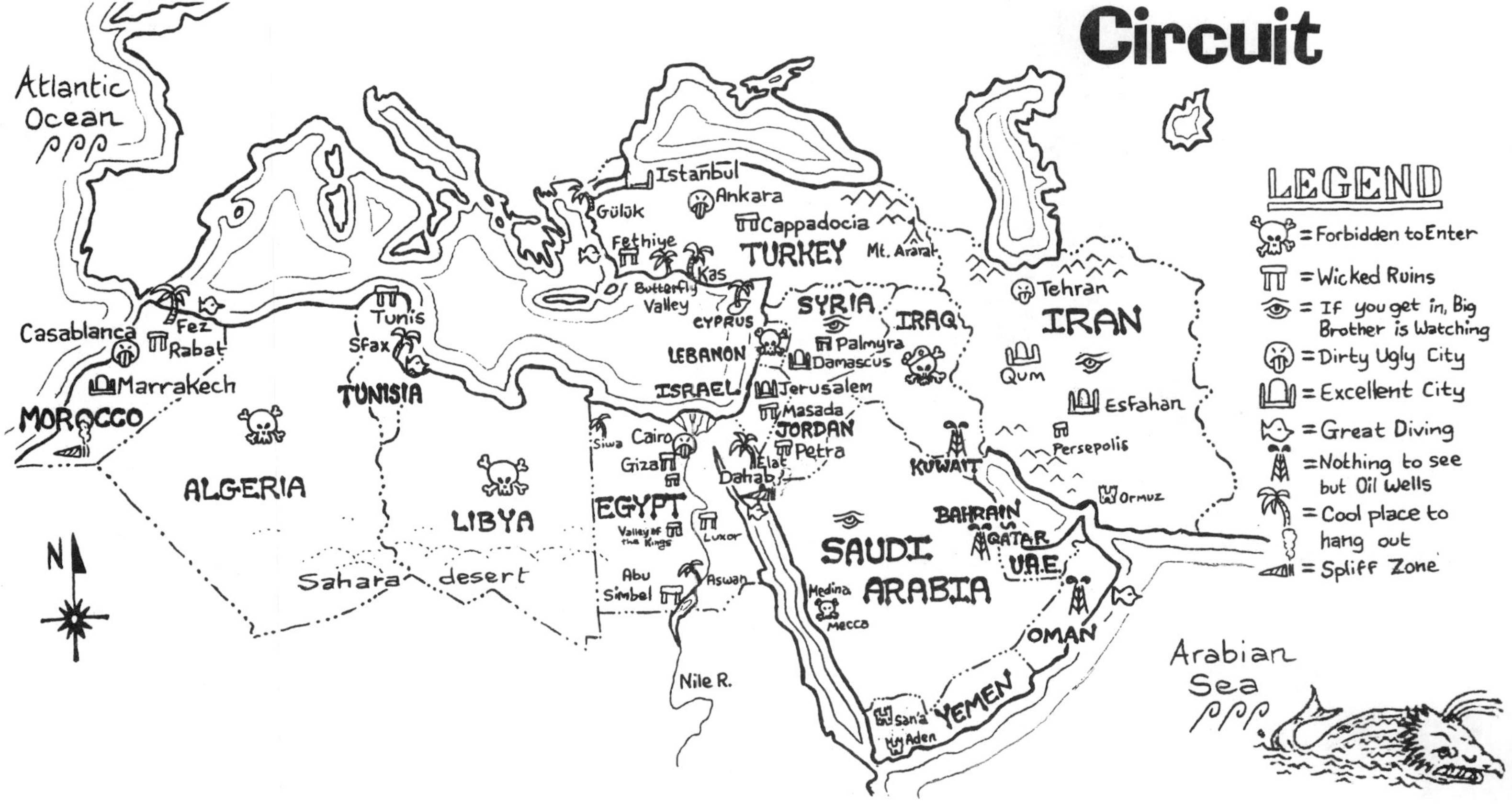

LEGEND

☠ = Forbidden to Enter
ᴫ = Wicked Ruins
👁 = If you get in, Big Brother is Watching
🏚 = Dirty Ugly City
🏛 = Excellent City
🐟 = Great Diving
♨ = Nothing to see but Oil Wells
🌴 = Cool place to hang out
♨ = Spiff Zone

Atlantic Ocean

MOROCCO
Casablanca
Fez
Rabat
Marrakech

ALGERIA

TUNISIA
Tunis
Sfax

LIBYA

Sahara desert

EGYPT
Cairo
Giza
Siwa
Valley of the Kings
Luxor
Aswan
Abu Simbel
Nile R.

TURKEY
Istanbul
Ankara
Cappadocia
Gulük
Fethiye
Butterfly Valley
Kas
Mt. Ararat

SYRIA
Palmyra
Damascus

IRAQ

LEBANON

CYPRUS

ISRAEL
Jerusalem
Masada
Elat
Dahab

JORDAN
Petra

IRAN
Tehran
Qum
Esfahan
Persepolis
Ormuz

KUWAIT

BAHRAIN
QATAR
U.A.E.

SAUDI ARABIA
Medina
Mecca

OMAN

YEMEN
Sana'a
Aden

Arabian Sea

N

North Africa and the Middle East Circuit

*To travel safely through the world, a man must
have a falcon's eye, an ass's ears, an ape's
face, a merchant's words, a camel's back,
a hog's mouth, and a hart's legs.*

– Arabic proverb

Tempers seem to flare very easily in North Africa and the Middle East. Internal strife continues to wreak havoc in Algeria, Cyprus, Lebanon, and Israel. Brutal dictators in Iraq and Libya like to push their weight around and sponsor terrorism. Countries like Kuwait, the U.A.E. and Saudi Arabia enjoy some of the highest incomes in the world, but create resentment and jealousy alongside dirt-poor neighbors. And almost all of them are fanatical about their religion. This is arguably the most dangerous circuit in the world, but rarely is the threat targeted at travelers, apart from Algeria and sometimes Egypt.

The land of Arabian nights and the birthplace of Western civilization has much to offer the intrepid Stomper. Long the historical crossroads between the East and the West, North Africa and the Middle East features many unique attractions and distinctions. Tied together mainly by a common religion (Islam) and common language (Arabic), this circuit delivers wicked ruins, cheap prices, great beaches, interesting people, and excellent diving in the Mediterranean and Red Sea. Some countries are quite volatile and outright dangerous, others hospitable and friendly. Thank goodness for strong international borders. Here are the visa requirements and a rundown on the circuit:

Algeria

Fundamentalists are killing foreigners these days. Just the color of your skin might be a one-way ticket home ... in a body bag. Bad scene, don't go.

Bahrain

The only island state in the Arab world, this country is quite stable and liberal compared to its tumultuous neighbors. Oil and banking are the drivers of the economy, so a visit here is very expensive. Over 150,000 foreigners live and work on the island and jobs can be found, but are usually arranged ahead of time. Visas can be obtained at the Bahrain airport or on the causeway coming in from Saudi Arabia for only 72 hours. Visas require a $50 fee and a letter from a Bahrain citizen guaranteeing full responsibility for all expenses.

Cyprus

An incredible historic collection of culture sits atop this Eastern Mediterranean island-nation. The ancient Phoenicians, Greeks, Romans, and European crusaders have all left their mark, complemented by beautiful mountains and coastline. As a strategic position militarily, Cyprus has been wracked by war and conflict over the centuries, and these problems still exist today. Deep hatred festers between the Turks and Greeks who inhabit the island and crossing over the militarized border is prohibited. Despite the animosity, large numbers of tourists come each year to visit (mainly the Greek side) for the fine beaches, warm sunny climate, and the cheap cost of travel. No visa required, but a passport is for 3 month stay, as well as an $8 departure tax.

Egypt

Egypt is home to one of the oldest civilizations on earth and some of the best monuments and ruins to be found anywhere. As of late, fundamentalists have taken to using tourist groups as target practice. Terrorism has devastated Egypt's tourist industry which has made it very cheap to travel. But get here quick before it becomes too poverty stricken and dangerous to Stomp. See: Egypt, below. Visas can be obtained ahead of time for $15, or at the airport for $20. Visas are valid for 1 month upon arrival.

Gulf States (Oman, Qatar, and United Arab Emirates)

Nobody goes to these countries for traveling because there is nothing to do. Oil wells and desert sums it up, with a notable exception of Oman's untamed wilderness and pristine beaches, and Qatar's Khor Al-Adaid estuary. Because these nations produce oil, they are rather expensive to Stomp within, as well as the cost of a visa ($36, $45, $30, respectively).

Iran

The only way to travel from Europe to India overland is by passing through Iran. Fortunately, the slogan "Death to America" is fading away, and could open to freestyle travel soon. Ironically, U.S. dollars are the preferred and accepted currency. Iran is full of warm and hospitable people, with exquisite food, interesting souvenirs and beautiful textiles. Aussies and Europeans (except U.K. citizens) can get 14-day transit visas, but they must be obtained before arriving at the border.

Iraq

Same story as Algeria, don't go. Unless, of course, you want to be one of Saddam's human shields.

Israel

In the eyes of most of its Arab neighbors, this country does not exist and is simply being occupied by the Jews. If you are traveling on from Israel, make sure you do not get a stamp in your passport because some Arab countries will not grant a visa. See: Israel, below. Visas are free upon arrival for 3 months and you can request the entry stamp be put on a separate piece of paper. A departure tax of $15 is charged when leaving the country.

Jordan

The peace process with Israel has drastically reduced travel restrictions, and crossing the border is no longer a problem these days, even if your passport contains an Israeli stamp. Visas are $44 and can be obtained at the border and allow the visitor a stay up to one month. Passports required. Jordan is now one of the most accessible Arab countries. Most travelers agree: the people are helpful, friendly, and considered the most hospitable in the region.

Not a whole lot is happening in the sleepy capital Amman, but three hours south is the rose-red city called Petra. Carved into a canyon by the ancient Nabateans, Petra is an archaeological site not to be missed. The nature reserve of Wadi Dana and Wadi Rum are another must-see.

Kuwait

After the Gulf War, Kuwait was one of the best work-countries to make a ton of cash quick. Now things have gotten back to normal and the temp jobs have all but dried up. Apart from working, there is not much reason to come here. The climate is extremely hot in the summer, the land is flat and full of oil rigs, the urban centers are drab and artificial, and the cost of everything is very high. No tourist visas are issued and one must have a local sponsor for a business visa. Transit visas are issued for 24 hour stays, for $8, and proof of an ongoing ticket must be presented.

Lebanon

Lebanon is quickly recovering from its long bout of civil anarchy and Westerner visitors are no longer considered fair game for terrorists. The Hezbullah (Party of God) in southern Lebanon has ceased military activity after Israeli troops pulled out of the southern buffer zone in May, 2000. Lebanon is now re-emerging at a frantic pace and has much to offer such as: nice beaches, fine restaurants, impressive ruins, the Jeita Caves, and even snow skiing. As a sign of the times, there are trendy shops and restaurants popping up all over Beirut again. A 3 month single-entry visa is available for $20 at the airport or land borders.

Libya

Nobody goes to Libya for vacation except wanted terrorists.

Morocco

The Moroccan government is eager to promote tourism because it is such a lucrative part of the national economy. The activities are what you come for: loads of sun, surf, archaeology, trekking in the Riff and Atlas Mountains, and a flamboyant culture. The cities are mostly exotic and well preserved.

Morocco is well accustomed to tourism, so watch out for scammers. Beware of locals who want to be your friend or act as a tour guide, they may rip you off in the end. Women should not travel here alone and groups of women should be accompanied by at least one male. Also, be careful about from whom you buy hash. Although it is legal in some parts of the country, other parts it is not, and you might find yourself being shaken down for all you money by corrupt police. No visas are required for stays up to 3 months; extendible.

Saudi Arabia

Good news and bad news. The good news is that the Saudis like Americans and the country has much to offer. It has one of the most beautiful expanses of desert wilderness in the world. Two holiest sites of Islam – Mecca and Medina. The legendary hospitality of the Bedouin. And for those with bizarre tastes, it even has public beheadings.

The bad news is the kingdom is closed to tourism. In the interest of screening out decadent Western influences, the Saudis have banned satellite dishes and travelers. The only way to get in the country is to travel on bona fide business and have a local sponsor. Tourist visas are not available for travel in Saudi Arabia.

Syria

This is a country that is still very much hostile with Israel, and the police-state mentality that prevails here can be a nightmare. On the other hand, Damascus, the capital, is right out of Arabian nights and has been fascinating travelers for centuries. An age-old custom in Syrian cities are the *hammam*, or steam baths, which welcome foreigners. Most Stompers have reported the Syrian people to be the most receptive in the Middle East and internal travel is not a problem, apart from a few road-blocks and check-points. Foreigners are treated with extreme courtesy.

Any slight evidence of having been to Israel, even holding a few shekel coins or a Jewish sounding name can get you booted from the country. Also, beware of being drawn into a political discussion by the secret police. This, too, can get you kicked out. Visas must be obtained before reaching the country. They are available in consulates and embassies in most large cities. You are given 3 months on a single-entry or double-entry visa. Both visa cost $61.

Tunisia

Landlocked between two hostile-to-Western nations, Tunisia welcomes tourists without fear of terrorism. Offering the usual sun, sand, and Roman ruins of most Mediterranean countries, Tunisia is usually overlooked by most travelers. It is only an overnight ferry ride from Italy or Malta. Visas are not required for stays up to 4 months.

Turkey

Rich in history, ancient ruins, and culture, Turkey also boasts some of the best beaches in the world on its Aegean and Mediterranean coasts. The most liberal and Western of the Arab countries, Turkey is a good testing ground and starting point for this circuit. Some women complain of chauvinistic men or squat toilets, but as a whole, it's the mellowest of the lot largely due to many years of foreign Stompers. Turkey is well equipped to meet the demands of tourism with loads of cheap hotels and traveler restaurants serving up some of the best food in the region.

In the cities and tourist areas English is widely spoken, and elsewhere you will still be understood, especially when spending money. Don't forget when shopping, haggling is the name of the game for everything here, and elsewhere in the Arab countries. Women should not travel alone in Turkey. Visas are available on arrival for $20 and are valid for 3 months.

Top Ten Mellow Party Scenes (#6)

Butterfly Valley on the Mediterranean Coast in Turkey is one of the mellowest party scenes in the world. The beautiful views and fantastic swimming are the attractions by day, while bonfires on the beach, guitar sing-alongs, and drinking beer are the draw card at night. A small cafe prepares all the meals, sells the beer, and runs the stilt platforms for sleeping. There are no roads in from Oludeniz, so catch one of the daily boats.

Yemen

The dust has just settled in Yemen after a bitter civil war tore the country apart. It is still a dangerous destination (most guns per capita in the world), but a few intrepid travelers are slowly trickling in. After arrival and away from trouble, Yemen is a laid back, unspoiled vestige of the authentic Arabia. The drug of choice is *qat*, a chewable leaf that induces a mildly narcotic trance. Some of the old medieval cities appear as they have for thousands of years. As the terminus of the Incense Road, Yemen is filled with history and culture. A visa will cost $50 and is valid for 30 days, but a letter of invitation is required.

Earthlings

The straw that broke the camel's back.

Egypt

"When Moses was alive, these pyramids were a thousand years old. ... Here began the history of architecture. Here people learned to measure time by a calendar, to plot the stars by astronomy and chart the earth by geometry. And here they developed that most awesome of all ideas — the idea of eternity.
— Walter Cronkite *"Eternal Egypt"*

The land of pharaohs and pyramids is a unique travel experience, one not to be missed. The monuments in this land are unprecedented in the world. If you have ever dreamed of going there, do it soon before it may become too risky. In recent years there has been an increase in the number of religious fundamentalists threatening tourists. Although the incidents are rare and quite low in proportion to the number of visitors annually, there is still a risk involved. Because of this threat, tourism has dropped dramatically from where it had been a decade ago. This has made the ego-centric merchants very desperate, and the "hassle factor" is way up as a result. A running joke is the only real attacks on tourists are the constant and frequent hawking from the merchants.

The population is going to explode in Egypt over the next few decades. From 56 million (1995) to projected 94 million (2025). Six out of ten Egyptians today are under the age of 21.

Greater Cairo is home to 13 million people, many of who live in shanty-towns or are homeless. One in five Egyptian workers is jobless. The fertile Nile delta is damaged because of reduced river flow from the Aswan High Dam, and if global warming continues to make sea levels rise, 15 percent of the land will become unfarmable and nearly 8 million people will become refugees. In what is highly regarded as the most volatile region of the world, Egyptian demographics are contributing to the prospects of future unrest year after year.

The good news is that until the Embassies of the world advise travelers not to go, Egypt is still relatively safe to Stomp. Statistically, you are in less danger of being shot in Egypt than you are in any major U.S. city. The terrorist scare has really opened the door for bargain hunters. Roughly expect to pay: five dollars a night for a double room; seven dollars for a full day camel or horseback ride out to the pyramids; four bucks to tour a monument (double without a student card); a dollar or two for a meal; fifty cents for a beer; and scuba dive the Red Sea on two tanks for $35.

On The Stoner's Trail (#9)

Dahab, Egypt: synonymous with laid back and stoned. This little village is situated on the shores of the Red Sea and offers some of the best scuba diving in the world. It is also a place where pot is sold and smoked openly on the beach terraces. Decent grade ganja can be bought from the multitude of camel-ride drivers in town, or ask the stoner in the cushion pile next to you where he got his. Chances are he will just toss you a stem off his shesha pipe (hookah). The Sphinx would be proud.

Egypt's Top Ten most Wicked Ruins

10. Habu temples. Relief sculptures galore in a huge nook and cranny complex build by Ramses III.

9. The Citadel in Cairo. A walled fortress surrounding the modern mosque of Mohammed Ali. Don't kiss or hold hands in the mosque or you will get kicked out.

8. Ramesseum. Massive statues of Ramses II and huge decorated pillars overwhelm any visitor.

7. The Valley of the Kings. King Tut and 61 other Pharaohs had been buried in this valley near a pyramidal mountain. The tombs were cut deep into the bedrock and the passages are finely sculpted and decorated.

6. Saqqara. King Zosar built this first pyramid complex 4700 years ago. Successive pharaohs built pyramids, temples, and tombs nearby.

5. Luxor. Giant entry pylons followed by large pillared halls. The three km Avenue of Sphinx's leads to ...

4. Karnak. Dedicated to Amun the sun god, it was built section by section by dozens of pharaohs, and even Alexander the Great when he conquered Egypt. Large obelisks and lakes add to the charm.

3. Deir El Banri. Queen Hatshepsut's marvelous temple beautifully incorporated into the mountain backdrop.

2. Abu Simbel. This gigantic temple of Ramses II had to be sawed out of the cliff it was carved into and reassembled up on the desert plateau before the Aswan High Dam flooded over.

1. Giza Plateau. The granddaddy of all pyramids where the Sphinx keeps watch over the whole complex. Exploring the tombs and chambers inside the Great Pyramids of Giza is arguably the wildest experience of any world tour.

Earthlings

The Persian Golfer

Full Moon Pyramid Climb

From the travel journal (26 Mar. '94)

I planned my flight from India to Egypt not on plane schedules or departure times, but on when the moon would be full in Cairo. My Dutch girlfriend Katja (from Holland, met in Goa) arrived at the airport on the same day and we had a week to relax and take in the sights before the big night. One day we road horses through the desert to the Third Dynasty (Old Kingdom) step pyramid of king Zosar. A very cool pyramid indeed, but not the one I had my eyes on. Certainly I wanted the best. The Great Pyramid of Cheops is the biggest and mightiest in all the land; the one shrouded in mysticism and wonder, the one with all the mathematical and astronomical equations, and the one I would dominate on full moon.

Katja and I caught the sound and light show (for free of course) on a dune near the Sphinx and that's when I plotted my route up. She waited in a Chinese restaurant and I approached the 50 story tall monument in a state of awe. A second light show began and the night was still early, so there were quite a few guards about. Yes, this could present a problem because climbing the pyramids is not allowed, unless of course you are willing to pay off half dozen guards. No *baksheesh* payments tonight, I wanted to do this alone.

When the pyramid lights went down on Cheops and up on Chepren I saw this as my big chance to go for it. I started quickly climbing up the meter high blocks until the lights came up again, and then had to dive for cover. This hiding in the lights and climbing in the darkness went on for a half hour until I finally reached the top. The light show was still in progress as I sat on the top and watched the monuments light up and fade back into the darkened void of the Sahara desert. The lights of Cairo blazed along the Nile as far as I could see, and a light breeze cooled my face. Strange feelings overcame me as the powers of the pyramids began to work their wonders. A religious experience for an atheist would be the best way to describe the intensity. Climbing down I rejoiced the night for its cover and the moon for enough illumination. So I wouldn't be spotted, I climbed down quickly and ran a zigzag course through some tombs and temples until I was safely out of the complex.

Israel

*We have always said that in our war with the Arabs we had a
secret weapon – no alternative.*
– Golda Meir, 1969

Three major world religions – Islam, Christianity and Judaism – all consider the state of Israel to be their Holy Land. The resulting collision zone of religion, trade routes, and politics have historically made this little piece of land a highly sought after prize. The age-old clash between Arab and Jew, East and West, Israeli and Palestinian remain as intense as ever, despite several recent peace treaties aimed at diffusing tensions.

Steeped in history of biblical proportions, travel through Israel constantly reminds you that this is an ancient land. Names like Bethlehem, Jericho, Jerusalem, and Masada seem rather odd on modern highway signs, but there they are, along with thousands of religious tourists seeking out the sacred sites and buildings of their faith.

Along the coast, Israel has a typical Mediterranean climate with hot and dry summers and cool and wet winters. The Dead Sea region and south to the Red Sea are desert climates year 'round. They can get extremely hot in the day and bitterly cold by night. Most of the country is relatively arid, and the Israelis have performed a miracle of irrigation to make this country the largest net exporter of produce in the region.

Big On Stomping

Some of the most widespread Stompers around the globe are young Israelis just out of the military. You can always tell the age of an Israeli traveler by the length of his hair. If it's a crewcut, he's 21 and fresh out of the army. Average length and he's 22 or 23. Hippie length and he's in his mid-twenties. This distinction is easy to make because every man and woman in Israel has to join the armed forces from 18 to 21, except for religious pacifists and physical misfits.

Israel is in a perpetual state of military alertness, so its citizens are a tough breed. When the young finish their obligations to the state, the only thing they want to do is travel the world and start enjoying life. Quite understandable after hearing some terrible fighting stories from Lebanon and the old occupied territories. With all their military training, and innate shrewdness that comes from being Jewish, the Israelis can come off as being brash or arrogant at times. But once you get to know the group they travel in, or have a chat with them one on one, you will come to realize the Hebrew facade is just an instinctive buffer – they all speak English quite well.

Israeli travelers have a real zest to see every corner of the world with their typical, total balls-out attitude. The classic story was in 1991 when seven Israeli tourists were held at gunpoint after being captured by Muslim terrorists in Kashmir, India. Fearing for their life, they quickly made a plan in Hebrew and charged the gunmen. In the ensuing struggle, one Israeli was killed and the others escaped after shooting down their captors. In other words, do not provoke an Israeli – even the women are tough.

Work and Money

There are two kinds of live/work arrangements in Israel that are very popular with travelers. The first is the kibbutz where you work several hours in the morning for your meals and housing, then have the rest of the afternoon free for fun or lounging poolside (if that kibbutz has a pool). A kibbutz is socialist-style communal living, so wages are almost nil. The second live/work arrangement is the moshav, which is more of a full-time job. Moshavs offer better work, more responsibility, contact with Israelis and fellow travelers, and wages! Both want you to stay for a while (3 months or so) but the pay-for-work-ratio is low, so the worker-turnover-ratio is high.

Most jobs are picking in the orchards or sorting on an assembly line. Minimum wage on a moshav is $5 an hour for at least 3 hours a day, 5 days a week. If you want to work 10 hours a day, 6 or 7 days a week, they will pay you more. Save yourself placement agency commission fees by locating and going directly to the kibbutz or moshav yourself. Most will put you to work straight away, or they will tell you about a neighbor down the road who is hiring.

City jobs include all the under-the-table favorites, such as construction cleanup, painting, moving, and other labor intensive tasks the Israelis don't want to do themselves. When working illegally for someone, and this is true everywhere, make sure you collect your wages after every day until you feel you can trust your boss. Illegal workers have no recourse after being burned by a boss who doesn't recognize their help a week later.

Earthlings

Coliseum Hecklers

The SUB-SAHARA AFRICA Circuit

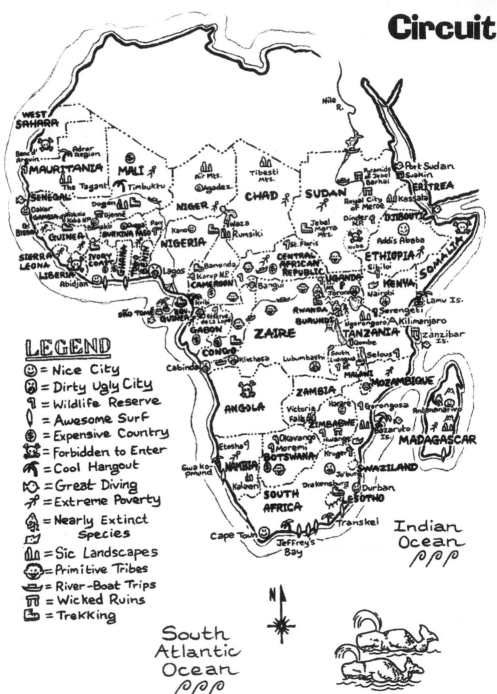

LEGEND

- ☺ = Nice City
- 🙁 = Dirty Ugly City
- ⚑ = Wildlife Reserve
- ◊ = Awesome Surf
- $ = Expensive Country
- 🚫 = Forbidden to Enter
- 🌴 = Cool Hangout
- ⋈ = Great Diving
- ✈ = Extreme Poverty
- 🐒 = Nearly Extinct Species
- ⛰ = Sic Landscapes
- 😊 = Primitive Tribes
- ⛵ = River-Boat Trips
- 🏛 = Wicked Ruins
- 🎒 = Trekking

South Atlantic Ocean

Indian Ocean

N

Sub-Sahara Africa Circuit

So geographers, in Afric-maps,
with savage-pictures fill their gaps;
And o'er unhabitable downs
Place elephants for want of towns.

— Jonathan Swift (1733)

Safaris. Jungles. Teeming wildlife. Extreme poverty. Active volcanoes. Ruthless dictators. Pygmies. Savannas. Tribal cultures. Mt. Kilimanjaro. Civil unrest. Migrating herds. African Queen boat trips. Grossly over-populated regions. Emerging democracies. Deserts. Old Arab trading posts. Lunar landscapes. The birthplace of Humanoids. However you want to look at it, one certainty exists; this is the circuit with the greatest contrast. Welcome to Africa south of the Sahara Desert, also known as the Dark Continent.

Despite "Third World" status for nearly all of the Sub-Sahara countries, the cost of visas and travel in general can be ridiculously high. The reason for this is most of these nations' economies are still tied to their former colonial masters, namely France. Thus, things like hotels, meals, transportation, and soft drinks are on par with prices found in Europe. A few breakaways exist, such as Zaire, Malawi, and Zimbabwe, which are a quarter in price to their neighbors. But economies in Africa tend to be as volatile as the dictators who exploit them, so no information can be truly updated until the day you arrive. Here's a rundown of the circuit:

All The Tiny West African Coastal Nations

Sharing a common coastline, race of people, and similar cultures, these 10 tiny coastal nations (Senegal, Gambia, Guinea-Bissau, Guinea, Sierra Leone, Liberia, Ivory Coast, Ghana, Togo, and Benin) are worlds apart politically and economically. In most of these countries the economic situation is pretty bleak and home to some of the poorest countries in the world. Top off this extreme poverty with a few ruthless dictators, such as Charles Taylor of Liberia, and you can see why most of these countries are considered "off the off beaten track."

But with every exception there is a rule, and in this case it's oil, agriculture, and pockets of tourism. The Ivory Coast and Ghana are the two success stories with highest per capita incomes in the region, while Senegal continues to attract many European tourists. Reports back from Stompers rate the area high in native friendliness, and exceptional for music, culture, and traditional art. The negative side is they can be expensive, are mostly French speaking, and high in hassles. Ghana is one of the few English speaking countries in Africa. The Ghanaians are just about the friendliest people on the planet, and their drumming is incredible. All countries except Senegal require American citizens to have a visa before arrival. Prices range from $13 to $45 and stays are granted for 30 days to 3 months.

Angola

An ongoing civil war has ravaged the cities and countryside over the last decade, but the dust is settling and there are talks of democratic elections. Angola is only for the serious Stomper and visas may or may not be issued. For those who get in, Angola is a beautiful country, especially the coastline. A knowledge of Portuguese is handy. Visa information can be found on www.angola.org

Botswana

Botswana is home to the vast, dry, and virtually un-populated Kalahari desert. This is safari country and last refuge of the !Kung Bushmen – a hunter and gatherer tribe still living in Paleolithic times. Distances are vast between tourist spots, but the Okavango Swamps, Moremi, and Chobe Game Reserves in the Northwest are absolutely stunning.

Botswana is a multilingual nation, but the official languages are Setswana and English. The democratic government is stable here and the economy is healthy which makes Botswana an expensive destination. Tourism is big business here, and so are diamond mining and cattle ranching. Visas not required for stays up to 90 days.

Burkina Faso

As one of the five poorest countries on earth, you would think life is pretty dismal here. Far from it. In the capital city of Ouagadougou mopeds cram the boulevards and the central market is a bustling uproar of commerce. However busy city life can be, Ouaga (for short) has a relaxed atmosphere and rates high among mellow African cities.

After you leave the city the standard of living gets pretty grim, yet the people maintain a miraculous sense of optimism. They will take you into their mud huts to live communally if you want. You can become part of their group and help out with everyday chores. Staying with a tribe is the best way to really understand how the other half lives, no matter how deprived of Western luxuries. A 3 month extendible visa costs $25.

Burundi

Many of the neighboring tribal conflicts in Rwanda have spilled into Burundi as well. This country may or may not be open, depending on the latest status of factional struggles. Not a whole lot to see or do here anyhow, apart from observing a textbook example of the devastating effect overpopulation has on nature, land, and people. Multiple-entry visas valid for 2 months cost $80.

Cameroon

Wealth has come to this Central African nation by default – oil. As one of the most prosperous nations on the circuit, it is also one of the most expensive. This is not to discourage anyone from visiting, Cameroon truly has some wonderful attractions. In the north, there are hobbit-like villages perched on rocky cliffs near the surrealistic landscapes of Rumsiki. The

"Fon of Kon" receives guests in his residence called the Laikom Palace in an *Alice in Wonderland* sort of way. Scattered around the country are great wildlife reserves, mountains to climb, and beautiful isolated beaches along the coastal region. A 90 day multiple-entry visa costs $65.22.

Central African Republic

Long regarded as one of the best places to go for hunting safaris, (the CAR) is now hoping tourists will be content with just looking instead of killing. As a result of over-hunting, the forest elephant population is nearly decimated, as are the unique bongos (spiral-horned antelope). This is also the land of butterflies, Pygmies, and muddy roads. The CAR is a good starting point for riverboats making the long journey down the Congo. Visas up to 90 day stays cost $60, over 90 days, $150. Visas can only be obtained by mail.

Chad

The long civil war and battles with Libya are finally over. While the far north may still be off limits, the rest of the country is open and beginning to thrive. As is true with the whole world, those people who are the poorest and have the least contact with travelers are always the friendliest – Chad being no exception. The country is lively and exotic, and certainly a momentous example of human's staying power to survive in the harshest of conditions. A single-entry visa valid for 30 days is $25.

Congo

As land and people go, the Congo is much like a twin to neighboring Zaire — only more relaxed with mellow police and fewer obstacles for getting around the interior. The locals are nice, the government is legit, and the overland safaris are a blast. Everybody usually finds something to like about the Congo. A multiple-entry visa will bust you for $70. It is valid for 3 months.

Djibouti

One of the newest independent countries in the world, Djibouti broke away from Ethiopia a few years ago because they had all the money. Affluent by African standards, it is chock full of culture and art, *without* the extreme poverty. A visa will cost $30 for 30 days.

Equatorial Guinea

Despite widespread poverty and a very backward nature, this is a country for extreme adventurers who want to stray way off the beaten track. What those who venture this far will find is lots of jungle terrain, surprised natives, deserted beaches, and maybe even Tarzan. This is truly the land of swinging from vine to vine. Local language in fang, but Spanish and French are also understood. Visas must be ordered in advance from the Ambassador of Equatorial Guinea in Washington DC.

Eritrea

Eritrea lies on the shores of the Red Sea. It is a rugged country of mountains, bush and desert. It seceded from Ethiopia in 1991 after a 30 year war of independence, which still senselessly rages on along the border of Ethiopia. Eritrea is not nearly as affluent as the other Ethiopian breakaway, Djibouti. For the very serious Stomper only. A 6 month visa costs $25 but is very difficult to obtain.

Ethiopia

Ethiopia has opened its door to overlanders, but travel is not allowed near the Eritrean border. Reports from Stompers rank it an incredibly beautiful country, very mountainous and green. The famine, as infamous as it became, was very localized. The people are friendly and eager to meet foreigners. In the south central part of the country is the famous "Historic Route" which includes the ancient capital Axum and the amazing rock-hewn churches of Lalibela. Apart from visas, prices are reasonable. A 2 year visa costs $70, or a transit visa for 72 hours costs $40.

Gabon

Since the discovery of oil and minerals, this country has become rather expensive and watered down culturally. There are some good jungle treks and primitive tribes the further east from the coast you go. Multiple-entry visas valid for 4 months cost $60.

Kenya

Perhaps the most famous destination on this circuit, Kenya is home to some of the best wildlife parks and game reserves on the planet. Kenya has become a rather expensive country compared to the rest of Africa, mainly due to the decades of tourism. The capital city, Nairobi, is a pleasant respite from the chaos of other African towns, but still dirty and ugly nonetheless. Widespread poverty has made Nairobi a dangerous city, especially if walking alone at night.

Head out of the city for the surrealistic view of lions, rhinos, cheetahs, and giraffes roaming free with skyscrapers as a backdrop. Venture into the hinterland for a safari, a camel trek, or a climb up Mt. Kenya. Enjoy picture-postcard beaches or a close-up look at the millions of migrating and integrating animals. It remains unclear whether the terrorist attack on the U.S. Embassy in August, 1998 was politically motivated or aimed at curbing Kenya's lucrative tourist industry. Single-entry visas valid up to 6 months cost $30 and must be obtained in advance.

Madagascar

Madagascar is an attractive destination because it is so different from the rest of Africa. Long the historic crossroads of colonizers near and far away, Madagascar has emerged as a multi-cultural treasure chest. Africans, Indonesians, East Indians, Asians, Arabs and Europeans have all come to this island at different points in history, which has resulted in the cross blended Malagasy people.

While rich in culture, the world's fourth largest island is economically one of the poorest. Shantytowns are popping up everywhere as the population grows exponentially. The big losers are the many varieties of endangered lemurs, which border on extinction as a result of deforestation and hunting. If you plan a trip here, expect to pay a lot for transportation, and high prices for everything else. Biking is a good ultra-budget option. Study some French before arriving because it is the primary language of Madagascar. Single-entry visas are valid for 30 days and cost $33.45.

Malawi

This narrow SE Central African nation bordering the long Lake Malawi is densely populated and poor. Bus service is good, the prices are very cheap, and the country has had a democratic government since 1994. A few National Parks around towering mountains bring in visitors, but the real attraction is the deep, majestic lake with its sandy beaches and exotic resorts. Stompers zone in on Cape Maclear to relax at one of the most beautiful places in Africa. Excellent treks exist all over the country, especially the highland wilderness area of Mulanje. No visas required for stays up to one year. Exit fee $20.

Mali

Everyone has heard of Timbuktu but didn't know where it was. Well, it's in Mali, along with a lot of sand. A few other things of interest include: the nomadic Tuareg people, primitive people living in hobbit-like homes, camel treks across the desert, and boat trips down the great Niger River. The people are friendly and the markets are lively and colorful. Despite extreme poverty, it is considered by many Stompers as the gem of West Africa. Visas must be obtained in advance for $20 and permit the holder to stay up to one month.

Mauritania

The Sahara desert covers everything in Mauritania, including many towns. Islam is the official religion. The Arabian Moors are the majority in government and regard the minority black people inferior. It is an openly racist government and clashes between the two are frequent. Getting around is rough and the heat can be unbearable. Despite government repression, there are some cool things to see. Check out the multitudes of migrating birds along the coast and the nomadic oasis tribes around the Adrar region. 3 month visas cost $20 and must be arranged ahead of time.

Mozambique

The war is officially over and a recent democratic election has calmed things down enough for the serious Stomper to break some new ground. Caution! There are still many unexploded land mines inland, but none around the coastal attractions. Mozambique has the largest population of one-legged people in the world.

The breathtaking coastline is the longest in Africa. Also stunning are the coral reefs. Seafood feasts of fresh fish and king prawns are cheap and available. Images of pristine beaches, calm lagoons, and deserted isles must be juxtaposed with extreme poverty, malnutrition, and human suffering. Ranking bottom or next to the lowest on all studies of the worst off nations in the world, Mozambique is a picture of pain amidst beautiful natural settings. Many parts of the country are closed, but those that are open are spectacular; that is, if you can turn a blind eye to starving children. As of late, affluent South Africans and other travelers have been making their way to Bazaruto Island every full moon for all-night rave parties. 30 day visas must be obtained in advance and cost $20.

Namibia

This dry country is home to some of the last great migrating herds in Africa, with over 10 enormous parks to protect them. Roads are good, distances are vast, and hitching is quite easy. There are only a few Bushmen tribes left in Namibia. Most have assimilated into shantytowns and all the trappings of a materialistic life.

Long annexed to South Africa, Namibia just achieved its independence in 1990. Much of the apartheid legacy remains, as the white minority communities live in luxury while the black majority is mostly poor and illiterate. Since independence, however, all areas of public life are now officially integrated. No visa required for stays up to 90 days.

Niger

Another dirt poor country bordering the Sahara Desert. About the only reason to come here is to see the lively cattle markets, and Curé Saleé – a colorful beauty pageant where unmarried men woo the opposite sex. To get in you must have a letter of invitation, proof of sufficient funds, a vaccination card and pay $35.58 for a one month visa, or $88.94 for 3 months.

Nigeria

The hands down winner for the dirtiest and ugliest city on the planet is the capital city Lagos. Avoid it at all costs. Not only is it a veritable shithole: congested; high crime rate; hot and muggy; nothing to see – it is also the most densely populated city on earth. In fact, the whole country is extremely overpopulated and home to 1 in 3 Africans. Basically, Nigeria is to Africa as China is to Asia, but in a much smaller space. Their only saving grace is oil production, which spares the people from mass starvation. Travelers be warned of banditry in the northern part of the country. One year visas cost $20 for a single-entry, and $40 for multiple-entry.

Rwanda

Rwanda recently came to the world's attention when hundreds of thousands of warring Hutu and Watutsi tribal members began systematically slaughtering each other. As one of the most densely populated countries of the world, almost every available piece of land is under cultivation to feed the people.

Between social chaos and encroaching farmers, the big loser in all this is the nearly extinct mountain gorilla. The largest primate is being poached for a horrible reason — their hands make nice souvenirs. One of the gorilla's last remaining sanctuaries is the Parc National des Volcans, which is now a war zone. *C'est la vie* cousin gorilla. Multiple-entry 3 month visas cost $90 but may or may not be issued depending on the current status of fighting.

São Tomé and Principe

These remote islands off the west coast of Africa are a virtual paradise on earth. The people are happy, friendly, and well educated. Picturesque little villages dot the lush jungle, shadowed by cloud capped volcanoes. Amazing beaches and incredible diving all welcome the intrepid Stomper. Best of all, nobody goes there, and this gem is relatively unknown to the outside world. If you're near Gabon to get a visa, by all means go! A 3 month tourist visa costs $35, and 6 months cost $40.

Somalia

If the U.S. Marines couldn't handle this unruly lot, don't think you can. It is very poor, poverty stricken, and dangerous. Don't go.

South Africa, Lesotho, and Swaziland

In general, these three countries at the southern tip of the continent all have fair climates, beautiful natural scenery, abundant wildlife, tribal culture, and ethnic strife. Long the subject of an international boycott over racist apartheid laws, South Africa is now governed by the black majority and is open for tourism and business. No visas are required for stays up to 90 days. See: South Africa, below.

Lesotho and Swaziland are both landlocked kingdoms that managed to retain their autonomy from colonizing Europeans. Visas are not required for Swaziland on stays up to 60 days, but Lesotho requires $7.50 for a single-entry, and $15 for a multiple-entry visa.

Sudan

In the vast expanses of the Sudan, just getting from one place to another is an ultra-adventure. This country is recommended only for the hardiest of world Stompers. The main travel arteries are open, but be prepared for unrelenting heat (March to September) and mud roads during the rainy season (winter). There is extreme poverty, a bankrupt government, pockets of civil war, bandits who torture and kill (mainly in the far west), famine, and drought. Yikes! For those willing to risk these obstacles, the traveler will find a fascinating place to visit. Within the population of 24 million people, there are more than 300 tribes who speak over 100 languages and dialects. Sudanese hospitality is legendary, and many consider this one of the world's last frontiers to be explored. A 3 month tourist visa costs $50.

Tanzania

Home to some of the best wildlife reserves on the planet, Tanzania offers up nature as few others can. Here is where Mt. Kilimanjaro soars into the sky, and wild animals roam the Serengeti. Complementing the inland animals are beautiful coral reefs and tropical fish just off the Tanzanian shore. Mellow towns and nice beaches also grace the coastline.

A popular side trip is out to the island of Zanzibar where you will observe the strong influence of the Arabs who came as traders and slavers. The old Stone Town on the island is a fascinating labyrinthine of ruined palaces, forts and Persian baths from the Omani period. Another adventure is to swim with the dolphins off Kizimkozi, or visit the ultra-beautiful Jambiani beach. Both are a short day trip from Stone Town.

It still remains unclear whether the terrorist attack on the U.S. Embassy in August, 1998 was politically motivated or aimed at curbing Tanzania's lucrative tourist industry. Tourist visas (valid 6 months from date of issuance) are good for 1 entry up to 30 days and may be extended after arrival. The cost is $45.

Uganda

After decades of brutal dictators such as Idi Amin, the years of terror and bloodshed have finally ended. Bouncing back, the Ugandan people are among the friendliest on the circuit, despite ongoing poverty and Christian suicide cults. The present government is honest and legit so don't be afraid to go there. You will find a beautiful country with a great deal to offer in the way of safaris and scenery, especially the Queen Elizabeth National Park and Maramagombo Forest. Maybe one day Uganda will once again be known as the "Pearl of Africa." Passports required for entry. Immunization certificates for yellow fever and cholera are also required.

West Sahara

Assimilated into Morocco by force after Spain withdrew in 1975, this dry land is closed for travel due to continued fighting between Algeria-backed rebels fighting for independence and the Moroccan government. Nothing much to see or do anyhow.

Zaire

Formerly known as the Belgian Congo, now called the Democratic Republic of the Congo, Zaire is basically one enormous jungle. The expansive rainforests of Zaire are to Africa as the Amazon rainforests of Brazil are to South America. The roads through the dense vegetation are horrendous, and driving from one end of the country to the other can take up to a month. Another mode of transport is to take a riverboat along the Zaire or Oubangui Rivers for the true jungle experience. Zaire is recommended only for the serious Stomper because travel is rough and the natives are intensely primitive. But this can have its rewards. Shooting a blow dart with a Pygmy tribal member could be a memory to tell your grandchildren.

The economy is recovering quickly from a civil war in the mid-90s, but is still quite poor. Travelers should carry a large amount of small denomination U.S. dollar bills because the Zairian currency isn't worth shit (well, maybe toilet paper). The cost of travel is super cheap, but the cost of a visa is ridiculously high. A one month single-entry visa is $75, double-entry $120. Travelers should pay very particular attention to current epidemics and where they are breaking out, namely the ebola virus and yellow fever..

Zambia

Another vast safari country full of wildlife and adventure. Yet, Zambia is unique because visitors can walk among the animals in the company of armed guards. Game is prolific throughout the many parks where elephants, antelopes, lions, giraffe, zebra, black rhino, and cape buffaloes roam free. Victoria Falls is a major attraction, along with whitewater rafting. Political unrest is common, yet travelers continue to visit. Tourism is about the only thing keeping the national economy afloat. A multiple-entry visa valid up to 3 years will cost $40.

Zimbabwe

As another former British colony in the southern part of the continent, Zimbabwe struggled for its independence, then fought to abolish apartheid. Today, blacks and whites work alongside each other and English is widely understood. Although racial tensions persist, the feeling is more of reconciliation. The people are determined to build a better country and live together harmoniously.

The capital city Harare is cosmopolitan and mellow, where the rural villages are rustic and retain their traditional ways. Most Zimbabweans get by on a subsistence living, but despite economic hardships, these people are proud of their past and eager to show a visiting traveler the beauty of their country. Zimbabwe is cheap, the roads are excellent, hitching is easy, and the scenery is some of the most spectacular in the world. All the best of Africa without the hassles – a Stompers favorite! Don't miss Victoria Falls, the abundant game parks, or the ruins of Great Zimbabwe – the old capital of a 14th century gold-trading empire. Visas are available upon entry for $30 and are valid for 3 months. There is also a $20 exit fee is paid at the airport.

EARTHLINGS

"Hey, wait! *Don't shoot!* We're just two guys in a leopard suit!"

South Africa

Africa is a paradox which illustrates and highlights neo-colonialism. Her earth is rich, yet the products that come from above and below the soil continue to enrich, not Africans predominantly, but groups and individuals who operate to Africa's impoverishment.

– Kwame Nkrumah, Ghanaian president (1965)

Three times the size of California, South Africa sits atop a treasure trove of underground wealth. It sells the world 54 different minerals, including nearly half of all gold produced on the planet. All this mining potential has established South Africa as one of the chief economic powers on the continent.

Extracting ores, minerals, and developing land require a highly centralized labor pool. This is where the trouble begins. White people began emigrating in large numbers at the end of the 18th century. With them they brought Malay slaves from Southeast Asia and East Indians from India to work on sugar plantations. Black Africans were brought in to work from their homelands, but were never allowed to settle. Hence, the white people established "White Areas" and amassed enormous amounts of the nation's capital.

South Africa is definitely a nation of haves and have nots. The Homeland areas of the blacks can be extremely poor and potentially dangerous. Avoid these areas, or travel with extreme caution.

Apartheid was formally implemented in South Africa in the late 1940's, but is today abolished. Apartheid is a concept of government that segregates the population along four main racial categories: black, white, "Coloured," and Asian. The new constitution drafted in 1993 and the election of Nelson Mandela as president has done much to dismantle apartheid, but racism still exists, as it does everywhere in the world.

Travelers should be forewarned that crime in Jo-burg continues to rise. There are still outbreaks of violence in the rural areas of Kwazulu / Natal, and car hijacking is rampant.

Beautiful Settings

South Africa is home to some of the finest coastlines, mountains, game reserves, colorful cultures, and beautiful cities (Cape Town) on the continent. The roads are excellent for renting a car, shared minibus taxi, bus, or hitchhiking. Perhaps the most famous road in Africa is the Garden Route along the Southern tip from Cape Town to Plettenberg Bay, and continuing on up to Durban. You will not be disappointed.

Top Ten Mellow Party Scenes (#7)

The bathing, surfing and scenery along the Garden Route is easily some of the finest in the world. The most famous hangout is Jeffrey's Bay (JB) where the surf breaks, and the locals live the relaxed beach life everyday. The seafood is awesome down here and the beach parties even better. Many compare the South African lifestyle to be much like that of Australia, only with a visible edge called inequality. Travelers usually come to JB for a day, and wind up staying a month.

From Durban, continue inland to the Drakensberg Mountains bordering Lesotho. This is Zulu country who named it *Quathlamba*, or Barrier of Spears because of the sheer and jagged escarpments. The trekking here is top notch, and an added value is the multitude of Bushmen rock painting sites to be encountered along the way.

For the nature enthusiast is Kruger National Park on the border with Mozambique. Here can be found more than 130 species of mammals, ranging from rhinoceros and elephant to impala and zebra. Naturalists claim Kruger N.P. has the most diverse range of animals in the world, including 450 species of birds. Near the Kruger National Park is the Eastern Transvaal escarpment, an area of breathtaking beauty.

Work and Money

Due to an ongoing recession and high unemployment in the home-lands, the government looks unfavorably on illegal foreign workers. Work visas or residence permits are rather difficult to obtain. On the other hand, casual work in restaurants and bars along the coast can be found, as well as under-the-table labor jobs in the wealthy white neigh-borhoods. The pay is nothing great, but enough to finance a Stompers lifestyle. Currently the South African rand is greatly devalued on the world currency market, making travel very affordable.

The
SUB-CONTINENT
Circuit

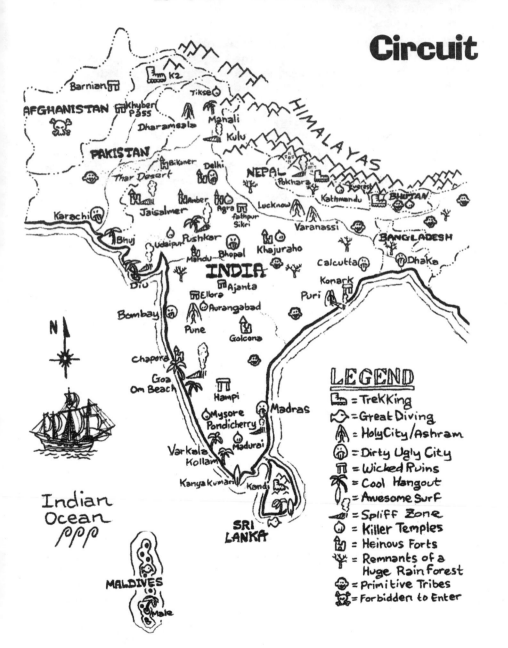

LEGEND

- ![] = Trekking
- ![] = Great Diving
- ![] = Holy City/Ashram
- ![] = Dirty Ugly City
- ![] = Wicked Ruins
- ![] = Cool Hangout
- ![] = Awesome Surf
- ![] = Spliff Zone
- ![] = Killer Temples
- ![] = Heinous Forts
- ![] = Remnants of a Huge Rain Forest
- ![] = Primitive Tribes
- ![] = Forbidden to Enter

The Sub-Continent Circuit

Life is a bridge. Cross over it, but build no house on it.
— Sanskrit proverb

The first pages of recorded human history began in this part of the world. One of the oldest ancient civilizations to emerge came fourth along the Indus River valley 4,500 years ago, in what is now present day Pakistan. Cities were planned, roads laid out, and a highly organized agriculture system was founded and supplemented by active commerce. Invading forces over the centuries ended this culture, but introduced many new ones. The last occupying force was the British empire, leaving behind its language, system of government, and a well-developed infrastructure. Today, this means ease of travel and communication on the Sub-Continent Circuit.

The mighty Himalayan mountain range, the only mountains in the world that continue to grow, separate this sub-continent from the rest of Asia. Dominated by India, but fringed in the north by Afghanistan, Pakistan, Nepal, Bhutan, Bangladesh, and the southern island-nations of Sri Lanka and Maldives. This circuit is a vibrant kaleidoscope of languages, people, cultures, and religions.

Afghanistan

Afghanistan is presently engaged in a nasty civil war. Crime, kidnapping, rape, murder, fighting and land mines are commonplace. Definitely off limits until real peace can be brought back, and that day looks distant. Besides, visas are not being issued at this time.

Bangladesh

Bangladesh is troubled by the triple whammy of over-population, droughts, and flooding on a fairly regular basis. This is the "basket case nation" of the Sub-Continent Circuit. Bangladesh lacks the cultural and geographical diversity of India, but represents all the problems of its dominating neighbor – amplified tenfold. Brave travelers in between disasters report a surprisingly interesting excursion where few others venture, despite hard-up Muslim men following Western women around and widespread poverty. Visas can be obtained in any capital city for two weeks, or ahead of time for 3 and 6 months. $45 fee for tourist or business visas.

241

Bhutan

This is a country that has forever been isolated from the West, but is just now opening up to freelance travel. An almost medieval country with close ties to Tibet, this Buddhist kingdom slopes up from the Indian rainforests to the precipitous peaks of the Himalayas. Being so fresh to tourism, the friendly people will be fascinated by the sight of any foreigner Stomping around their country. Leave a good impression! If available, visas for 15 and 30 days must be obtained in advance in New Delhi, India for $20. Most visitors arrive via all expenses paid trips arranged by a private Bhutanese travel agency for at least $200 per day.

India

Some turmoil between Muslims, Sikhs, and Hindus has erupted in India over the past few years, but it is almost always centered in the big cities, the places you don't want to be anyhow. Stay away from the separatist state of Kashmir; travelers run the risk of being kidnapped by Muslim extremists.

India is plagued by one of the largest and fastest growing populations on the globe. The environment is in shambles and appears to be heading toward complete eco-breakdown. Despite these major problems, India definitely grows on you after a while, and ranks high on many Stomper's favorite destination list. Out in the remote mountain, desert, forest, and beach regions you will discover an ancient land that has been attracting travelers since history began. See: India, below. Passport and visa required for entry. Visas are available three months for $40, six months for $50, or one year for $70. Apply for your visa at embassies or consulates in major cities around the world. 30 day permits are now being issued upon entry to the Andaman Islands with an Indian visa, but are not extendible.

Maldives

This tiny country consists of a long string of tropical islands just north and south of the equator. It can only be reached by air or a hitched ride on a cargo ship. The main shipping ports for the Maldives are from Titicorin, India, or Colombo, Sri Lanka. When you get there be ready to do nothing but lounge under a palm tree, scuba dive into amazing coral reefs, or hang out with some primitive tribes. No visas are required for the first month, $30 for each extended month.

Nepal

Nepal, the Hindu kingdom of the Himalayas, remains one of the top Asian attractions for trekking Stompers. The way of life in the villages and mountains has hardly changed since medieval times. Slavery, and the practice of burning wives alive when their husbands passed away, was not totally abolished until 1926. Still today, all vital supplies are carried up the extensive network of trails by porters and donkeys. A very popular alternative to trekking are the many thrilling rivers for white-water rafting. Also amazing is the Royal Chitwan National Park where Asian rhinos roam freely.

On The Stoner's Trail (#5)

The little hippie town of Pokhara on the banks of Phewa Lake is one of the most scenic places in the world. The town itself is blah, but the nearby mountains towering into the clouds above are absolutely awe inspiring. And it's cool to score and smoke toasty oats too. The pot is a bit standard, the charas better, the prices great. Several people a day will ask you if you want to buy weed or hash on the street. The people are poor, yet friendly, so negotiate tactfully. Do not pay more than a few dollars for a healthy bag of ganja or a sizable chunk of charas.

If you are going trekking in the fall (the best time of year to go), keep your eyes peeled for 3 meter high pot plants growing right off the trails. Many Stompers report finding such plants, stuffing their pockets full of the glorious green, and having a fresh stash for the remainder of their time in Nepal.

Himalayan High Times!

Tourism is the big draw card of foreign currency into Nepal, and the overall cost of travel is ridiculously cheap. Just about everything revolves around the travel industry, so finding lodging, trekking supplies, cool souvenirs, and decent food is hardly ever a problem. The only downside is that the country can be swamped with other Stompers during trekking season, and there is a 10 pm curfew in Katmandu because of recent political uprisings. Visas are valid for 30 days (extendible to 150 days) and can be obtained at the border, or the Katmandu airport for $40. 60 day visas must be applied for in advance at of cost $60.

Pakistan

"Wacky Packy" as it's known in the Stomper's glossary, refers pretty much to the intensely Islamic and heavily populated southern part. Up north is like another country altogether. The north is sparsely populated, and the ancient ways of life persist. The soaring Himalayas are a mellow and interesting alternative to the full-on south. Spend some time with a nomadic tribe in the Thar Desert and you'll feel as if you've taken a journey back in time. Travel is considered dangerous in the Sindh province and in the city Karachi. Be careful. 3 month visas cost $45 and must be applied for ahead of time.

Sri Lanka

There is an ongoing "tit for tat" terrorist conflict happening in certain pockets of the country, and that, not surprisingly, has scared away many visitors. The intrepid Stomper avoids the clashes and heads to the secure areas of the west coast and hill country. There are many treks in the mountains to do, wicked ruins, sic surfing in the south, and easy living on the beach; all for ultra-cheap. Visas are not required for stays up to 3 months. Passports, onward ticket, and sufficient funds required for entry.

India

There exists no politician in India daring enough to attempt to explain to the masses that cows can be eaten.
— Indira Gandhi, 1975

There is no country in the world where the sublime and horrible aspects of traveling collide so dramatically. Some of the scenes of poverty and human inequality will shock you so hard you won't know why you came. The "in-your-face" urban pollution and rural eco-catastrophes of India are almost beyond belief, and you'll probably hate the place with a passion upon first arrival.

But alas, you escape the cities and head up to the Himalayas, or the wonderful beaches, or the hippie stoner towns, or visit the magnificent monuments, and you will finally be glad you came. The Indians are generally a happy and curious lot of people, and their multifaceted culture is as diverse as the land they live on. Furthermore, the Stompers who survive (and thrive) after the initial shock-initiation, are some of the hardiest and most diverse travelers on any circuit in the world. India is a learning experience like none other.

Top Ten Mellow Party Scenes (#8)

Varkala Beach, down near the southern tip of India, is one of the slowest moving places on earth. Get here and just do nothing on the seashore every day. When you find it in yourself to finally leave, check out the backwater boat trip along the coast, or some of the ghats and rainforests up in the mountains of Kerala.

If you go to India, get ready for a crash course in life. It will rattle your foundations to the core.

Horrors

Be prepared to see starving children dressed in rags and living like animals under train cars. They beg for an apple core, or any scrap of food, and then scramble like rats to get it. Not uncommon sights in India include enormous oceans of people living in shantytowns, old people dying on the streets, and dead bodies floating in the Ganges river. Some beggars look so absolutely pathetic, like a midget with a deliberate leg cut off (families do this to deformed children because they are considered worthless otherwise), or a diseased person covered in hives, it is not hard to feel that dying painlessly would not be more humane than a scrap of food or Rupee donation.

The burden of overpopulation in India, as everywhere else, is taking its toll. This vast sub-continent, with its mighty forests and abundance of wildlife once rivaling Africa, is nearly wiped out. More than 75 percent of the trees in India have been cut down since 1900 and they are not coming back because of inadequate reforestation programs. All fourteen major rivers, which provide 85 percent of the country's drinking water, are polluted. What's more, the erosion from deforestation is not only contaminating the waterways but silting up the bottom and setting up the dominos for catastrophic flash flooding. When traversing the country by train you cannot help but notice how barren it all seems. The land is visibly turning to desert from the resulting soil erosion, yet the population is growing so out of control it will soon surpass China as the most populous nation in the world. But don't blame the uneducated Indians (only 43% can read and write), even former Prime Minister Rajiv Gandhi claimed, "Mass poverty was forcing the poor to degrade the environment on which they depend for sheer survival." Everyone has a right to eke out a living.

Bizarre Evolution

In the River Ganges, near the holiest city of the Hindus, Varanasi, something strange is happening in the water. After decades of pollution and centuries of bodies being thrown into the Ganges, the aquatic life in the river is nearly decimated. However, there is one notable survivor who has adapted and even thrived in these new conditions — that being a snapping turtle. Rather than feeding on fish and birds anymore, it lives off discarded human corpses.

Culture

For thousands of years, India has been sacked and invaded by foreign forces. The Persians, Greeks, Moguls, Muslims, Turks, and finally the Europeans all had a go at it. Because the British were the latest and most prolific colonizers, English is widely spoken today.

Although 83 percent of Indians are Hindu, (the worlds oldest religion, founded 5,000 years ago) India is home to other creeds including Islam, Sikhism, Christianity, Jainism, Buddhism, and Zoroastrianism. Religion is very powerful in India and rules the lives of people everyday through action and thought. Karl Marx was correct when he stigmatized religion as "the opium of the people." With over two million gods in Hindu lore, Indians are reputed to have the most festivals of any nation. All this religion makes your average Indian quite jolly and goofy, despite the widespread poverty.

Perhaps the most visible (and hilarious) aspect of Indian culture are the millions of holy cows roaming the countryside and urban areas. Bovines are considered sacred animals – incarnations of Hindu Indians – so they are not to be killed and eaten. In fact, most Indians do not eat meat, so this is a great country to try out vegetarianism. Your intake of meat and dairy products will fall drastically due to its lack of availability.

The legacy of the invading forces, and pervasive religious beliefs, have graced India with some of the finest monuments in the world. Famous places such the deserted ancient cities of Fathpur Sikri and Hampi, the Taj Mahal, the Agra Fort, the erotic sculptures of Khajuraho, the Konarak sun temple, the caves of Ajanta, and the opulent Mysore Palace evoke fantastical images of glorious past cultures. Traveling around, you will also discover thousands of smaller temples, shrines, and palaces at just about every turn.

On The Stoner's Trail (#3)

Marijuana has been an intrinsic part of the Brahmin life (priestly caste) for centuries, and remains to be. Indian *sadhus* on pilgrimage to the sacred Ganges river need ganja for proper worshipping duties to *Lord Boomshankar* (the god of pot). Weed to the Shaivaite holy man is like wine to the Catholic priest.

All the sacred sites (Varanassi, Puri, Jaisalmer, etc.) sell doobage in government run Banga shops. The price is laughably cheap, about a buck for a nickel bag, but the quality is low grade ditch weed. The stuff gets you pretty stoned, but you just have to smoke a lot. Another favorite is bang lassie shakes.

Other "freak centers" like Goa, Pushkar, Kerala, and the mountain region of Manali, have loads of excellent hash, or *charas* as it's called. *Charas* is readily available from just about any given hippie traveler. Be discrete about smoking fat in the Indian cities, the cops just love sniffing out a shake-down. *Boom!*

Welcome to Osho's Ashram

This virtual oasis of lush green beauty is in the middle of a large and drab city called Pune, (near Bombay). It is an experience not to be missed. Over 4,000 people a day come to the ashram (commune) for mind enhancement, meditations in the numerous Zen gardens, excellent vegetarian cuisine, dancing in The Great Buddha Hall, painting and sculpting in the art gallery, alternative courses at the Multiversity, drinking in the Bistro, and many sport activities in Club Meditation (including six Zennis courts). Outside the ashram there is the German Bakery, nude sunbathing, and the Pyramids where techno and tribal dance parties are held.

There are only two requirements to enter the ashram. One, you must wear a matching robe like everyone else, and two, you must have an AIDS test. Osho (formally known as Bhagwan Shree Rajneesh before he left his body in 1990) preached no-inhibitions, so if you want to party like Zorba the Greek, do it, if you want to sculpt like Henry Moore, give it a go, if you want to sleep around and expand your sexual chakara, well then okay. The key is to do whatever feels good to you. Basically, everyone lives by Oshos three L's philosophy: Life, Love, and Laughter. The love vibe is very strong here, and it's not uncommon to see two people standing in the main plaza embracing in a ten-minute hug.

If you get into the new age scene of the commune and feel an affinity towards Osho, you can take the Sanyassin Ceremony whereby you will receive a new Indian "ashram" name. Most of the long-term people of the ashram are Sanyassins. They are very cool people and want to help others grow as individuals. The only hard part is remembering all those Indian names. Call me Swami Dyhan Santosh.

Top Ten Best Bashes (#3)

Forget Santa, snow, and Christmas presents; come to Vagator in Goa (an old Portuguese colony) and dance on the beaches for your next holiday season! Rave parties last all night and into the next morning to the strange and humorous sounds of techno music. It's like a tripper's fantasyland of fluorescent decorations, colors, and glowing people under the black lights. It'll ring in your New Year like none other!

Work and money

There are no real wage earning jobs for foreigners in India because the locals work for next to nothing. Some travelers buy and sell in the flea markets in the state of Goa (Mapsua and Anjuna towns). The foreigners make money by selling haircuts, jewelry, massages, home cooked meals, and clothes (hats from Nepal, T-shirts from America, Lycra shorts from Europe, vests from Thailand, etc.) Another (not recommended) way people make money is by bringing hash and opium down from the mountains in the north to sell to the freaks in Goa. Hard-core travelers pick their own ganja in Manali during the fall harvest season for free smoke, and to earn a few extra rupees as well.

Some restaurants and guesthouses which cater mostly to Westerners will hire a traveler to deal with the customers in exchange for free food and a place to live. For the most part however, nearly everyone just holidays in India because the cost of everything is so incredibly cheap. Why bother with the hassles of working when it is quite easy to live well on six or seven dollars a day.

Earthlings

The cost of travel in India is the lowest of all the circuits. The ultra-budget country of choice.

Another attempt to get on a higher train of thought.

Earthlings

The winds of change.

Part

4

Every Good Thing Comes

to an End

Down the Gehenna or the Throne,
He travels fastest who travels alone.
— Rudyard Kipling

Most kinds of power require a substantial sacrifice by
whoever wants the power. There is an apprenticeship, a
discipline lasting many years. Whatever kind of power you
want. President of a company. Black belt in karate.
Spiritual Guru. Whatever it is you seek, you have to put in
the time, the practice, the effort. You must give up a lot to
get it. It has to be very important to you. And once you
have obtained it, it is your power. It can't be given away: it
resides in you. It is literally the result of your discipline.
— Michael Chrichton, *Jurassic Park*

Objects in motion tend to stay in motion, objects
at rest tend to stay at rest.
— Isaac Newton

To travel is better than to arrive.
— Robert Pirsig, *Zen and the Art of Motorcycle Maintenance*

Nothing happens unless first a dream.
— Carl Sandburg

Fitting Back In

And the end of all our exploring
Will be to arrive where we started
And know the place for the first time.
– T.S. Eliot, Little Gidding

The ancient Chinese observed long ago that the person who returns from a long journey is not quite the same person as the one who began it. How could that person be the same? Traveling opens your eyes to the real world as it is while you are living within it, and changes that inevitably transpire within you.

Only traveling can evoke impressions of the world as unique as your own fingerprint, impressions the mass media cannot entirely deliver. Thoreau writes, "Only that traveling is good which reveals to me the value of home and enables me to enjoy it better."

Rejoice. You have just seen the beauty and the ugliness
of the world that most people never will.

Upon return from the Stomp, you will naturally be full of enthusiasm and stories you'll want to share with friends and family. Telling your tales is a normal extension of your trip, and some people genuinely want to listen. However, do not be too disappointed if interest wanes after a few days or weeks. People don't want to hear about it too much, even intimate family members or close friends. Too many glorious stories of living life to its fullest can make their lives seem dull or inferior.

This unique personal experience will be yours to recall
for the rest of your life.

Most people will find it hard to identify with your new experiences. After a while, even the most open mind switches to overload. Short stories or anecdotes are best. Wait to see if questions or interests are aroused, then continue.

Don't undermine yourself by talking about your trip too much. If people don't want to hear about your adventures, forget about it while you are with them. Take this advice from ol' Grenville Kleiser: "Discreetly keep the most radical opinions to yourself. When with people be a listener a large part of the time. Be considerate in every word and act, and resist the tendency to say clever things. The best evidence of your culture is the tone and temper of your conversation."

A few tips from another Stomper

An American named Paul S. did a world tour and we met and traveled together in India. He arrived back in the States a few months before I did and wrote me a letter to help alleviate the nasty effects of reverse culture shock. His advice for fitting back in:

1. Live in a place with a large freak population. They remind you how incredibly diverse the world is, and help you forget the narrow Democrat/Republican, Coke/Pepsi, McDonalds/Burger King mentality that rules this place.

2. Never get near a TV, unless it's playing a good video or *The Simpsons*. The commercials particularly can be most disturbing.

3. Try not to get bogged down in national politics. My defense mechanism to keep the lamentable state of our country from dumping its negativity on me is to remain blissfully uninformed, except on issues near and dear to my heart like pot legalization.

4. Don't worry about the fact that nobody gives a fuck where you've been.

When the welcome home celebrations simmer down and people become used to seeing you around again, suddenly the realities of starting life anew and getting a job come back into play. This is when support from your family and close friends is most important. If you are returning from your world tour broke, this situation can be all the more stressful. But never quite so bad when you reflect upon how incredibly good you really have it in this world. A Chinese sage once said, "A wise person can never be poor, only broke. Being poor is a frame of mind. Being broke is only a temporary situation."

Sock a few bones away before the Stomp so you will have something to live off of when you return.

Once you let the bird out of the cage, it will never be satisfied going back in again. As time goes by, however, the bird will become accustomed to its old environs, and slowly begin conforming. There is no doubt that this bird will always be a little bit different than the rest of flock. It had stretched its wings and discovered the amazing beauty of flight and therefore will never lose the power to reflect on that most incredible time of freedom.

Redefine yourself and your role in life. You now have the capacity to dream, plan, and execute – so use it! Make a blueprint for another Stomp, or take this into a career if it feels right. The important thing is to be content with yourself and what you have accomplished. Be happy and others will pick up on it. There is no doubt that a positive attitude is infectious.

EARTHLINGS

(Batman and Robin are hanging precariously over a cauldron of boiling wax)

Robin: "Holy paraffin, Batman! This is going to be a close one!"

Batman: "Too close!"

Riddler: "This is my dream come true! With you two out of the way, nothing can stand between me and the lost treasure of the Incas ... and it's worth millions ... millions! Hear me Batman? *Millions!*"

Batman: "Just remember, Riddler, you can't buy friends with money."

Conclusion

Well, there you have it, a Global Travel Manifesto. Action now can only come from you. Wait too long, and it may never come. After all, the future's uncertain and the end is always near. That is why you should waste no time and start thinking in real terms about making a world tour of your own happen A.S.A.P.

Ask yourself, what is life for anyway, *but to live?*

Generations of young people have been traveling around the known world pretty much since history began. Transportation was primitive, but the desire to see new lands was equally as strong as it is for young people today. From the ancient Greeks, like Herodotus who traveled extensively in Asia Minor and Egypt, to young Roman foot soldiers who conquered all of the Mediterranean region and most of Europe. If it wasn't for the intrepid young crew members aboard the *Nina, Pinta,* and *Santa Maria,* Christopher Columbus could not have journeyed to the New World. Charles Darwin was only 22 years old when he set sail around the world on the *H. M. S. Beagle* for his history-changing voyage. Much of the inspiration Thomas Jefferson had for a representative government and freedom of speech came from observations made while traveling in Europe, especially France. In 1787 Jefferson wrote the following letter to his nephew Peter:

"When men of a sober age travel, they gather knowledge, which they may apply usefully to their country; but they are subject ever after to recollections mixed with regret; their affections are weakened by being extended over more objects; & they learn new habits which they cannot be gratified when they return home. Young men who travel are exposed to all these inconveniences in a higher degree, to others still more serious, and do not acquire that wisdom for which a previous foundation is requisite, by repeated and just observations at home. ... Be good, be learned, and be industrious."

The Young generation of today has much in common with the young generation of the 1950s and 60s. Both personify restlessness and experimentation. While the Baby Boomers exemplified these traits as well, the United States was at war in Vietnam when they were young, and Stomping was not popular in a turbulent world. The generation before them, the Beat Generation, was the first to turn on to the concept of leaving the country and living out of a backpack. The most famous was Jack Kerouac and his tales of being on the road. An excerpt from his book, *The Dharma Bums:*

CONCLUSION

"I've been reading Whitman, know what he says, cheer up slaves, and horrify foreign despots, he means that's the attitude for the Bard, the Zen Lunacy bards of old desert paths, see the whole thing is a world full of rucksack wanderers, Dharma Bums refusing to subscribe to the general demand that they consume production and therefore have to work for the privilege of consuming, all that crap they didn't really want anyway such as TV sets, refrigerators, cars, at least new fancy cars, certain hair oils and deodorants and general junk you finally always see a week later in the garbage anyway, all of them imprisoned in a system of work, produce, consume, work, produce, consume, I see a vision of a great rucksack revolution thousands or even millions of young Americans wandering around with rucksacks, going up to the mountains to pray, making children laugh and old men glad, making young girls happy and older girls happier, all of 'em Zen Lunatics who go about writing poems that happen to appear in their heads for no reason and also by being kind and also by strange unexpected acts keep giving visions of eternal freedom to everybody and to all living creatures ... "

The generation coming of age right now has more opportunities to travel the planet than any other generation before them. International air routes cover the globe, untold opportunities present themselves in our wealthy nation, there is no draft, no Cold War, higher (proportional) college attendance, and more leisure time. Ultimate freedom can only come to those who seek it. When sought, the consequences will last a lifetime. Business columnist Tom Peters writes in the *San Jose Mercury News*:

"How about a new Rule No. 1: No hiring him or her unless there is a gap in the résumé? Don't we want the kid who dropped out of MIT in the middle of her sophomore year to travel around the world for 24 months? On a lark? Don't we want to look for people who, short of chainsaw murders in their past, were discipline problems? These days, I worry about the young person with the lifelong 4.0 grade-point average who has never been a problem. Bland yesterday, bland tomorrow. It will not do ... At least go down swinging. Don't hunker down. Try something. Try anything. Be alive, for heaven's sake!"

Today's young generation will experience dilemmas in their adulthood like no other generation before them. The planet is being destroyed at an exponential rate, while the population doubles every 50 years. Weather patterns are changing and the planet is heating up. Russia is leaking nuclear secrets to terrorists and hostile nations. Who is going to pay the trillions of dollars in National Debt our country owes? Do you really think you or I will ever see a nickel of Social Security in our old age? With so much change in the world today, and the growing disparity of haves and have-nots, we, like no other generation before, *must* learn the ways of the world. There may never be another chance.

Sir Francis Bacon wrote in the 16th century, "Travel, in the younger sort, is a part of education; in the elder a part of experience. He that travelleth into a country before he hath some entrance into the language, goeth to school, and not to travel."

How things change. In Bacon's time they haveth no television or Hollywood that maketh English the most trendy and universally spoken language. Education is still very important to the traveler, but in other ways. Geography, math, modern and ancient history, art, music, reading, writing, sociology, cultures of the world, communications, psychology, and economics all tie heavily into the Stomp. Traveling is an extended, advanced degree in all of these subjects. It also gives hands-on experience in responsibility, patience, and open-mindedness.

Most of all, World Stomping is for you to enjoy. Go out and have a blast! Ralph Waldo Emerson observed long ago, "Life is a festival only to the wise." So very true today. Ever notice how some people are content with just the little things in life? Or, how miserable people always find something to complain about? Maybe they complain simply because their life lacks a foundation.

The man who follows the crowd,
will usually get no further than the crowd.
The man who walks alone is likely to find himself
in places no one has ever been before.
Creativity in living is not without its attendant difficulties,
for peculiarity breeds contempt.
And the unfortunate thing about being ahead of your time
is that when people finally realize you were right,
they'll say it was obvious all along.
You have two choices in life:
You can dissolve into the mainstream, or you can be distinct.
To be distinct is to be different.
To be different, you must strive to be what no one else but you can be.

– Alan Ashley-Pitt

Expand yourself, reach out, observe the planet as it is right now, and take in as much as you can handle. The only benefactor can be you. The only one who can make it happen is you. And it's all so easy, accessible and out there waiting, just for you. To sum it up ever so concisely, this book ends with five words from the enlightened Zen mystic, Osho:

"The journey is the goal."

Osho International Foundation

Earthlings

Mood Swings

"Captain's log, final entry. We have tried to explore strange new worlds, to seek out new civilizations, to boldly go where no man has gone before. And except for one television network, we have found intelligent life everywhere in the galaxy."
Captain Kirk (John Belushi),
Saturday Night Live

Appendix

Travel is one way of lengthening life, at least in appearance.
–Ben Franklin

Free Information and References for Travelers

American Automobile Association (AAA)

1-800-222-4357
Information and emergency hotline.

American Express Information

1-800-528-4800
Missing cards and checks, billing statements, frequent-flier plans.
Members only.

Auto Driveaway Company

1-800-346-2277
For auto driveaways in the U.S. and Canada

Centers for Disease Control (CDC)

US Department of Health and Human Services
1600 Clifton Road, N.E., Atlanta, GA 30333
(888) 232-3228
The CDC provides the latest worldwide health information on
diseases, epidemics, immunizations and precautionary measures
for travelers.

Council Travel (CIEE)

1-800-226-8624
Travel destinations to U.S. and abroad, travel gear, insurance,
brochures, ID cards, European rail passes. Students only or under
26 years of age. Cheap airfares to mainly Europe. No age
restrictions.Also ask about the free travel zine called *Student
Travels.*

Eurail Passes & Information

1-800-4-EURAIL

Hostelling International Reservations for the U.S.

1-800-909-4776

A P P E N D I X

International Association of Medical Assistance to Travelers (IAMAT)
(716) 754 4883
This organization provides valuable, free information on climate, disease risk, sanitation conditions and a list of doctors who can help you if you become hurt or sick abroad.

International Telephone Information
AT&T 1-800-225-5288 (calling cards)
MCI World Com 1-800-950-5555 (general and card information)
Sprint International 1-800-877-4000 (general and card information)

Patagonia's Guidelines
1-800-523-9597
A free service offering travel tips and what outfitters to use.

Peace Corps Volunteers
1-800-424-8580

Rail Europe
1-888-382-7245
Information for planning European rail trips,to purchase passes, or individual tickets.

Ticket Planet
1-800-799-8888 (Reservations and Information)
Airfare consolidator for around the world and circuit to circult trips.

United States Center for Disease Control and Prevention
(404) 639-3311 (general information)
(404) 332-4555 (recorded options)

United States Department of State
Passport Services Correspondence Branch, Room 386, 1425 K Street NW, Washington, DC 20524
(202) 647-5225 (information)
(202) 647-3000 (fax-direct)

United States Customs Service
P.O. Box 7407, Washington, DC 20044 (to order publications)
(202) 927-6724 (directory to publications)

United States Printing Office
Superintendent of Documents, Washington, DC 20402
(202) 512-1800

Appendix II

Free Internet Resources for Travelers

Airfare and budget travel www.1travel.com
Good deals on international flights, cruises, hotels, and all-inclusive resorts. The onetravel.com "farebeater" feature searches several databases and gives you a deal instantly.

American Express *www.americanexpress.com*
A multi-user website for American Express Traveler's Checks and cardholders. The "last minute travel bargains" feature is worth exploring.

Bureau of Consular Affairs *http://travel.state.gov*
This site includes consular Information sheets, travel warnings, and public announcements, passport and visa information, travel publications, legal assistance and general travel information.

Center for Disease Control (CDC) *www.cdc.gov/travel*
The U.S. government's CDC travel information site offers advice on vaccinations, immunizations, and general health conditions abroad.

Central Intelligence Agency *www.odci.gov/cia/publications/factbook*
The CIA World Factbook has basic unclassified information on nearly all the countries of the world.

Courier flights *www.courier.com*
The International Association of Air Travel Couriers charges a fee to get the best available courier flights.

Dive destinations *www.diverplanet.com*
The best travel options and cheap scuba dive destinations worldwide.

Hostel listings worldwide *www.hostels.com*
Thousands of mostly private hostel listings in North America and international.

Hostelling International *www.iyhf.org*
All official HI listings worldwide.

Lonely Planet Thorntree *www.lonelyplanet.com/thorn/thorn.htm*
A computer bulletin board organized by region, where traveling
companions meet in one of several forums.

Map sites
Restaurants maps *www.mapquest.com* or *www.lycos.com.*
General mapping at www.*mapblast.com, www.mapsonus.com,
www.excite.com* or AOL users can use the Keyword: *mapping* to
the Maps and Directions page.

Online booking engines
Many top contenders: *www.expedia.com, www.travelocity.com,
www.ticketplanet.com*

Ship employment *www.shipjobs.com*
A resource site on all the inside details of the cruise ship industry.

Train information
Schedules, fares, and schedules for U.S. travel on can be found on
www.amtrak.com European travel on *www.raileurope.com* and
worldwide on *www.railserve.com*

Travel guidebooks *http://travel.roughguides.com*
The Rough Guide travel series put the full text of some of its most
popular titles online in 1995, and a search engine accesses any
destination.

Travel vaccination locations *www.tmvc.com*
Traveller's Medical and Vaccination Centres

United States Customs Service *www.customs.gov*
Customs regulations for the U.S. and international governments.

United States Department of State *www.state.gov*
The U.S. State Department's main web site contains current
foreign affair information,potential hazards and a wealth of
resources.

World Wildlife Fund *www.worldwildlife.org*
The World Wildlife Fund ((WWF) is a nonprofit organization
specializing in the preservation of natural environments and
wildlife. The WWF offers a wide range of trips, the "Buyer Beware"
booklet, a FAQ section on world travel and information on
endangered species.

Glossary

*Slang is a language that rolls up its sleeves, spits on
its hands, and goes to work.*
– Carl Sandburg, 1959

Advoyage n. exciting experience over land, air, and sea; travel encounters in this game called life.
Advoyager n. person who seeks advoyages; one living by his or her wits.

Babe n. attractive person of the opposite sex.
Babealoynia n. place where there is a high concentration of attractive members of the opposite sex.
Bail v. to leave quickly; go.
Bash n. a social gathering; large amounts of people getting trashed in one place.
Bluehair n. elderly person; old fogie.
Bogart n. one who takes without giving; selfish person; hog of a joint.
Bonehead n. mentally deficient person incapable of rational conduct; very stupid person; idiot.
Bones n. dollars; U.S. currency; wealth.
Brutal adj. very hard or difficult; not easy to bear; harsh.
Bunk adj. of poor quality; lousy; low value.
Busker n. entertainer performing in the street.
Buzzkill v. cause slight anger to; loss of one's high; troublesome.

Cabbage n. money; any nation's coin or currency.
Check interj. all right; all correct; expressing approval.
Cheese adj. loss of memory; tending to forget.
Cheesehead n. one who forgets often; spacy; a person from Wisconsin.
Chill-out adj. relaxed and mellow; down time.
Chow down v. eat heartily; chew and swallow (food); have a meal.
Circuit n. one of ten travel zones in the world; a customary route of travel.
Commando-crash n. to camp somewhere not allowed; sleeping wherever one ends up.
Cowboy adj. naked; without underwear under jeans.
Crash n. sleep; natural condition of rest with unconsciousness and relaxation of muscles; spell of this.

Doable adj. possible; capable of happening or being done.
Doobage n. ganja, marijuana, dried hemp.
Dude n. male friend; guy.
Dudette n. female friend; girl.

Epsilon n. lowest caste of person; stunted in mental and physical growth.

Fat n. ganja; marijuana; dried hemp.
Fatty n. large joint; generously rolled marijuana cigarette.
Flounder v. become weak, cease functioning; be unsuccessful.
Freelance travel unrestricted exploration of Planet Earth.

GLOSSARY

Freestyle *adj.* method of travel with no restrictions or limitations; exclusive use of one's own ideas.

Ganja *n.* marijuana; Jamaican word for pot.
GOBL *acronym* Guild Of Beaver Lickers.

Hammered *adj.* extremely drunk; intoxicated with alcohol; inebriated.
Hang out *n.* cool place to relax, meet interesting people and enjoy life; not to do much of anything.
Hard-ass *n.* uncompromising person, one with an attitude problem.
Heinous *v.* most highly exalted; supremely sic.

Joint *n.* marijuana cigarette; spliff.
Joppi *adj.* retarded; backward in mental or physical development.

Leech *n.* one who clings to others; nuisance.

Mac *v.* to eat a large meal. Chow down.
McGyver *v.* handle in a skillful or cunning way; the art of making things happen; taking advantage of situations and opportunities.
Mobile *adj.* able to pack up and move quickly; complete freedom to travel.
Mofo *n.* mother fucker; bad and evil person.
Mooch *n.* accepting or imposing without intention of payback; freeloader.

Procrastivegiac *v.* to put off and space simultaneously; postpone action, forget.

Retrench *v.* cutting off unnecessary spending; reorganizing your personal finances and budget.
Runt *n.* small or stunted person; annoying child.

Sap *n.* foolish person; chump; mawkish demeanor.
Sausagefest *n.* place with an overabundance of men; party with few girls, mostly dudes.
Scam *n.* dishonest deception; person or thing that is not what he or it pretends to be; fraud.
Shanty *n.* of very poor quality; dilapidated.
Sic *adj.* much above average in size or amount or intensity; highly exalted; great.
Sick *adj.* unwell; vomiting; finding amusement in misfortune or morbid subjects; disgusted.
Sir-Talk-A-Lot *n.* one who talks too much; never shuts up.
Slop *adj.* contemptible; lousy; inferior; poor.
Spliff *n.* doobie; marijuana cigarette.
Spliff Zone *n.* area or region of the world where marijuana is smoked openly and freely.
Sponch *n.* nutritionless yet filling food; eatable; chow lacking flavor.
Stoked *adj.* to arouse enthusiastically into being or activity; evoke.
Stomp *v.* to go from one place to another; to move swiftly; travel.
Stomping *n.* the act of traveling; a series of journeys.

Toke *n.* short inhale of smoking substance; puff.

Void *n.* hard to reach; unknown whereabouts; in the Twilight Zone.

Wake 'n' bake *n.* arise to get high; bong hits for breakfast.

Wasteoid *n.* one who is perpetually high on drugs; stoner.

Weasel *n.* the ability to manipulate and overcome; scammer; sly or sneaky.

Whiner *n.* one who complains in a childish fashion.

Wicked *adj.* very fine; totally awesome.

Words from Australia

Aussie *a. & n. (colloq.)* Australia(n).

Barbie *n.* barbecue; outdoor grill.

Billies *n.* bongs; water pipes for smoking marijuana.

Bloke *n.* male friend; guy.

Boomerang *n.* Aboriginal hunting device; missile of curved wood that can be thrown so as to return to the thrower.

Bush *n.* outback; scrub desert; anywhere away from the city.

Cobber *n.* friend; mate; best buddy.

Cones *n.* buds of marijuana; pot.

Didgeridoo *n.* Aboriginal musical instrument in the form of a long wooden tube.

Dinkum *a.* true, genuine, real; honestly.

Loo *n.* toilet; rest room.

Oz *n.* Australia.

Piss-up *adj.* extremely drunk; hammered; drinking binge.

Poofter *n.* gay person; homosexual.

POME *acronym n.* Prisoner Of Mother England; derogatory term for a British person.

Ratbag *n.* friendly term of abuse; unpleasant person.

Root *n.* sex; screw; fuck; to engage in intercourse.

Seppos *n.* derogatory term for an American; derived from 'Yank septic tank'.

Sickie *n.* day's sick leave; free day from work.

Suss *v.* To figure out; come to understand.

Tinny *n.* can of beer; as in 'crack a tinny.'

Whinge *v.i.* complain; be querulous.

Yank *n.* common reference for an American; Yankee.

Words From India

Acha *adv. & adj.* okay, or 'I understand.'

Ashram *n.* a commune style residence of a guru and his or her community of followers.

Bhanga *n.* marijuana; weed sold in government run shops.

Bhang lassie *n.* shake made from curd, fruit, and charas.

Boom *v.* word shouted before toking on a chillum; exclamation paying homage to Lord Boomshankar.

Boomshankar *n.* Hindu god of marijuana; Shankar is a feminine aspect of Lord Shiva.

Brahmin *n.* member of the Hindu priestly caste.

Charas *n.* hash; packed marijuana and resin.

Chillum *n.* slightly funnel shaped smoking device used for smoking charas and tobacco mixtures.

Duney *n.* sheets set up in tent formations, usually found on beaches.

Dyhan *v.* meditate; to reflect upon; contemplate.

Ghat *n.* steps down to a river; sacred place for cremating bodies and bathing; landing-place.

Om meditation chant; sacred invocation representing the absolute essence of the divine principle.

Sadhu *n.* Hindu holy man; spiritual seeker.
Sanyassin *n.* spiritual seeker like a sadhu; disciple of Osho.
Shanti-shanti *adj.* slow and easy; no rush.
Shaivaite *n.* disciple of Lord Shiva; holy man who smokes chillum.
Shiva *n.* a principal Hindu god; the destroyer and restorer of worlds.
Shree Sai Baba *n.* Hindu god of moderation, appears to be saying, 'No thank you, I'm already very stoned.'

Words From Japan

Ahoka *n.* foolish person.
Bosozoku *n.* motorcycle gang; rebellious one who races motorbikes.
Domo arigato *v.* great appreciation; to express gratitude.
Donjon *n.* top floor of a Japanese castle; residence of a Shogun.
Gaijin *n.* outside person; foreigner.
Gargoyle *adj.* ugly waiter or waitress.
Genki *adj.* cheerful; willing; happy.
Gombate *adj.* occurring by or having good fortune; good luck.
Gomi *n.* junk; reusable items that have been discarded.
Haiku *n.* an unrhymed poem having three lines of five, seven, and five syllables.
Karoshi *n.* employment related stress culminating in demise; death from overwork.
Koroshitaroka *adj.* threat to do bodily harm; kill you.
Mabui *adj.* sexy person; lust attraction.
Nippon *n.* Japan.
Nihonjin *n.* Japanese.
Salaryman *n.* one who works for a company 50+ hours a week; corporate employee.
Shibakuzo *adj.* derogatory comment requesting one to depart; fuck off.
Shikataganai *n.* circumstance or event that cannot be helped; shit happens.
Shinkansen *n.* bullet train; high speed railway network.
Shinjinrui *n.* new generation; radical youth.
Shogun *n.* the hereditary commander of the Japanese army who until 1867 exercised absolute rule.
Yarooka *adj.* horny; ones request for sex.
Yakuza *n.* member of the Japanese Mafia; organized crime.
Yellow cab *adj.* loose female; girl who is easy to pick up and take home (for sex).

"Claustrophobia? It's a dreadful fear of Santa Claus."
Vinnie Barbarino
Welcome Back, Kotter

Index

INDEX

CCC PUBLISHING ORDER FORM

Send to: CCC Publishing
1559 Howard Street, San Francisco, CA 94103

_____

NAME

_____

ADDRESS

_____

CITY, STATE, POSTAL CODE, COUNTRY

PAYMENT METHOD (CIRCLE ONE)

       CHECK   **MONEY ORDER**   **VISA**   **MASTERCARD**

_____

CREDIT CARD NUMBER, EXPIRATION DATE

_____

NAME AS IT APPEARS ON THE CREDIT CARD

_____

SIGNATURE OF CARDHOLDER

Circle book of choice:

World Stompers, In Search of Adventure, Sacred Places, both *Extreme* guides

Please send me:———————————————————————

_____ each book(s) @ **$17.95** each =   **$**_____

Shipping ($2.00 for the first book, $1 for each additional book)   _____

Tax ($1.70 per book for California residents only)   _____

                               TOTAL $_____

Credit card orders will be shipped within 24 hours.

CCC PUBLISHING ORDER FORM

Send to: CCC Publishing
1559 Howard Street, San Francisco, CA 94103

_____

NAME

_____

ADDRESS

_____

CITY, STATE, POSTAL CODE, COUNTRY

PAYMENT METHOD (CIRCLE ONE)

     CHECK   MONEY ORDER   VISA   MASTERCARD

_____

CREDIT CARD NUMBER, EXPIRATION DATE

_____

NAME AS IT APPEARS ON THE CREDIT CARD

_____

SIGNATURE OF CARDHOLDER

Circle book of choice:

World Stompers, In Search of Adventure, Sacred Places, both *Extreme* guides

Please send me:—————————————————————

____ each book(s) @ $17.95 each = $_____

Shipping ($2.00 for the first book, $1 for each additional book)   _____

Tax ($1.70 per book for California residents only)   _____

                     TOTAL $_____

Credit card orders will be shipped within 24 hours.

TRAVEL NOTES

TRAVEL NOTES

TRAVEL NOTES

W O R L D 🕊 S T O M P E R S
World Stompers Seeks Your Help!

The world is constantly changing. Prices fluctuate, schedules change, new places open up and bad ones close down. Cool hangouts emerge every day and previously good ones turn sour. Nothing stays the same. The Consortium of Collective Consciousness and *World Stompers* want to hear your views and opinions about traveling the planet. Your letters will be used to help update future editions and ensure publication objectivity. All information is greatly appreciated and the best input letters will receive a free copy of the next edition.

Since *World Stompers* remains a renegade publication, every edition should be read by as many people as possible. Pass this copy around. Order new ones and keep them going around. Ask your local bookstore to order copies.

World consciousness is like the 100th monkey effect: A study group in Japan observed one monkey who found a way to clean a potato and he demonstrated the new technique to another. They continued their practice and showed a few others. Soon enough, every monkey in the tribe, the 100th monkey, learned the new way and it became collective consciousness.

Order signed copies of *World Stompers V, In Search of Adventure, Sacred Places,* or both *Extreme Adventure* guides by sending a check or money order for $17.95 + $2 shipping & handling ($3 outside the U.S.) to:

C.C.C. Publishing
1559 Howard Street
San Francisco, CA 94103
Phone (415) 552-3628
Fax (415) 552-9ccc (9222)

Check out our Web sites!
http://www.stompers.com
http://www.bradolsen.com
http://www.peacetour.org